P.W.J. Howard.

STRATEGIES FOR PROGRAMMED INSTRUCTION:
AN EDUCATIONAL TECHNOLOGY

STRATEGIES FOR PROGRAMMED INSTRUCTION:
AN EDUCATIONAL TECHNOLOGY

Edited by:
J. HARTLEY, B.A., Ph.D.
Lecturer in Psychology, University of Keele, Staffordshire

LONDON BUTTERWORTHS

THE BUTTERWORTH GROUP

ENGLAND
Butterworth & Co (Publishers) Ltd
London: 88 Kingsway, WC2B 6AB

AUSTRALIA
Butterworth & Co (Australia) Ltd
Sydney: 586 Pacific Highway Chatswood, NSW 2067
Melbourne: 343 Little Collins Street, 3000
Brisbane: 240 Queen Street, 4000

CANADA
Butterworth & Co (Canada) Ltd
Toronto: 14 Curity Avenue, 374

NEW ZEALAND
Butterworth & Co (New Zealand) Ltd
Wellington: 26-28 Waring Taylor Street, 1

SOUTH AFRICA
Butterworth & Co (South Africa) (Pty) Ltd
Durban: 152-154 Gale Street

First published in 1972

© Various authors mentioned in contents, 1972

ISBN 0 408 70252 4

Printed in England by Willmer Brothers Limited
Birkenhead

PREFACE

The argument of this book is relatively simple: educational problems can be tackled by the development of an educational technology, and to do this requires the application of certain basic principles. Because these principles underline programmed instruction, it is with programmed instruction that this book is primarily concerned. A number of different ways of implementing these principles have now been devised, and the purpose of this book is to compare, contrast and evaluate such strategies. To achieve this each chapter has been written by an expert in a particular 'strategic' area.

In the *Introduction* the view is expressed that programmed instruction is seen by the authors as implying a systematic methodological approach to education and training, an approach which bases its decisions on facts rather than value judgments. The view that a systematic or scientific method should be applied to education is not, however, new. Thorndike (1906) wrote, 'The efficiency of any profession depends in large measure upon the degree to which it becomes scientific. The profession of teaching will improve (a) in proportion as its members direct their daily work by the scientific spirit and methods; that is, by honest, open-minded consideration of facts, by freedom from superstitions, fancies or unverified guesses, and (b) in proportion as the leaders in education direct their choice of methods by the results of scientific investigation rather than by general opinion.'

Thorndike was one of the few men who, almost single-handed, influenced educational practice, but it would seem that his belief in the virtues of applying a systematic methodology to education did not commend itself to the teaching profession. Today, however, the problems facing education and training are more acute, and for some the application of scientific methods now seems more attractive.

Preparing instructional material is not a simple task. Objectives have to be decided, techniques of presentation worked out, and an assessment made of the efficiency of resulting methods. This book reminds instructors and research workers of the *varieties* of approach in each of these stages. In pursuing this theme, this book has perhaps concentrated too much on comparing individual strategies and too little on considering their possible interaction. Further research is needed to see how individual strategies, although interesting in themselves, can best be integrated.

This book has been written to encourage members of the teaching profession, at whatever level of education, to experiment with their teaching, and to evaluate their results. Several strategies of approach to preparing instructional materials have been collected, compared and assessed. It is hoped that this book will help the reader to translate some of this research into action.

In the preparation of this text I have had much assistance from many friends. I would like here to thank particularly my colleagues who have furnished basic chapters, and Professor Peter McKellar —without whom this book would not have been written.

J.H.

University of Keele,
1972

FOREWORD

by Professor Peter McKellar, Department of Psychology, University of Otago, New Zealand

The teaching-learning situation, both in education and in industry, merits the best strategies of teaching that science can devise. This book is devoted to this theme. Its authors comprise four psychologists active in the discipline of Programmed Instruction. Scientific understanding of the learning process—of the ways in which human beings are modified in their behaviour as a result of the events of their own life histories—is today playing an active part in education, business, and the armed forces. This applies in many of the most developed countries of the world. It applies also in some of the countries of Africa, Asia, and South America, where teachers are few and learners are many, and the fullest mobilisation of scientific knowledge in the service of education is doubly necessary.

It was in the mid 1920s that Sidney L. Pressey, at Ohio State University, first introduced the teaching machine as a device which presented information, tested comprehension, and gave prompt knowledge of results in the learning situation. By the 1930s Pressey was writing about 'a coming revolution in education'. Education and commerce soon began to make use of these devices, and this new teaching movement. Many other psychologists joined Pressey in this work. By the mid 1950s one of the most important theorists of the psychology of learning, B. F. Skinner, had become active in the field. A more self-conscious approach to the process of imparting information, and a clearer realisation of the goals of the process of instruction, was beginning to influence the foundations of scientific psychology in one of its most fundamental areas: the theory of learning.

The four contributors to this book, Dr. Hartley, Dr. Annett, Professor Davies, and Mr. Duncan all write about the areas of which they have specialised knowledge. A companion volume *'Contributions to an Educational Technology'*, is edited by Professor Davies and Dr. Hartley. Cross references to this carefully selected set of readings which comprise the companion volume have been incorporated in the present book. Both have been designed to provide information on this area of research, and its applications, for those who wish to keep up to date with work in this field.

CONTENTS

PREFACE

FOREWORD

ACKNOWLEDGMENTS

ACKNOWLEDGMENTS

For permission to reproduce various figures, the Editor and Authors would like gratefully to acknowledge the following :

Figure 1.1. Professor R. Revelle, and IPC Business Press
Figure 1.2. Professor H. Ozbekhan, and IPC Business Press
Table 1.2. Professor W. A. C. Stewart, University of Keele
Figure 1.3. Professors F. Harbison, C. A. Myers, J. Vaizey, and McGraw Hill Ltd
Figure 1.5. Messrs. P. B. Warr, M. Bird and N. Rackham, and Gower Press

Figure 2.1. Dr. L. F. Thomas, Brunel University, London
Table 2.2. Dr. T. F. Gilbert, Praxeonomy Institute, New York
Figure 2.3. Messrs. C. A. Thomas, I. K. Davies, D. Openshaw and J. Bird
Figure 2.4. Professor R. M. Gagné, and Holt, Rinehart and Winston
Figure 2.5. Dr. A. E. Hickey, Entelek Ltd., Massachusetts
Table 2.3. Professor R. M. Gagné, and The National Education Association of the United States
Figure 2.6. Professor R. M. Gagné, and the Editor of the *Psychological Review*
Table 2.4. Professor R. M. Gagné, and Dunod Press
Tables 2.5 and 2.6. Dr. G. O. M. Leith, University of Sussex
Figures 2.7, 2.8 and 2.9. Professor R. M. Gagné, and the Editor of the *Psychological Review*

Table 3.1. Professors N. T. Bell, J. F. Feldhusen, D. D. Starks, Purdue University
Figure 3.1. Messrs. R. J. Hughes, P. Pipe, and The English Universities Press and Doubleday & Co.
Table 3.2. Dr. J. Holland, Professor B. F. Skinner, and McGraw Hill Ltd
Table 3.3. Dr. T. F. Gilbert, Praxeonomy Institute, New York
Table 3.6. Dr. E. C. Poulton, and the Editor of *Ergonomics*
Figure 3.3. Dr. F. W. Stainer, and the Editor of the *Proceedings of the Institution of Electrical Engineers*
Figure 3.4. Dr. F. Mechner, Basic Systems, New York

Table 4.1. Professor A. Anastasi, and Macmillan Ltd

Table 4.2. Mr. J. McGregor, The Regis School, Tettenhall, Wolverhampton

Table 4.3. Mr. J. McGregor, The Regis School, Tettenhall, Wolverhampton

Table 4.4. Messrs. C. Hall and K. N. Fletcher, and H.M.S.O.

Figure 4.3. Professors C. O. Neidt and D. D. Sjogren, and the Editor of *Audio-Visual Communication Review*

Figure 4.4. Mr. W. J. Thomas, Pitmans, London

Figure 4.5. Professors H. F. McCusker, P. H. Sorensen, and Aldine Publishing Company

Table 4.9. Mr. J. F. Duke, and the Editor of *New Education*

Figure 5.1. Professor E. R. Hilgard, and Appleton-Century-Crofts

I

Introduction

JAMES HARTLEY

This chapter explains the need for new technological approaches in education and training, and shows how one of these, programmed instruction, contains certain principles basic to the development of appropriate strategies leading to an educational technology. To do this the chapter is divided into four sections. Section 1 briefly outlines some of the problems facing educational systems today, while Section 2 introduces some of the solutions that have been proposed to help overcome these problems. This is followed by a section which examines programmed instruction in more detail, and the final section introduces the concept of an educational technology. Because programmed instruction utilises principles basic to the development of an educational technology, it is important therefore to examine the different strategies that are evolving from the application of these principles. This chapter, therefore, puts programmed learning in perspective.

SOME PROBLEMS FACING EDUCATIONAL SYSTEMS

Many problems face the many different educational systems of the world, but some of these problems, although different in scale, are international. It is proposed to examine briefly only five such problems here:

(a) The 'population explosion'.
(b) The 'information explosion'.

1

(c) The demand for higher education.
(d) The teacher shortage.
(e) Restrictions on change imposed by present-day existing situations and priorities.

When these problems are considered *in combination*, then the implications for education and training become more apparent.

The 'population explosion'

At the time of writing it is estimated that if the present rates continue, then the world's population will double by the year 2000 to some 7 000 million (Revelle, 1967). What is important to note (*see Figure 1.1*) is that this is a steadily increasing growth curve, and that the rate of growth is much faster for developing countries —where, generally speaking, there are the highest rates of illiteracy and the poorest educational facilities. In Great Britain and the U.S.A. these latter problems present less difficulty, but nevertheless the estimates for the expected population increases (*see Table 1.1*) still provide educators with disturbing food for thought.

Table 1.1 Estimated populations of the United Kingdom and the U.S.A., 1965–80. (Data from O.E.C.D. 1966)

Year	*U.K.*	*U.S.A.*
1965	54 000 000	193 000 000
1970	56 000 000	205 000 000
1980	60 000 000	237 000 000

A related problem in this area is that increases in population are not expected to be parallel in all age groups. Thus in Great Britain and the U.S.A. it is expected that by 1980 there will be significantly more older people than there are today, as well as significantly more younger. Such developments, it has been argued, when related to expected social and industrial changes, will change the emphasis of many educational problems. Retraining, and continuing education will be needed for adults (E. and R. M. Belbin, 1969): a different kind of education or training will be needed for the young. Such conclusions, however, anticipate other problem areas.

The 'information explosion'

It is now becoming commonplace to state that there is a considerable and a growing increase in the amount of material to communicate, particularly material of a scientific nature. It has been estimated, for example, that 90 per cent of the world's scientists who have ever lived are alive today, that something like two million scientific journals appear in the world every day, and that two-

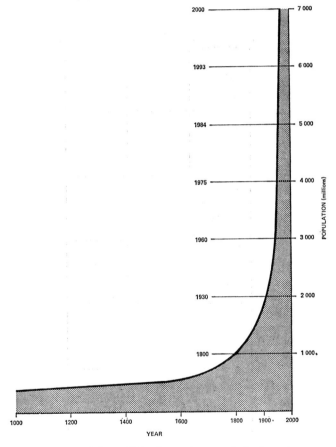

Figure 1.1. Population of the world has increased enormously in the past 300 years. By 1800—about a million years since his beginnings—man had built up a population of 1 000 million. Since then, however, the periods between successive increases of 1 000 million have progressively shortened. For the population to increase from 6 000 million to 7 000 million could take only seven years (1993–2000). Such explosive growth can be attributed at least in part to improved nutrition and standards of hygiene in the developing countries (From Revelle, 1967, Courtesy: IPC Business Press.)

thirds of scientific knowledge known to man has been discovered since World War II. Indeed, it has been argued that the sum total of human knowledge will soon be doubling every year. The increase in scientific knowledge and its applications must lead to radical social changes (*see Figure 1.2*). Facts like the ones just stated lead one to expect and to predict dramatic changes in our methods of storing and retrieving information; direct access to computers for both pupils and teachers seems inevitable.

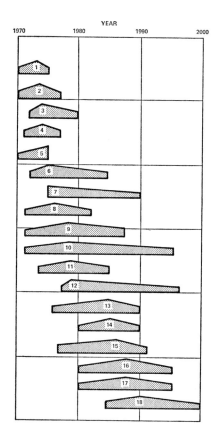

Figure 1.2. Technological progress in automation as predicted by a panel of experts. The length of each bar represents various estimates put forward by the 'middle half' of the panel. In each case one quarter—the 'lower quartile'—proposed dates earlier than that at which the bar begins and another quarter—the 'upper quartile'—give dates beyond that marking the end of the bar. Each bar has a peak value which represents the median date estimated (From, Ozbekhan, 1967, Courtesy: IPC Business Press)

The information explosion is thus likely to affect our social and industrial lives as well as our educational systems. As Bowden (1968) has remarked, 'There was a time when a man could be educated for life before he left university, but that is quite impossible today because no man can master a subject and go out having learnt it once and for all. Education must be a continuing process and a process of discovery.'

The demand for higher education

One result of the information explosion has been the increasing demand for higher education. Compared with the population growth, there has been an even greater rate of expansion in the demand for higher and further education. In 1955, in Great Britain, one in six 16-year-olds remained in full-time education; by 1960 this was one in five, and by 1965 it was one in four. The Government Report *Higher Education* (1963) (more popularly known as the Robbins Report) showed that in Great Britain in 1960 there were 179 000 students pursuing higher education: it was estimated that this figure would be 344 000 in 1970, and 558 000 in 1980. Present-day numbers are already exceeding these projections. The Robbins Report, accepted by the Government, aimed to expand the university intake of Great Britain by no less than 50 per cent in five years, and in fact this was achieved. In the last ten years the number of universities and the number of students have doubled and the cost of university education has

---

1 *Increase by a factor of 10 in capital investment in computers for automated process control*
2 *Air traffic control—positive and predictive track on all aircraft*
3 *Direct link from stores to banks to check credit and to record transactions*
4 *Widespread use of simple teaching machines*
5 *Automation of office work and services, leading to displacement of 25 per cent of current work force*
6 *Education becoming a respectable leisure pastime*
7 *Widespread use of sophisticated teaching machines*
8 *Automatic libraries looking up and reproducing copy*
9 *Automated looking up of legal information*
10 *Automatic language translator—correct grammar*
11 *Automated rapid transit*
12 *Widespread use of automatic decision making at management level for planning*
13 *Electronic prosthesis (radar for the blind, servo-mechanical limbs)*
14 *Automated interpretation of medical symptoms*
15 *Construction on a production line of computers with motivation by 'education'*
16 *Widespread use of robot services*
17 *Widespread use of computers in tax collection*
18 *Availability of a machine which 'comprehends' standard I.Q. tests and scores above 150*

B

risen enormously (*see Table 1.2*). Together with this increase has come a widespread dissatisfaction with the present system, both from students and from government administrators. The situation

Table 1.2 Estimated university expansion in the United Kingdom. (Data from figures presented by Stewart, 1968)

Year	No. of Universities	Approximate Number of Students	Approximate Expenditure
1958	23	100 000	£36 000 000
1970–71	46	220 000 (Robbins: 204 000)	£200 000 000

is not helped by the mutually contradictory tasks facing universities: on the one hand they are told to increase their efficiency, and yet on the other to increase student participation on important committees.

When the Robbins Report was made, little account was taken of the Industrial Training Act (1964), which was passed by the Government the following year. This Act was designed to ensure that there would be an adequate supply of properly trained men and women at all levels of industry and to secure a general improvement in the quality and efficiency of industrial training. This Act has strengthened the demand for further education, particularly in technical colleges, for management is now seeking better educated and better trained employees. Belbin (1965) noted that in America workers may be expected to change their jobs at least twice after the age of forty, and predicted that this will soon occur in Britain too. Furthermore, better educated parents are insisting on better education for their children, realising that, without higher or further education, career prospects may be diminished. Indeed, the demand for education has been termed yet another 'explosion'—the 'explosion of human aspirations' (Richmond, 1967).

This picture of rapid expansion in higher and further education in Great Britain is reflected in the U.S.A., the U.S.S.R. and other developed countries. The link between education and economics is a complex one (*see* Vaizey, 1967), but undoubtedly (*see Figure 1.3*) until the present day there has been a close relationship between economic development, education in general, and higher education in particular. This relationship, however, is to some extent more complicated today by increases in the rates of migration of trained personnel. To quote Bowden again, 'There is a new mobility of educated people throughout the whole world: it is tending all the time to take people to the U.S.A.'

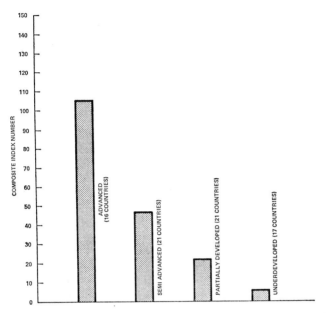

Figure 1.3. The average composite index of 'human resource development' for a variety of countries showing the relevant availability of skills related to education. At the lowest level are mainly African countries where the national income is low and the educational levels are also low. At the other extreme is a group of developed countries (led by the U.S.A., whose index number is 261.3—well beyond the page boundary) (By permission from, Education, Manpower and Economic Growth, HARBISON F. and MYERS C.A. Copyright 1966. McGraw Hill Ltd)

The teacher shortage

Migration, it may be argued, except for the United States, may lead to an increase in the shortage of trained men at the top of their professions. In terms of teaching, a loss of top men may be most important. Even without migration there are (as Kay *et al.* (1968) point out) only a few who can teach the more advanced subjects it is necessary to teach in a highly developed technological community, and there is already a grave problem of teacher shortage. Vaizey (1966) commented, 'To staff (British) schools adequately at this moment we need at least 100 000 more teachers.' This British need is shared in other countries. Apart from the general shortage, there are particular shortages which pose more acute problems. There is in Britain, for example, a shortage of qualified mathematics and science teachers at secondary level— precisely where, following the 'information' and 'aspiration' explosions, they are most needed; there is a problem of 'wastage', particularly of women teachers at primary level (there is a loss of almost 25 per cent of trained women aged between 24 and 29); and a considerable shortage of appropriate personnel has revealed itself consequent upon the Industrial Training Act (1964).

There is much debate, in view of the problems outlined above, as to whether the general and the particular shortages will continue, grow worse, or improve. In England, the Secretary of State for Education estimated in 1966, that by 1971 a target of no more than forty pupils in each secondary school class would be achieved. Many, however, would consider these figures still too high. Furthermore, it is predicted, with the raising of the school leaving age to sixteen in 1972–73, and possibly to seventeen in 1980, that the problem of large classes will not disappear. It is interesting to note, in this respect, that the Robbins Committee did not foresee the staff position in higher education getting worse, and it is encouraging to observe the considerable increases in the number of students being trained for teaching. Nevertheless, overall, there seem little grounds for optimism.

Thus here we have a dilemma: on the one hand there is an acknowledged teacher shortage; on the other, the combination of problems already discussed suggests that there must be an increase in the demand for teaching. To resolve this dilemma means that the teachers of *tomorrow* cannot be like the teachers of today: their functions and their roles must change. Teacher-training and re-training thus present new problems and demand new solutions, and this is an area of expanding concern (*see* Taylor, 1969).

Existing limitations and priorities

In 1962 it was reported that almost a quarter of the school buildings in Great Britain contained some parts that were built before 1875. The Labour Government of 1966–70 placed the provision of more staff and more buildings at the top of its list of educational priorities, but in view of the problems discussed above it may be questioned whether these are, in fact, the right ones. Nations have other priorities apart from education, and indeed, one questions how seriously in fact they take education. Systems of priorities imply financial restriction and control, and the amount spent per item indicates its importance. It was not until 1969 in the United Kingdom, for example, that a greater proportion of the gross national product was spent on education than on defence: indeed, in 1970 the Labour Minister of Defence was able to state that the lowest paid private in the Army earned more than his daughter did teaching! It is well known, too, that in England more is spent on industrial chemical research into 'whitewash' than on research in education: indeed, of the money spent on education less than one per cent is spent on educational research (Wall, 1968) —although, happily, this figure is rising. Until the last few years or so Governments have seemed to be unaware of the educational crises they are running into. As Kay *et al.* conclude, 'The challenge is to design educational systems whereby we can teach our communities to live, to think and to learn at a higher level than they have done at any time in recorded history.... We have now within our grasp the tools to help us as never before, yet we are showing neither insight nor enthusiasm for this work.' The existing educational system (in Great Britain) has been said to be decentralised, inefficient, and engendering apathy. None of these factors are conducive to rapid progress in terms of educational reform.

SOME PROPOSED SOLUTIONS

Five major problems facing educational systems have been outlined: many more solutions to these problems have been suggested. *Table 1.3* summarises some of these. The problems listed above are unlikely ever to be completely resolved, the solutions listed aim at reducing the urgency that they create: and the solutions themselves, of course, raise further problems.

It is perhaps worth noting at this stage of the discussion that a multiplicity of long-term solutions is possibly more easy to introduce and is more relevant to a developed rather than to a developing country, where the problems are more acute and are thus perceived differently. It is likely, for example, that a poor country with few qualified teachers will look to a more radical solution for its problems, possibly in terms of *one* new method of instruction (e.g. television) rather than in terms of a combination of methods. A rich country, by contrast, can afford to diversify its resources. These problems have been discussed further elsewhere (e.g. by Bienveniste, 1967). Strategies for introducing new methods and techniques in education into developing countries are described by Schramm *et al.* (1967). Developing countries, it can be argued, may profit by learning from the initial mistakes made by more advanced countries.

Table 1.3 Problems and proposed solutions

Problems
Population growth
Information growth
Demand for higher and further education
Teacher shortage
Existing limitations and resources

Immediate Solutions	*Long-term Solutions*
Increase class size.	Carry out curricular reform.
Increase hours teachers teach.	Carry out manpower forecasting.
Eliminate, reduce courses.	Improve teaching materials, aids, etc.
Lower standards.	Utilise new methods of instruction.
Employ teachers with poorer qualifications.	Research into teaching methods, systems and factors affecting their
Utilise unqualified assistants.	efficiency.
Improve teachers' pay/conditions.	Improve teacher training.
Train more teachers.	Introduce in-service teacher training.
Utilise existing plant better.	Make innovations in architectural design.

To return, however, to the main discussion. The solutions listed in *Table 1.3* have been categorised as immediate (but largely negative) and long-term (but positive). The short-term solutions are largely peripheral, and none of them probe the basic ideas and methods of teaching which have been employed for so long. Clearly it may be easier to adopt the immediate solutions, but this book is concerned with the long-term, more significant solutions, and in particular with one aspect of one of them (one new teaching method).

One main conclusion that can be drawn from the first part of this chapter is that teachers of the future will be required to impart more information to more people in approximately the same amount of time: solutions which suggest factors such as increasing class size and making more efficient use of plant, emphasise this view. This conclusion can, however, be stated another way: if teachers have to communicate more in the same time, then it may be concluded that they must communicate more efficiently. Solutions which suggest changes in teacher-training, and the introduction of new methods and techniques—with related research—emphasise this.

Yet there is a third but related conclusion that can be drawn. This conclusion is that, rather than impart more, what needs to be taught must change. Because of the information explosion and expected concomitant social changes, it is argued that children

of the future must learn at least two things: they must be able to adapt readily to change, and they must be able to abstract the underlying principles of subjects (their 'structure', as Bruner (1966) termed it). Such objectives are easier to state than to achieve, but solutions which emphasise curricula reform are perhaps most relevant here.
To summarise:

(a) Educational systems face great problems.
(b) Considering these problems in combination leads to certain conclusions.
(c) Each long-term solution listed in *Table 1.3* is relevant to these conclusions.

The general conclusion reached, however, is that education will have to be more efficient. It is in terms of an efficient communication system that programmed instruction may now be considered.

PROGRAMMED INSTRUCTION

As shown by implication in *Table 1.3*, programmed instruction is only one of many solutions listed, for it is only one of a general group headed 'new methods'. This point is illustrated further in *Table 1.4*, which lists new methods and techniques designed to assist the efficiency of communication, and classifies them in terms of communication systems. It must be acknowledged that the classification system used in *Table 1.4* over-simplifies the issues involved, for the methods and techniques listed there can be modified to cut across the basic distinctions drawn. Furthermore, teaching *aids* have been omitted—the blackboard, projection aids, maps, wallcharts, models, textbooks—these can all be used by the teacher to increase the effectiveness of his communication. Nor is it intended to suggest that because of its position in *Table 1.4* as a flexible two-way communication system, programmed instruction is necessarily superior to other teaching methods; each method has its own objectives and its own advantages and disadvantages. Indeed, it will be shown by Davies later in this book, Chapter 3, that some of the basic ideas from different methods can be integrated with each other. However, it is argued here that a system which modifies its presentation according to what students say and do, and in itself learns from this, is a system that is likely to be more efficient than one that does not do this.

Table 1.4 Teaching methods considered as communication systems

	One-way[1] Communication Systems	Two-way[2] Communication Systems	

Fixed presentation[3]	Radio
	Tape-recordings
	Film — loop
	    — strip
	    — radio
	        vision
	    — moving
	    — silent/
	        sound
	Television (open)
	Television (*c.c.t.v.*)
		Films } with
		T.V. } students
		Radio } responses
		
		Language Laboratories
		
		Linear programmed
		instruction
			Team teaching[5]
			A systems approach

Flexible presentation[4]	—	Programmed
		instruction
		Adaptive
		    mechanisms
		Computer-assisted
		    instruction	

Key:
1. No interaction between communicator and receiver.
2. Interaction between communicator and receiver.
3. Presentation order does not alter (despite 2).
4. Presentation order depends on student responses.
5. Methods integrating 'appropriate' techniques.

Programmed learning and programmed instruction

The reader may feel that it is a little premature to be discussing programmed instruction in terms of communication systems before learning a little more about it. However, it is assumed in this book that the reader will be familiar with the general notions of programmed learning and programmed instruction, and that distinctions to be drawn in this section will suffice to review them.

Like any distinction between teaching and learning, it is clear that two sides of the same coin are being discussed, and that definitions must to a certain extent overlap. In the early days of programming, programmed *learning* was stressed. Programmed learning can be characterised in terms of what students do when faced with a teaching machine or programmed text. The basic principles may be listed as follows:

(a) The student works with a machine, or programmed book individually, and at his own rate.

(b) He works through a carefully ordered sequence of items (usually short) which ask him to respond in some way (by writing answers down, pressing appropriate buttons, etc.).

(c) The material (or program) is so designed that the student makes few errors.

(d) At each stage the student is immediately informed whether or not his responses are correct.

Thus, the student works from the familiar to the unfamiliar at a speed which allows him to assimilate new information, knowing at each stage that he has understood the material.

These principles are the characteristics of programming that are relevant to the success of the pupil in learning: it can be seen that a number of well-known principles have been combined into one system, hence its success. Each principle listed, however, has been subjected to much research and scrutiny, in order to determine its importance (*see* Holland, 1965).

More recently, however, attention has been directed from research on programmed learning (what students do) to research on programmed *instruction* (what program writers do). This antithesis is somewhat false, but it serves to make the distinction clear. It is with the strategies used in the construction of programs that this book is mainly concerned. The process of programming is

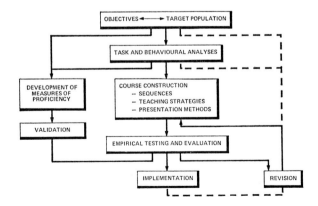

Figure 1.4. The 'process' of programmed instruction

typically that shown in *Figure 1.4*. In more detail, the main steps may be characterised as follows:

(a) The objectives or aims of the program are specified precisely and in a way that can be measured. The objectives of a program state what it is that the student will be able to do when he has completed the program.
(b) The prior knowledge, skills and abilities of the students who are to use the program are similarly specified.
(c) The material to be taught, and the skills to be acquired by the learner, are painstakingly analysed.
(d) From these analyses are determined (i) optimum teaching sequences, (ii) appropriate teaching strategies, and (iii) appropriate presentation methods (one of which may be programmed *learning* in the sense described above).
(e) The program is tested on students for whom it is intended.
(f) On the basis of results obtained from empirical tryouts, the program is revised, retested, and revised again until it can be seen to be 'working' satisfactorily.

Not all program writers go through all of these processes: some take a simpler path (*see* Kay *et al.*, 1968); some do steps (b) and (c) before step (a); and some place more weight on the evaluation instrument for determining teaching strategies and objectives (*see* Markle, 1968). Clearly, whatever sequence is used, it is a time-consuming task to program a whole course, and in many cases (e.g. in commerical companies) experts develop in specific areas (e.g. analysers, writers, illustrators, editors). In brief, however, the key stages are:

(a) Objectives.
(b) Tests of objectives.
(c) Analysis.
(d) Presentation.
(e) Evaluation and revision.

These stages form the subject matter of the following chapters.
   Figure 1.4 shows the 'process' of programmed instruction. In principle it looks rigorous, in practice it is not—not yet—but the basic ideas behind programmed instruction mean that one day it may be so. Programmed instruction requires that objectives must be determined and that the achievement of these objectives must

be assessed. If the objectives are not achieved, then this implies that there must be a revision of the strategies initially adopted until the objectives are satisfactorily reached. In terms of communication systems, programmed instruction can thus be seen as a *self-correcting* system. In the words of Kay *et al.*, 'Every part of a teaching system is subject to the rule that whatever fails to do its job should be replaced.'

Figure 1.5 shows the results of applying a self-correcting system. In this experiment in industrial training reported by Warr *et al.*

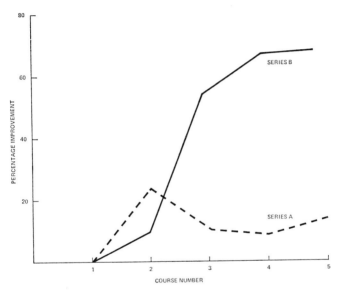

Figure 1.5. Comparison of course series with and without self-correction. Percentage improvement beyond the first course in each series. (From Warr et al., 1970, Courtesy: Gower Press)

(1970), information was available at the end of each course on several measures—including pre-knowledge, post-test scores, and student attitudes. In the first series of courses (Series A) although these measures were taken, they were not revealed to the instructors. In the second series (Series B) the results were supplied to the instructors and they were incorporated into plans for improving the course. *Figure 1.5* shows that the average knowledge improvement (post-test minus pretest) for Series A was some 10 per cent above the level of the first course, whereas for Series B the equivalent improvement was 70 per cent.

PROGRAMMED INSTRUCTION AND AN EDUCATIONAL TECHNOLOGY

The concept of programmed instruction developed in this chapter is much broader than has been usually the case. Programmed instruction is defined in this chapter not as a way of teaching without a teacher, but as a method of instruction which has measurable objectives, pre-arranged sequences and methods of presenting materials, and which is self-correcting. Often this can or will involve a computer. It is argued here that the wider application of such principles could result in the development of an 'educational technology', that, 'this offers the real possibility of a revolution in the organisation, content, methods and achievements of an education system' (Davies, 1965a).

'Educational technology' is, for the authors of this book, synonymous with 'scientific improvement', where 'scientific' implies a systematic methodological approach which bases its decisions on facts rather than value judgments. Educational technology is not, therefore, just concerned (as some people appear to think) with new techniques such as projectors and language laboratories: it embraces more than this. Indeed, each long-term solution listed in *Table 1.3* is viable under its heading. An educational technologist is concerned with improving education by using concepts such as measurement, efficiency, productivity and cost effectiveness. These concepts are equally relevant to such things as curriculum reform and school counselling as they are to technological innovation. It is suggested here, indeed, that a full-scale educational technology cannot be developed if *any* of the long-term solutions listed in *Table 1.3* is ignored: solutions must be considered in combination and in relation to the educational system as a whole.

Thus it is argued in this book that the problems listed in the first section can only be tackled by the development of an educational technology—where this embraces in a *total* system, or complete 'package deal' as it were, the solutions separately proposed. Although full-scale educational technologies of the kind envisaged here have not yet been realised, it is perhaps worth noting that progress has been made in some schools in America towards providing a separate course of instruction for every child (Cogswell *et al.*, 1966; Esbensen, 1968), and more miniature systems have been described, e.g. by Sullivan (1969) and Banks (1969). The possible impact of such an educational technology on American society is well discussed in a book edited by Rossi and Biddle (1966).

This 'overall solution' is clearly an idealised one, fraught with many problems, and the prospects of progress towards it in Britain are most gloomy. Some immediate objections are that:

(a) There is a shortage of suitable information, materials and reasearch knowledge about each long-term solution proposed, let alone a combination of them.
(b) Few people will take kindly to such a global view: problems concerning the demarcation of areas of interest and role conflict seem inevitable.
(c) The limitations of the present-day system discussed above (and elsewhere, *see* Richmond, 1967) will operate to prevent the rapid growth of an educational technology.

Despite this, the argument of this book is that educational systems can try to meet the problems facing them by the development of an educational technology; that all areas in education can be improved by the application of basically simple principles; and that, because these principles underlie programmed instruction, it is with programmed instruction that this book is concerned.

CONCLUSION

It may appear in this chapter that instruction has been stressed at the expense of learning. If this is the case, it was not intended. The important things to bear in mind are the objectives of any system. If, for example, the student or trainee is required to learn through discovery methods, then this is the teaching strategy that must be adopted: discovery methods are not inconsistent with the principles of programmed instruction (*see* Covington and Crutchfield, 1965; Tucker and Hartley, 1967). If, for example, the student wishes to be responsible for his own learning, then (particularly by using computers) this is quite possible (*see* Mager, 1961; Grubb, 1968). Restating the argument, an educational technology must arrange the conditions of learning in such a way that learning is more efficient, and that the abilities of learners are extended, not restricted. The use of terminology such as 'cost effectiveness' does not imply that broader educational aims will be ignored. If this were the case, then the objectives of such a system would need restating, and by definition, the system would not be 'effective'. The development of an educational technology thus does not imply, as many seem to think, that a rigid and sterile education system will result: on the contrary, it should mean that our children will be better taught, and that they will be able to advance further. The social implications of an efficient educational technology are startling.

Yet in a sense this discussion is naive. The argument so far has tacitly assumed that there is a static set of problems, and a static set of solutions. It is clear that this is not the case. The information explosion places great strain on the concepts of programmed instruction and educational technology developed here. Problems will engender solutions which will engender further problems. Long-term educational objectives may change slowly, but more limited objectives are likely to change more rapidly. Such changing objectives imply that cost effectiveness must be an important constraint to use when developing methods of instruction. A lecture may not be so inefficient if it can be easily adapted to rapidly changing conditions: text books, on the other hand, are often out of date before their publication. Certainly, many of the techniques discussed in the following chapters may well have disappeared in the next few years. So, although programmed instruction allows an objective examination of its success, it is questionable whether a self-correcting system can, in a dynamic social and educational context, ever be 'correct'. There is always room for improvement.

2

Strategies for Analysis of the Task

KEITH DUNCAN

INTRODUCTION

The last few years have seen an erosion of confidence in some of the clearcut propositions of the early protagonists of programmed instruction. The first generation of teaching machines achieved little which cannot, with a little ingenuity, be achieved without resorting to hardware (Goldstein and Gotkin, 1962; Annett, 1964; Duncan, 1964; Knight, 1964). More important, evidence has accumulated suggesting that those features which distinguish one style of programmed instruction from another may not be so critical as was supposed. Experiments which have deliberately 'mutilated' the styles of Skinner (Pressey and Kinzer, 1964), Crowder (Senter *et al.* 1964; Kaufman, 1964; Biran and Pickering, 1968; Duncan and Gilbert, 1967) and *Mathetics* (Davies, 1969a) are among the most persuasive. For all these findings are consistent with the view that the major contribution to learning has been, not from superficial features of programming style, such as response mode and sequencing, but from the initial stages, common to all programming, of defining and ordering what the learner must master—i.e. from *task analysis*.

Unfortunately, task analysis is not without its difficulties. The techniques which have been advocated are legion (Annett and Duncan, 1967) and poorly developed. Nonetheless, in the emerging educational technology task analysis is an essential stage in the cycle of development, not only of programmed materials, but of any well designed course of instruction (Wallis, 1965).

It is extremely difficult to give an adequate definition of what the various writers who use the term *task*, mean by it. A fundamental difficulty, to be met by any satisfactory operational definition, is that most, perhaps all, human performance may be recorded, for instructional purposes, at many levels of description, ranging from gross statements of procedure, to microscopic details of limb or finger movement. This is a systematic difficulty to which we will return. Meanwhile, we may accept that 'task' is only a 'partially defined term' standing for 'any group of activities performed at about the same time, or in close sequence, and sharing a common work objective' (Miller, 1962b).

It is useful to distinguish between *job*, which is a person-oriented concept, and *task*, which is a system-oriented concept (Singleton, 1968). A job is a set of tasks, which have been assigned to one person on some more or less rational assessment of his capabilities, and which he contracts to carry out, usually in return for some reward or to avoid sanctions. The set of tasks typically has a title, e.g. Quality Control Inspector, Lathe Operator, Assistant Librarian, Shift Charge Engineer. Fifth Former and Undergraduate are also jobs in this sense.

The tasks themselves, be they machine operations, translation exercises or essays, arise in the first instance because they, hopefully, enable the objectives of some system to be realised—such as manufacturing electric light bulbs or ensuring that school leavers achieve some mastery of French. It will always be open to question whether a task should exist in its current form, or for that matter, be performed at all. Indeed, a thoroughgoing instructional technology will closely examine the justification for all tasks requiring instruction; it will also specify tasks which a system's objectives entail but which at some stage have been ignored or overlooked. For these reasons, system objectives should be explicit and detailed. It should be clear, e.g. what percentage of sub-standard light bulbs is acceptable in consignments leaving the factory and on the retailer's shelf; whether the school leaver is expected to pass written translation papers or, perhaps, to converse proficiently with a Frenchman in defined situations such as ordering and paying for meals, car repairs and other similar circumstances.

Before beginning analysis, then, one first establishes that tasks are consistent with what the system, which gave rise to them, is trying to achieve. This much is common to both education and occupational training. There are, however, differences in emphasis and approach which make it convenient to consider separately the strategies for task analysis developed in support of 'teachers', on the one hand, and 'training officers' on the other.

EDUCATIONAL APPROACHES TO TASK ANALYSIS

One of the earliest pleas for an instructional technology was made by Tyler in 1932. For adequate measurement of instruction, which was his main concern, Tyler stipulated that course objectives must first be stated by instructors and specified *in terms of the different kinds of behaviour required*. This done, the next steps are to devise test situations which sample and permit these different kinds of behaviour to be measured.

The argument is illustrated by a college zoology course. According-ing to Tyler, teachers' marks did not distinguish clearly between the several different attainments implicit in the course objectives which, when separately measured, yielded scores which were not closely related. Among the different kinds of behaviour which were operationally distinct were:

(a) Skill in the use of a microscope.
(b) Memory of information.
(c) Understanding of technical terms.
(d) Ability to draw inference from facts.
(e) Ability to apply principles to concrete situations (Tyler, 1961).

Tyler's argument is that there are different kinds of competence and that identifying these is a prerequisite for any adequate testing of course attainment. This essentially is the argument taken up some twenty years later by Bloom and his associates at the University of Chicago when work was undertaken on the now well known 'Taxonomy of Educational Objectives' (Bloom, 1956). Development of the taxonomy, or method of classifying the various sorts of behaviour which may be developed by an education system, was begun by scrutinising the curriculum plans, instructional materials and instructional methods of a number of teaching institutions. From these sources a list of educational objectives was compiled.

In developing the Taxonomy from these data, Bloom and his team were guided by the following principles:

(a) The major distinctions between classes would reflect the distinctions implied by the ways in which teachers state their objectives.
(b) Logical considerations such as precision and consistency would be met by the classification scheme, especially by any division into sub-categories.

C

Table 2.1a The three domains of the 'Taxonomy of Educational Objectives,
(From Bloom, 1956)

COGNITIVE DOMAIN	'Recall or recognition of knowledge and the development of intellectual abilities and skills.'
AFFECTIVE DOMAIN	'Includes objectives which describe changes in interest, attitudes and values, and the development of appreciations and adequate adjustment.'
PSYCHOMOTOR DOMAIN	'The manipulative or motor skill area.'

(c) Distinctions consistent with psychological research would be observed and other distinctions discarded—whether made by teachers or not.

The resulting taxonomy is outlined in *Table 2.1*. Each subdivision is defined in words and by examples of objectives and illustrative test questions.

Table 2.1b The Cognitive Domain (condensed). (From Bloom, 1956)

Knowledge
  Knowledge of specifics
    Knowledge of terminology
    Knowledge of specific facts
  Knowledge of ways and means of dealing with specifics
    Knowledge of conventions
    Knowledge of trends and sequences
    Knowledge of classifications and categories
    Knowledge of criteria
    Knowledge of methodology
  Knowledge of the universals and abstractions in a field
    Knowledge of principles and generalisations
    Knowledge of theories and structures
                  Intellectual Abilities and Skills
Comprehension
  Translation
  Interpretation
  Extrapolation
Application
Analysis
  Analysis of elements
  Analyses of relationships
  Analysis of organisational principles
Synthesis
  Production of a unique communication
  Production of a plan, or proposed set of operations
  Derivation of a set of abstract relations
Evaluation
  Judgments in terms of internal evidence
  Judgments in terms of external criteria

At the beginning of this chapter it was emphasised that a crucial component of an adequate technology is the statement of instructional objectives in performance terms. Tyler and Bloom make the major point that the variety of performance which may be specified is considerable, and that this implies a similar variety of measures by which performance must be tested. The Taxonomy of Educational Objectives indicates the extent of this variety and one strategy for course design may be to use it for classifying objectives. For objectives successfully classified, this procedure would provide useful indications of the type of testing required.

Furthermore there is evidence that the taxonomy may be reliably used (in the statistical sense) in classifying test questions (Stanley and Bolton, 1957). Indeed, use of it for classifying questions may constitute a useful check on validity of test content when the final version of the test is compiled from a large pool of possible questions (Cox, 1965). However, what is contestable is whether the Taxonomy is of use in the *formulation* of objectives. More important than classifying *existing* statements of objectives may be the question of what requirements should be met when formulating objectives in the first place? For the answer to this question we can turn to approaches to the problem in a rather different context.

TASK ANALYSIS IN MILITARY AND INDUSTRIAL TRAINING

To survive, military and industrial systems must be efficient—if only during the limited periods required to eliminate their competitors. Not surprisingly one encounters in such systems a rather widespread concern with what the various system components—men and machines alike—are for, what they do, whether they do it effectively and how economically. This view, despised by some, is held by others to have had a salutary effect on research directed to improving the processes of instruction.

The operationism of Miller and Mager

The approach to the problem of instructional objectives, in particular by military psychologists, tends to be critical of existing training assumptions and seeks to establish criteria by which any statement of instructional objectives may be judged. This approach first became widely known outside military training research circles with the publication of a short, lucid and down-to-earth text by

Robert Mager (Mager, 1962). Its origins, however, are certainly much earlier, for example earlier by at least a decade in the case of R. B. Miller's sustained attack on the problems of task analysis (e.g. Miller, 1953, 1954, 1956, 1962a, 1966). Miller's approach was based on the 'simple-minded premise (which turned out to be a revolutionary one, and still is today)... that training should be based on what the operator or maintenance man had to do, rather than on the theory of operation of the machine or the physics of the phenomena' (Miller, 1966). The requirements for an adequate statement of what the trained man should be able to do—i.e. of training objectives—are quite explicit. In common with 'any sound procedure for behavioural description' the statement should specify 'what criterion responses should be made to what task stimuli and under what ranges of conditions'. The standards proposed by Mager for adequate instructional objectives (Mager, 1962) are rather similar, namely:

(a) Specification of the kind of behaviour which is acceptable as evidence of successful instruction.
(b) Statement of the conditions under which the behaviour is to occur, e.g. whether translation is to be performed with or without a dictionary or, to take an industrial example, whether a repair task is to be supported by a fault-location guide.
(c) Specification of performance standards, usually specification of acceptable accuracy and speed.

Mager emphasises that these components of the statements are necessary if a major criterion is to be met, that is, if the instructional objective is to be *communicable*. Statements which do not meet these standards will leave the instructor, the student, or any one else, in doubt as to just what the student should be able to do after instruction. Taking one of Mager's examples, 'knowing how an amplifier works' is an inadequate expression of an objective since it could mean different things to different people. Should the student be able to draw a circuit diagram of an amplifier? build one? list its components? or repair it? The ambiguity in this and many other statements of instructional objectives lies in the way the word know and others like it are used. The core of a well stated objective will be a verb such as to 'classify', 'distinguish', 'calculate', 'mend', which indicates the kind of behaviour required and hence is less open to misinterpretation. Relatively abstract words like 'understand', 'know', 'realise' or 'appreciate' have too many possible meanings to be useful (and sometimes so many as to be meaningless). However, it should be noted that several words which have been favourites in statements of objectives are apparently not so clear to teachers as might be supposed (Deno and Jenkins, 1969). Just which action words *are* useful, in the sense that there is good agreement about the behaviour to which they refer, is an empirical question. Miller's and Mager's criteria provide useful guidance on stating objectives in behavioural terms. There remains, however, the problem—particularly acutely felt in industrial and military training—of determining exactly *what* behaviour should be the endproduct of training. For instance, some electronic theory is frequently included in training courses for electronic maintenance technicians. The evidence that such training is associated with effective fault-finding performance after the training course is meagre, and occasionally negative (Williams and Whitmore, 1959). Now it is perfectly possible to state what behaviour constitutes satisfactory evidence of mastery of electronic theory, i.e. training objectives meeting Miller's and Mager's criteria could probably be stated in this case. However, to state objectives in this way does not mean that instruction which meets them will be relevant or in some way valuable, only that the extent to which it achieves what it sets out to do may be readily assessed.

How, then, does one determine what behaviour *is* relevant or valuable and therefore to be achieved under instruction? It is sometimes said that this is easier to do in the case of occupational training than in the case of education. The goals of education are certainly complex, embracing highly generalised skills and techniques and also perhaps responses to the ideals of society at large. Consider, for example, the possible ways in which students' behaviour might be shaped by studying the reign of Henry VIII. Any assessment of what behaviour is relevant or valuable objective of general education, will inevitably be controversial. On the other hand, so the argument goes, in occupational training the question is settled by appealing to what performance is expected in the job situation. Selecting training objectives on the basis of what the man does in that situation is in fact the advice of Miller and Mager. However, to do so is, in this writer's view, to become involved in a superficially simple exercise which may in practice be far from straightforward.

Data collection problems

The archetypal industrial task is performed by an operator at a bench or on an assembly line; it consists of a series of movements—mainly manual, which are more or less 'skilled'—and is

completed in minutes, or exceptionally in hours. The *job* consists
of a *single* 'short cycle, repetitive' *task*. In fact many jobs are more
varied and less easily specified. Well known examples are the
supervisor and the maintenance man, especially in their 'troubleshooting' as opposed to daily routine roles. The unplanned content
of such jobs tends to increase as the systems they are helping to
control become more complex, and departures from fixed procedures in both contingent and regularly occurring tasks become
more prevalent. The jobs of operators on semi-automatic plant
are also changing in this way and such jobs are increasing in
number. Recording by direct observation (e.g. by objective
techniques such as high speed photography) becomes less feasible
as jobs become more varied.

Also discernible is a tendency in recent years for training
requirements to shift from skilled movement to skill in distinguishing critical changes in the work situation, and skill in selecting
one course of action from several alternatives. Again, it may be
less easy to record from direct observation what is required in the
increasing number of perceptual and decision-making tasks than it
is in the case of recording skilled movement. There has always
been this problem in the case of emergencies—which the analyst
is by definition unlikely to observe—and the tasks to be carried
out in emergency situations are for that reason easily overlooked.
Furthermore, jobs in some industries, especially those involved in
controlling continuous process plant, consist very largely of irregu-
lar or infrequent actions to remedy unpredictable events, such as
changes in feedstock or ambient conditions, and varying degrees of
emergency occasioned by plant failures.

For jobs which present these problems—i.e. a variety of tasks
such as infrequent emergency tasks, tasks involving not only motor
skills but also perceptual and decision skills—the series of studies
by Rupe and his associates in the early 1950s present what is still
possibly the best evidence on the relative merits of techniques for
gathering job information. Rupe considered five techniques:
questionnaire survey, group interview, individual interview, observation interview and technical conference; and his studies
embraced a wide range of jobs in the U.S. Air Force, including
weather observer, different types of repairmen, instrument
mechanic, policeman, cook, firefighter and 'personnel specialist'.
While there were differences between jobs in the efficiency of each
of these techniques, the individual interview proved to be the most
efficient overall when account is taken both of the dependable,
useful job information obtained and the cost (mostly man-hours)

involved in obtaining it (Rupe, 1952, 1956; Rupe and Westen, 1955a, 1955b).

Thus, how to determine in useful detail what a man actually does in the job situation is one problem created by the decision to establish job-oriented training. It also entails the problem of what information, for training purposes, should be included in the analysis, what information should be excluded, and the more subtle problem of the detail in which training information should be recorded.

There are two general criteria, *frequency* and *criticality*, which may be applied in deciding what activities to include in the analysis. The associated techniques of 'activity sampling' and the 'critical incident technique' have been successfully employed in both industrial and military situations. Barnes's text on activity sampling (Barnes, 1957) is classical, although for many training purposes the excellent summary by Chapanis may be preferred (Chapanis, 1959). For an account of the critical incident technique Flanagan (1954) may be consulted, as well as the adaptation of this approach to the job of supervisors recently made by Warr and Bird (1968). These techniques are especially useful when describing jobs which embrace a wide variety of tasks, e.g. supervisors, salesmen, or private secretaries. It is probably generally true that the smaller the organisation, the more varied will be the tasks which are the responsibility of a single job encumbent, and therefore the more appropriate will be the use of some activity sampling or critical incident technique.

Describing occupational skill

That skilled performance may be described at several levels of detail is widely recognised. Thus the task of folding a shirt may be described as a series of 'major steps' such as setting the collar, placing the collar in the head of the presser, and each 'major step' may in turn be further described, e.g. setting the collar involves positioning the shirt correctly on the table, inserting stiffeners and so forth (King, 1964). Some writers specify the levels of description to be employed. A recent guide to course design produced for the U.S. Army recognises the following four levels of description. *Jobs*, e.g. motor mechanic, comprise *duties* or 'distinct major activities', e.g. tuning the motor. At the next level are sets of *tasks* (in the sense of R. B. Miller) which form 'a logical and necessary part of the performance of a duty', e.g. adjusting the carburettor, removing, cleaning, adjusting, or replacing spark plugs. Tasks in turn may be broken down into *elements* or 'single simple acts', e.g. turning a screwdriver adjustment anticlockwise (Smith, 1964). Similarly, a document produced for the U.S. Navy, setting out guide lines for task analysis, proceeds from the identification of *task blocks* to their constituent *tasks* and finally to the isolation, within tasks, of *behaviour details* (Folley, 1964a). More recently Mager and Beach (1967) have distinguished three levels of description, namely *vocations* (Painter, X-Ray Technician, Landscape Gardener), *tasks* (preparing a surface, mixing paint) and *steps in performing the task* (selecting appropriate paint, removing old finish). The Mager and Beach booklet is a more useful contribution than most, since the levels of description they propose are extensively exemplified.

Indeed, the several levels of description of performance which have been proposed in the literature are at best exemplified rather than defined. Not surprisingly agreement is less than perfect as to the terms for designating different levels or the number of levels to be distinguished, although a *fixed* number is generally assumed. One obvious strategy for the training course designer is to select a level of description which *prima facie* suits his situation and which he finds most easy to distinguish. This approach has been adopted by several of the Training Boards recently formed to implement the Industrial Training Act (1964).

It will be argued later that any *fixed number of levels* of description should be explicitly rejected in favour of a strategy of progressively redescribing the different components of a task as many times as is useful. At this point it is simply noted that the number of levels which proves useful in a particular case may be only one or two—as in the example of folding shirts—or several levels of description may be necessary to obtain all the information needed for training—as in the description of preparing an omelette put forward by Thomas *et al.* (1968) in the course of their research for the Hotel and Catering Industry Training Board (*see Figure 2.1*).

The fallacy of the 'Experienced Worker Standard'

To base training on what the man does in the job situation involves the analyst in choosing appropriate levels of detail to record job information, and this information may often have to be obtained at second-hand, i.e. by interview rather than by direct observation. The analyst may also encounter a third problem, namely whether what the expert, craftsman, master or experienced worker does is an adequate criterion for training objectives. For a number of

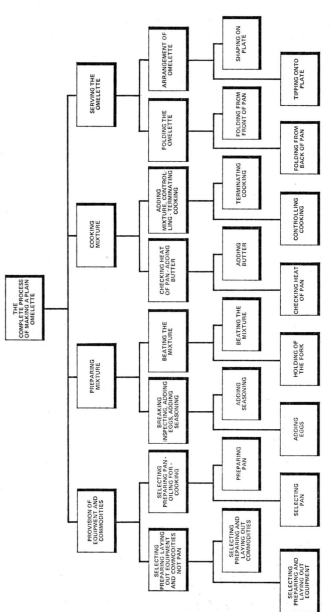

Figure 2.1. Analysis of Making a Plain Omelette (From Thomas, 1968)

reasons current job holders may perform in sub-optimal fashion and the question for the analyst may not be what does the experienced man do, but rather what *should* a man do in this situation.

One reason for sub-optimal performance may be that the experienced man has only his experience to guide him in a situation where experience alone is not enough. A case in point is a search task encountered by the writer in a study of the job of controlling a continuous chemical process plant. A typical search task is represented in *Figure 2.2*. The boxes represent steam or cold water heat exchangers through which acids pass in a purification process. Quality control sampling of the product, i.e. after it has passed through all eight heat exchangers, may report water contamination indicating that one of them is leaking.

The task consists of taking further samples of the product at certain of the sampling points a–g to locate the unit which has failed, i.e. is leaking. Then numbers corresponding indicate relative costs of obtaining samples at different points on the plant (e.g. sampling acids in liquid form at a pump's drain valve is less costly than sampling where the acids are in vapour form and under vacuum). The numbers in the boxes are the approximate probabilities of failure. The task is to minimise sampling costs in locating such failures. An efficient search strategy which is diagrammed in the lower part of *Figure 2.2,* is to take the first sample at e, then if it is contaminated to sample next at d, otherwise at f, and so on.

In tasks such as this, there are many possible sample sequences which, whether more or less efficient, will all locate the fault, and an experienced operator will not necessarily discover the most efficient strategy, or even improve on his initial strategy, if his only training has been by exposure to the situation—on the familiar assumption that practice makes perfect. Indeed, one supervisor, whose plant experience and understanding of process control was acknowledged in his firm to be outstanding, used a strategy in a problem of this type which was one of the more efficient but not the most efficient.

There is by now evidence that in a number of situations a man may make sub-optimal judgments when he has to estimate probabilities or choose a course of action yielding most information towards the solution of a problem e.g. Dale, 1958; Cohen, 1960; Edwards *et al.*, 1965). The fault location task represented in *Figure 2.2,* is only one of many in which it would be hazardous for the task analyst to regard performance of an experienced operator as a criterion for deriving training objectives.

Another reason for caution in taking operator performance as

the sole criterion for training objectives is that the task in its
current form may be such that the operator cannot *in principle*
perform efficiently. It has been pointed out that not even designers
of electronic equipment can do what the maintenance man is

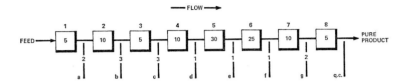

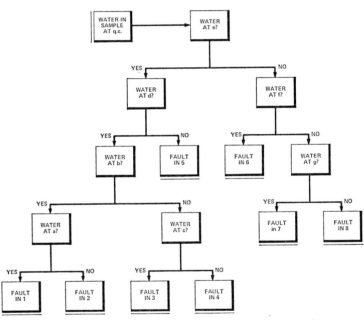

*Figure 2.2. The flow diagram illustrates one feature of an industrial acid purification process.
The acid passes through a series of heat exchangers, boxes 1 to 8, anyone of which may leak.
The consequent water contamination is initially detected at the quality control sampling
point, q.c. A leaking heat exchanger is isolated by taking further samples at points a to g,
thus a sample at d, for instance, that is not contaminated, eliminates boxes 1 to 4 leaving
boxes 5 to 8 still suspect. Because cost of sampling varies in chemical plant, each sampling
point has a corresponding cost index of 1, 2 or 3. The figure inside each box is the approximate
failure probability. The decision tree minimises sampling costs over a random series of faults
occurring with frequencies corresponding to their specified probabilities*

sometimes expected to do in fault location, that is, from his under-standing of electronics theory determine what a waveform or volt-age at a check point should be, or specify the set of components which, if malfunctioning, could produce a given out-of-tolerance reading. In design work, engineers recognise that theory alone is not sufficient—that "bread boarding" (i.e. the temporary assembly of prototype circuits) is also needed—because the components in real equipment do not correspond exactly to theory. For example, there is some capacitance in resistors and inductors, some inductance in resistors and wire, and some resistance in inductors (Shriver, Fink and Trexler, 1964).

The solution proposed by Shriver for electronic fault finding tasks is to 'pre-troubleshoot' the equipment. The typical analysis which is time consuming and exhaustive establishes:

(a) How a functional diagram of the equipment can be divided into blocks, such that whenever the signals entering a block where the boundary is drawn are all 'good' and a signal leaving the block is 'bad', then the fault will always be in that block.

(b) The limits of what constitutes a good signal, e.g. voltages, wave forms, wherever a signal crosses a block boundary.

(c) What symptoms are produced by failures in each of the blocks.

(d) Within each block, the resistance of small sets of components, generally a chain of five or six condensers, resistors, etc. between an accessible test point and earth.

With this information, performance aids are developed which realise the central feature of this powerful technique—that *at every stage* of fault location the *cues* which the repairman must recog-nise and the *responses* which he must make are clearly specified. Thus a symptom list provides the cue indicating which blocks to check. Another guide specifying 'good' signals for the boundaries of these blocks provides the cues indicating within which block to search. Finally, during within-block search, a list of resistances provides cues indicating which half-dozen or so components include the faulty one (Shriver, 1960; Shriver, Fink and Trexler, 1964; Shriver and Trexler, 1965).

Decisions, decisions, decisions . . .

The Shriver technique of task analysis, which effectively reduces to procedure-following what were formerly judgment and decision making tasks, has been paralleled in this country by the technique of ordering problem solving tasks in a branching sequence of binary decisions known as 'logical trees' or 'algorithms' (Jones, 1964; Horabin, Gane and Lewis, 1967). The diagram at the bottom of *Figure 2.2* is, in fact, an algorithm, or, as the writer would prefer, *decision tree,* for locating the origin of contaminant in the acid purification plant. One need only provide the operator with such a decision tree to guarantee perfect or near-perfect performance.

It is, however, important to realise that the analysis of problem solving or complex procedural tasks to yield decision trees, or detailed procedural guides of the kind developed by Shriver is, in effect, programming performance rather than programming learning. In an evaluation of the decision tree in *Figure 2.2* and a decision tree for interpreting control alarms and instrument readings on the same plant, the performance of trainees proved markedly superior to that obtained from a comparable group practised in fault location based on explanations and diagrams of the flow of product through the plant. Use of decision trees in this way was, however, at the expense of retention and transfer which were observed in the second group of trainees—the loss of transfer effect being the more serious of the two, in the sense that the data suggest that these effects are more stable over time (Duncan, 1969).

The analyst of problem solving and decision making tasks is thus likely to be closely involved in the overall personnel policy of the system in which he is working. In some situations it may be highly desirable to proceduralise such tasks, in other situations the need to train for retention or transfer, for 'flexibility', may be more important. Widespread and indiscriminate use of decision trees might present more problems than it solved. However, the writer is not simply siding with those critics of decision trees who are happy to score silly debating points about the possible reduction of human performance to that of an unthinking puppet.

Whether or not a particular problem solving or decision making task could with advantage be reduced to a procedure, will depend on several factors. As already implied, one of the more important of these will be the trainee population. Less able groups may be expected to follow procedures with more success than general principles. For more able populations, highly procedural instruction might prove boring and would largely exclude transfer of learning which might otherwise be obtained over a range of tasks. At the same time, procedure-following would fail to exploit transfer from previous learning to the present task. Secondly, the stability of the population to be instructed will also be important. High labour turnover will tend to make procedural training more economic, since mastery of general principles will usually entail longer periods of instruction, or more sophisticated instructional techniques.

In short, task analysis for industrial or military training often involves problems, the solution of which depends on factors other than training considerations *per se*. The same performance may be achieved by different techniques of training, by use of job aids, or by combinations of these, and in consequence be more or less exacting, more or less boring. At one extreme, method study may so fragment a production process that the tasks of individual work-people become simple, repetitive, and undemanding. An intriguing question facing the training psychologist is how tasks may be designed to involve, arouse and maintain interest without unacceptable losses in production efficiency (Davis, 1957, 1966; Scott, 1966). There is some evidence that it may be possible to do this, although it is not easily achieved and maintained (Hill and Thickett, 1966).

CONTRIBUTION OF PROGRAMMED INSTRUCTION

After some initial hesitations programmed instruction has gained widespread support in education and occupational training alike. The influence of Skinner in promoting programmed instruction is now part of the history of the movement. Directly and indirectly his influence on approaches to task analysis has been considerable.

Emphasising that the first concern of education is the behaviour of students rather than the behaviour of teachers, Skinner focused attention on 'entry' and 'terminal' behaviour. Both must be specified—that is, responses already 'in the repertory' and the responses which define mastery—if progress from the one to the other is to be programmed. One of the basic programming concepts advanced by Skinner was 'shaping', that is, selectively reinforcing the variety of responses initially emitted, and in this way shifting the pattern of responses by successive approximations towards the desired terminal performance.

It has been argued, notably by Lumsdaine (1962) and Cook (1963) that this emphasis on reinforcing *emitted* (i.e. spontaneously occurring) responses is misplaced when considering human learning, and that the programmer's problem is how to *elicit* required responses. A more appropriate model, therefore, might be classical or *respondent* conditioning rather than *operant* conditioning with

which Skinner is mainly concerned. Possibly because of his preoccupation with manipulating reinforcement, Skinner has contribu-
ted little to the problem of eliciting the variety of novel responses
entailed in most human learning under programmed instruction.
His emphasis on the specification of entry and terminal behaviour
has, however, been a crucial contribution.

Behavioural analysis

Systematic attempts to bridge the gap between stated entry and
terminal behaviour were soon made. One approach retains operant
conditioning as the basic model and attempts to characterise
different kinds of behaviour in these terms. Thus programmed
learning of a *concept* involves *specifying* a set of exemplars, a
set of stimuli to which the student must make the *same* response,
e.g. 'is a vertebrate', 'is an equilateral triangle'. It also involves
specifying instances which novices may mistakenly take as
exemplars and for which they must learn alternative responses or
discriminations, e.g. 'is an invertebrate', 'is an isosceles triangle'.
Conceptual learning is thus operationally defined as generalisation within a class and discrimination between classes. This is
illustrated by Mechner's (1965) analysis of one of the skills of
interpreting electrocardiograph traces, an example of which
concludes Chapter 3. According to this view, learning to solve
problems entails learning the concepts at each choice point in a
branching sequence, and mastery is reached when the links between each choice have been learned or when the correct 'chaining'
of concepts has been established (Mechner, 1965 and 1967).

Chaining and the identification of chains, i.e. of sequences of
responses, is a central idea in the system described by Gilbert,
another writer who seeks to extend the model of operant conditioning to task, or *behavioural* analysis, to use the term preferred
by those whose orientation is primarily to Skinnerian reinforcement principles. *Table 2.2* illustrates the chaining of responses
involved in performing long division. An important point is
Gilbert's insistence that the responses in a chain should be brought
to mastery *retrogressively*. That is to say, that prompts should be
withdrawn from the last response, then from the next to the last
response, and so on. (Note that the idea is not that the student
should perform responses backwards, in fact responses are always
performed, prompted or not, in the correct order.) Gilbert relies on
reinforcement theory to support this recommendation. He argues
that the last response is the one which is most easily reinforced
initially because completing the sequence is rewarding. Similarly,

the response which is most easily reinforced once the final one is mastered is the immediately preceding response, because it is then most directly linked to the rewarding experience of completing the sequence (Gilbert, 1962).

Table 2.2 Exercises in long division (simplified) designed
on the mathetical exercise model. (Gilbert, 1962)

---

1. DIVIDE 45 BY 11
   Here is what you do: (a) Since 4 × 11 is 44,   4
                              the 44 is placed   11)45
                              under the dividend ⟶   44
   Now complete the long division: ⟶
                          (b) Subtract 44 from 45
                              to get the remainder ....

---

2. DIVIDE 28 BY 12
   Here is what you do: (a) 12 goes into 28 *2 whole times*
                          (b) Multiply the divisor   2
                              by the quotient (12 × 2)   12)28
                              and put the product
                              under the dividend
                          (c) Subtract to get the remainder

---

3. DIVIDE 33 BY 15
                          (a) 15 goes into 33 *2 whole times*
                          (b) Put the 2 in place above the line
                          (c) Multiply the divisor
                              by the quotient and   15)33
                              put the product in
                              its place
                          (d) Complete the division

The principle of retrogressive chaining has not, in the event, been supported by empirical studies (Cox and Boren, 1965; Johnson and Senter, 1965; Hartley and Woods, 1968; Duncan, 1969). Nevertheless, inherent in Gilbert's system for analysing tasks, (which he calls Mathetics), is the important principle that specific conditions may be required for the most efficient learning of a *class* of tasks or task components, in this case the retrogressive withdrawal of prompts for learning chains. This point is taken up later, when the whole question is discussed of a 'task taxonomy' to specify training methods.

Subject matter structure

Behaviour analysis as expounded by such writers as Gilbert and Mechner seems to imply that learning concepts and rules simply entails mastering a 'behavioural catalogue' of exemplars and non-exemplars—'A concept is defined in terms of its instances, members and manifestations . . . behavioural analysis of a concept lists appropriate instances and non-instances' (Mechner and Cook, 1964). That rules, as such, may be learned, together with suitable exemplification, and may therefore be programmed, was proposed by a more eclectic group of programmers (Evans, Homme and Glaser, 1962) in their account of the 'ruleg' system of programming. The ruleg system was the first significant attempt at fragmenting and structuring major learning tasks without necessarily having recourse to existing laboratory based models of learning. Structure, and hence sequencing, is sought in the subject matter itself. All subject matter, it is proposed, may be said to consist of rules (*ru's*), and examples (*e.g's*). Glaser (1962) writes:

> The rules should, after a preliminary ordering, be arranged in a matrix. . . . This matrix is based on the conception that an expert in a particular domain of knowledge manifests his expertness by an ability to integrate the concepts in his field. The *ru* matrix permits the examination of similarities, differences, and possible confusions between the rules and other interverbal connections which must be learned by the student. Upon this matrix we can impose different operators for interrelating the *ru's*. For example a very general operator is *relation*. We might ask how rule 1 is related to rule 2 and how rule 2 is related to rule 1. Some cells will be of no consequence and some cells will be redundant, but we might attain some systematic structuring of the knowledge domain. The diagonal cells, which relate each rule to itself, can be called *definition* cells, in which a particular rule is explained in terms of previous behaviour that exists in the student, so that the definition can be made meaningful in terms of his existing repertoire. Another operator might be *discrimination,* in which we can ask, for any particular cell, how one rule is different from another; this may facilitate discrimination training.

In the United Kingdom, the ruleg system is best known from the version presented by Thomas *et al.* (1963). This contains many worked examples illustrating the central importance of the *ru* matrix (*see Figure 2.3*). The exposition is so well done that no further comment is necessary, except perhaps to say that the generality of the original notion, i.e. that there may be many possible operators on a matrix, seems to have been lost in Thomas and his associates' account.

D

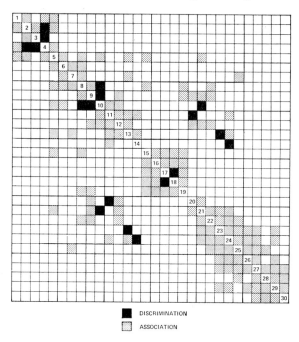

Figure 2.3. The final matrix for an electricity program (Thomas et al., 1963)

At about the same time as the ruleg system was being developed, Gagné (1962) set out another approach to the problem of the macro-structure of subject-matter and the deduction of learning sequences. Perhaps the most important feature of Gagné's method is that it proceeds from a general statement of what is required from the student to enquire what sub-tasks he must be capable of performing to meet this requirement. By successively applying this enquiry to the sub-tasks, and then to their sub-tasks and so on, Gagné finally arrives at those basic abilities which he suggests underlie most complex learned behaviour. Be that as it may, Gagné's technique lays bare the learning which must intervene between terminal behaviour and any given entry behaviour. The technique is also said to indicate the sequence of learning which, in general, is the *reverse* of the sequence of the analysis.

Deriving learning sequences

This intriguing notion that the learning sequence may be prescribed by the structure of the subject-mattter is common to

1 An electric charge is produced by friction
2 The electron is the basic unit of charge
3 The electron is an impractical unit of charge
4 The coulomb is the practical unit of charge
5 Current is a flow of charge
6 Current is measured in coulombs per second
7 One coulomb per second is called an ampere
8 When current flows work is done
9 Energy is used when work is done
10 Energy must be supplied for current to flow
11 Electromotive force is a measure of the rate at which energy is supplied
12 Energy is measured in joules
13 Electromotive force is the rate of supply of energy per unit current
14 The unit of electromotive force is the volt
15 Current meets resistance in flowing through a load
16 The resistance depends upon the nature of the load
17 Materials offering little resistance are termed conductors
18 Materials offering very great resistance are termed insulators
19 In overcoming resistance work is done
20 The energy used in moving a charge is proportional to the size of the charge
21 The rate at which energy is used is proportional to the rate at which charge flows
22 The rate at which energy is used is proportional to the current
23 Potential difference is the rate at which energy is used per unit current
24 The unit of potential difference must be the volt
25 Experiment
26 Potential difference is proportional to current
27 Potential difference equals current multiplied by a constant
28 The constant is resistance
29 Resistance equals potential difference divided by current
30 Unit of resistance is the ohm

Gagné's technique and the ruleg system. However, it needs some qualification. In the first place, the prescription of a *unique* sequence will not always be possible. It seems reasonable to assert that (a) oral production of words and (b) recognition of printed letters by sound must both precede (c) recognition of printed words by sound (*see Figure 2.4*). However, there is no requirement in Gagné's representation for (a) to precede (b) or *vice versa*. Indeed, there may sometimes be several possible sequences for the same subject-matter—for example, work at Birmingham University (Leith, 1968) found several possible pathways through an Ohm's Law lesson represented in the *ru* matrix by Thomas *et al.* (1963).

What happens if the order which the structure of the subject-matter seems to indicate is in some way violated in an instructional sequence? Part of the difficulty in designing experiments to answer this general question is that it is often difficult, if not impossible, to find sequences which may be taken as adequate controls. Such control sequences should both be intelligible and yet violate the sequence indicated by the subject-matter structure. Some investigators have simply compared structured with random sequences; others have checked that their control sequences were in some sense reasonable learning tasks. An impressive number of

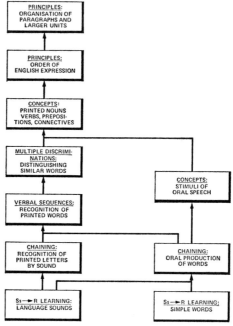

Figure 2.4. A learning structure for the basic skills of reading (From The Conditions of Learning *by Robert M. Gagné. Copyright © 1965 by Holt, Rinehart and Winston, Inc. Reprinted by permission of Holt, Rinehart and Winston, Inc., Publishers, New York)*

such investigations have failed to demonstrate the effect of differences between sequences in overall learning efficiency (e.g., Roe, Case and Roe, 1962; Levine and Baker, 1963; Payne, Krathwohl and Gordon, 1967; Pyatte, 1969).

One of the most thoroughgoing investigations of the relation between subject-matter structure and learning sequence was carried out by Hickey and Newton (1964). These authors report that throughout the analysis of the 'logic space' (*see Figure 2.5*), and the specifications of sequence variables, they were haunted by the question 'Will it make any difference?' In the event, this degree of thoroughness did generate sequences in an economics program which differed significantly. In this case sequences which stated principles first were superior, and the evidence suggested that learning several sub-concepts first was hazardous, especially if some were learned at a point in the sequence remote from the learning of the major concept. The impression from Hickey and Newton's work, which persists in the face of subsequent experimentation, is that although deriving improved sequences from subject-matter structure is undoubtedly possible, the analysis of structure must probably be very sophisticated indeed if it is to reveal useful differences in sequencing.

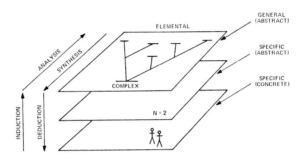

Figure 2.5. A model of the logic space (From Hickey and Newton, 1964, Courtesy: Entelek Ltd)

If deriving a sequence from subject-matter structure is not at all easy, and if there are sometimes several sequences indicated by the structure, is there any other criterion by which a sequence may be selected? In a now famous investigation Mager demonstrated that *the sequence preferred by the learner* may depart dramatically from that considered by the instructor to be inherent in the logic of the subject-matter (Mager, 1961). Students of electronics who were persuaded to control the order in which this subject was taught to them wanted to learn something about the 'vacuum tube' at or near the beginning of the sequence. As Mager points out, the 'logical' beginning to an electronics course from the point of view of the instructor, i.e. with magnetism or electron theory, is not the 'logical' beginning for the novice. For the novice it *is* logical to begin with the vacuum tube 'because to him vacuum tube and electronics mean one and the same thing'. Mager's subjects had other preferences which one suspects are fairly general and are fairly generally ignored when courses are planned. They were primarily interested in function and only secondarily in structure, e.g.

> ... learners wanted to hear that a picture was formed by causing an electron beam to be pulled back and forth across the screen many times a second, and that the light and dark portions of

the picture were caused by turning the electron beam on and
off at the appropriate time. Only when this general description
was offered would S show any interest in the fact that this
electron beam is moved back and forth by deflection coils located
on the neck of the picture tube (Mager, 1961).

Taxonomies

It was noted in the references to *Mathetics* that an important
feature of this system was its assumption of category-specific learning conditions, that is, the notion that components of performance
can be classified in such a way as to identify the conditions under
which they will best be learned. It will be remembered that, for
'chains', i.e. tasks or sub-tasks in which responses are required in
an invariant sequence, Gilbert (1962) advocated a specific
programming technique, namely the retrogressive fading of prompts.

A taxonomy or scheme of performance classification, which
would *specify the ideal learning conditions for each of its categories,*
is an extremely attractive proposition. For instance, it seems plausible to assume that the formal similarities between the skill of a
doctor and a radio repairman—symptom interpretation, search,
component adjustment, replacement and repair—should require
essentially similar training techniques. Manifestly the *content* of
training would differ, but it seems reasonable to expect instructional *method* which succeeds with electronic troubleshooting to
be equally successful with medical diagnosis.

Unfortunately, the promise of the taxonomic strategy of task
analysis has not yet been fulfilled. Taxonomies have proliferated
alarmingly (for a bibliography the reader is referred to Annett
and Duncan, 1967), so it is important to be clear about the
criteria to be met by a satisfactory taxonomy. Clearly, the major
criterion to be met is a set of categories which have demonstrably
different optimum learning conditions. Less important, though
nevertheless desirable, are two main *systematic* criteria which should
be met by a taxonomy, namely, that the categories should be
mutually exclusive and *exhaustive.*

It is questionable whether even the systematic criteria have been
met in the various attempts at a workable taxonomy. Cotterman
(1959), E. E. Miller (1963), Stolurow (1964), and Gagné (1965a
and 1965b), have all attempted to meet the criterion that categories
should be mutually exclusive by careful formal definition. Gagné,
for instance, defines his categories in language of this sort: 'Upon
presentation of two or more potentially confusable stimuli (physically defined), make an equal number of different responses which

differentially identify these stimuli, and no other responses' (*multiple discrimination*). The second systematic criterion, exhaustiveness of the list of categories, has been dealt with in two main ways. An approach taken by Cotterman (1959) and Stolurow (1964) was to carry out massive surveys of the range of tasks in the learning and training research literature. Folley (1964b) and E. E. Miller (1963) adopted another, less effortful, expedient of including a catch-all category defined to include any behaviour not otherwise classified. It seems that, for some time at least, any attempts at classification will, in the event, be subject to inevitable additions and re-formulations. Thus, the four categories proposed by Gagné and Bolles (1959) were later increased by Gagné (1965a and 1965b), first to six and then to eight.

Of the many attempts to meet the major criterion for a training taxonomy, the longstanding attack on the problem by R. B. Miller (1953, 1962a, 1966) is especially deserving of attention, particularly from military and industrial training officers. Over the years, Miller has proposed several slightly varying schemes for codifying the processes which may intervene between environmental events and the responses of skilled men, e.g. *scanning, search* and *detection* of cues; *identification* of cues; *short* and *long-term retention* of task information; *interpretation, decision making* and *problem solving*.

Miller avowedly adopts utility over other criteria for his categories. He is not concerned if the training implications are the same for more than one category provided that they are *identified*. Thus, the notion of time sharing is one with a training implication which *cuts across* his categories. Only procedure-following and 'automatised' components of tasks will not suffer interference when time shared, and he argues, probably rightly, that task components which do suffer, e.g. scanning and searching, short-term recall and decision making, should all be proceduralised when time shared with another activity. Again, much of Miller's discussion of the training implications of his categories amounts to illustrating difficulties rather than pointing to category-specific learning conditions. Thus Miller's system presents a detailed annotation of different task difficulties and possible training solutions rather than a system in which training recommendations distinguish sharply or systematically between behaviour categories. For example, the main point of his discussion of 'search for job relevant cues' and 'short-term recall' (1962a) is in both cases simply to *practise* with those materials and in those situations which are peculiar to the task in question.

Perhaps the most thorough attempt to meet the major criterion

Table 2.3 Categories of behaviour differing in formal characteristics relating to ease of learning, including preconditions of the learner and conditions of the instructional situation. (From Gagné, 1965a, Courtesy: National Education Association)

Behaviour Category	Behaviour Description	Preconditions of the Learner	Conditions of Instructional Situation
Response Differentiation	Response controlled by discriminated stimulus (most frequently, echoic)		Contiguity of S^D and R
Association	Specific stimulus related by coding to a particular response	Discrimination of stimulus by observing response: differentiation of response; a pre-learned coding	Contiguity of S^D, coding stimulus, and R
Multiple Discrimination (Identification)	Two or more specific stimuli call out an equal number of different responses	Individual associations; differentiation of responses	Make the stimuli highly distinctive
Behaviour Chains (Sequences)	Two or more acts to be completed in a specific order	Individual associations; multiple discriminations among members of the chain	Begin with high-strength acts, associate these with low-strength acts in order
Class Concepts	Responses made to stimuli of a class, differing in appearance	Individual associations; multiple discriminations as necessary	Present sufficient variety of stimuli to insure generalisation
Principles	Chaining of at least two concepts: if a, then b	Concepts	Insure availability of concepts, encourage constructed responses
Strategies	Chaining of concepts	Concepts which determine selective attention and mediate responses	Insure availability of concepts, encourage constructed responses

for a task taxonomy is the scheme worked out by Gagné (1965a) (*see Table 2.3*). In a more extensive treatment (Gagné, 1965b) the relative positions of *multiple discriminations* and *chains* in the hierarchy are reversed. The model was later represented (Gagné, 1968) by the diagram in *Figure 2.6*, and the abridged statements in *Table 2.4* were taken from a more recent paper by Gagné (1969) in which he summarises the main features of his categories.

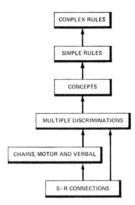

Figure 2.6. A general sequence for cumulative learning (From Gagné, 1968, Courtesy: American Psychological Association)

Gagné's taxonomy places categories in a hierarchy. Each category has not only different optimum learning conditions, but also different *preconditions*, e.g. learning a rule of the form 'if *a* then *b*' should be preceded by learning the concepts *a* and *b*. So again we encounter an important feature of Gagné's strategy of task analysis, namely, the appeal to a hierarchy to indicate the *sequencing* of instruction. Learning is usually slow, he argues, only because several levels of performance are typically being trained at the same time, which, since optimum conditions differ between levels, must necessarily be inefficient.

The work of Miller and Gagné on task taxonomy has been described because, of the numerous classification schemes which have been proposed, theirs are representative and possibly the best worked out. However, one more is included because it is concise, rich in category specific instructional suggestions, and fairly recent (Leith, 1968). *Table 2.5* shows Leith's proposed classification of learning tasks and the panel (*Table 2.6*) contains extracts from his discussion of the instructional problems of the categories.

Good agreement between independent analysts specifying train-

Table 2.4 Categories of learning. (From Gagné, 1969, Courtesy: Dunod Press)

1. *Motor Skill*

This kind of learning may be exemplified by the task undertaken by an adult learning to pronounce a letter sound which does not occur in his native language. An American . . . acquiring the proper pronunciation of the French 'u', . . . is acquiring a new motor skill. The capacity for making this sound correctly is present, but the particular movements of throat and facial muscles has not previously been used to make this sound. There appears to be no formal difference between such learning and other motor skills, such as, the skill of firing a gun . . .

2. *Verbal Sequences*

. . . 'verbal rules' and 'verbal maxims' are learned, and may be of some usefulness to us in remembering things, and in communication with other people. For example, a rule for automobile driving is, 'car on the right has the right of way'. The easy recall of this verbal statement may be quite useful in many situations, and widely generalisable in this verbal form as a memorised rule. Another kind of rule is the verbal sequence of numerals that gives the value of pi—three point one four one six—obviously a widely memorised verbal sequence which has only one meaning and many uses.

3. *Discriminations*

. . . children learn to make finer and finer distinctions among colours, shapes, textures, and many other object properties . . . adults can, and often do, learn new discriminations also—when called upon, they are quite capable of learning to make finer discriminations of colours, tones, tactile stimuli, odours, tastes, and many other kinds of discriminations. Children must apparently learn at an early age a number of common discriminations to a reasonable degree of fineness, and then they can function quite well in pursuing further learning . . .

4. *Concepts*

In its fundamental meaning, one learns a concept when one acquires a common response (often, a name) for an entire class of objects or events, the individual members of which may not be physically similar to each other.

A concept is learned when the individual is able to identify object properties,

Table 2.4 (con't)

for example, such as blue, round, hard, heavy, etc. Each of these properties, which may occur in some particular combinations in any given object, must previously have been discriminated, in order for it to function as an effective stimulus in the learning of a concept. Concepts are learned when a sufficient variety of instances of the class have been presented to the learner and he has responded to each with a common response (or class name).

It is necessary also to recognise . . . abstract concepts, sometimes characterised as relationships, that are learned by means of definition . . . abstract concepts are formally similar to principles . . . Examples of abstract concepts are 'father', 'uncle', also physical concepts like 'mass' and 'density'.

5. *Principles*

The learning of a principle involves the formation of a sequence of concepts or similar principles. The principle 'Fish live in water' to take a simple example, is a combination of the concepts 'fish,' 'live,' 'in' and 'water,' and may be considered to be learned when the individual can identify each of these concepts and put them in the proper order. The principle that force is a product of mass and acceleration is similarly composed of concepts that must be placed in the proper sequence. Usually, the test of whether a learner has acquired a principle is carried out by asking him to demonstrate with a particular example. For instance, one may present him with a particular mass and a particular acceleration, and ask him to find the particular force. . . .

6. *Problem Solving*

. . problem solving is an event in which two or more subordinate principles are 'put together' to achieve a more general principle. For example, the learner who knows what multiplying means, as one principle, and what an exponent means, as another principle, may be able to solve the problem, 'What is X^3 times X^2' for himself. He may be able to 'figure out' the more complex principle that 'to express the power to which a variable must be raised when it is the product of identical variables each raised to a power, add the exponents.' . . . an important category of principle called a *strategy* . . . governs the individual's own behaviour. Strategies can guide thinking . . . can guide learning . . . can be of unusual significance for education, one of whose aims must surely be to make the individual into an independent learner and thinker.

ing for the same job should be made possible by an adequate
taxonomy. To some extent careful definition of behaviour categories should help to reduce variations from analyst to analyst—
though it is for serious consideration whether the language used in
some definitions will make them unambiguous to an industrial or

Table 2.5 Suggestions for a taxonomy of learning (From Leith, 1968)

Types of Learning Activities	Methods of Facilitating Learning	
1. Stimulus discrimination	(a)	Emphatic cues
	(b)	Distinctive names
	(c)	Fading
2. Response learning	(a)	Practice with feedback
	(b)	Tips on how to make the response
	(c)	Errors to be avoided
3. Response integration	(a)	Practice
	(b)	Symbolic mediators (learner's own are best)
4. Trial and error learning	(a)	Personal trials
	(b)	Errors important to eliminate inappropriate responses
	(c)	Feedback
5. Learning set formation	(a)	Personal discovery
	(b)	Feedback
	(c)	Practice on each problem to criterion of mastery
	(d)	Variety of problems
	(e)	Making errors important (response elimination)
6. Concept learning		Trials with feedback to learner
7. Concept integration	(a)	Structuring of sequence
	(b)	Direct instruction/individual construction with feedback
	(c)	Sometimes random presentation helpful
8. Hypothetico-deductive inference (problem-solving)	(a)	Practice in framing and testing hypotheses
	(b)	Feedback
	(c)	Guidance
9. Learning schemata		Presentation of conflict situations needed to promote formation of higher-order structures

military training officer. Of the many advocates of task analysis
only Stolurow (1964), as far as the writer is aware, has made an
attempt to assess the reliability of his scheme. Stolurow had eight
psychologists, all distinguished in the training research field, independently analyse descriptions of tasks taken from the 'method'
sections of journal articles. Their agreement was less than perfect!
More studies of this kind, using descriptions of real-life tasks, are

Table 2.6 Learning conditions for the different categories (From Leith, 1968)

1. *Stimulus Discrimination* for example can be made easier by emphasising differences, fading cues . . . by giving distinctive names to the stimuli to be distinguished.

2. *Response Learning* needs practice and feedback. It is at this level of learning that shaping . . . is helpful . . . advice on how to achieve the response (both do's and dont's) . . . Examples would be making the 'll' sound in Welsh, the Xhosa 'click', or teaching a child to whistle.

3. *Response Integration* . . . assembling already learned responses in particular ways is also a case for practice. Interference from previously learned integrations may have to be overcome. Hook-up . . . can be facilitated by the use of mediating associations but these should probably be the learner's own.

4. *Trial and Error Learning*—by definition falls outside the discussion of programmed instruction . . . is a component of learning set formation. It can give rise to superstitious behaviour as in the case of a gorilla learning to open a box . . . By accident the animal nudged the hasp with its rear end and opened the box. The response learned was that of backing towards the box.

5. *Learning Set Formation* . . . is effected by giving (a) sufficient trials to solve individual problems and (b) a wide range of different problems . . . Whether order of problems is important is not clear. Some types of learner, I have found, learn to transfer if given a random arrangement of problems (i.e. those within a set being distributed also) while others respond best to a high degree of organisation. It can also be suggested that learning to learn involves the making of errors (to eliminate incorrect responses).

6. *Concepts* . . . The possession of a concept can be demonstrated by correct discrimination of exemplars and non-exemplars (i.e. implicit use of a rule) and also by explicit formulation of rules. As with a learning set one may acquire the 'know how' to operate correctly without being able to explain the criteria used. On the other hand it may be possible to give concise symbolic formulation of the rules involved . . .

7. *Concept Integration.* Concepts may overlap, be complementary, or mutually exclusive. They can be joined together to form additive, disjunctive and implicative concepts as well as having hierarchical relationships . . . The point is that networks and hierarchies of concepts forming propositions having logical and contingent relationships to each other, are capable of being learned and remembered with precision or of becoming confused and telescoped . . . . Their existence may help or hinder the learning of new concepts and integrations . . .

8. *Hypothetico-deductive Inference.* This is the kind of problem-solving in which a hypothesis is put forward, testable inferences are made and their validity is assessed . . . Availability of relevant notions, flexibility in interrelating them and ability to evaluate are prerequisites . . . review of related concepts practice forming relationships and learning of techniques, like leaving a problem for a time may be helpful.

9. *Learning Schemata.* 'Schema' is used in the Piaget sense to mean a general framework of mental operations . . . There is some evidence that in learning a schema conflict with existing schemes is beneficial.

badly needed, since no method, however valid on logical grounds or in the light of research, will be *empirically* valid unless it is reliable.

Performance hierarchies

The notion of performance hierarchies provides one of the most powerful models for the systematic analysis of tasks. A detailed justification of this assertion will be attempted in the last sections of this chapter. Meanwhile, something of the scope of this approach may be conveyed by a brief digression in which a hierarchical model is compared and contrasted with a rival view of the development of mental skills. In recent years, Anglo-Saxon educationists have discovered Piaget, so it may be illuminating to examine an argument in which Gagné (1968) sets out to explain how, in his terms, a child may master tasks which Piaget has used as demonstrations of the principle of 'conservation'. Gagné begins by asking:

> Can a cumulative learning sequence be described for a task like the conservation of liquid, as studied by Piaget (*see* Piaget and Inhelder, 1964)? Suppose we consider as a task the matching of volumes of liquids in rectangular containers like those shown. ... (*see Figure 2.7*)
> ... When the liquid in A is poured into Container B, many children (at some particular age levels) say that the taller Container B has more liquid. Similarly, in the second line of the figure, children of particular ages have been found to say that the volume in the shallower Container B, exhibiting a larger surface area, is the greater.
> What is it these children need to have learned, in order to respond correctly to such situations as these? From the standpoint of the cumulative learning model, they need to have learned a great many things. ... (*see Figure 2.8*)

Gagné goes on to point out that 'conservation of liquid' is not, as it stands, an operational statement of behaviour. However, it may be given a particular behavioural *interpretation,* as Gagné has done in this case, i.e. 'judging equalities and inequalities of volumes of liquids in rectangular containers'. He is also careful to point out that the cumulative learning of the task in *Figure 2.8* is not the only possible structure for mastery of the task. However, once the learning task has been stated in this general form it seems clear that *how* children learn to master such problems, or how mastery is best trained, are essentially *empirical* questions. It remains to be seen whether the work of Piaget or Gagné (or, more likely, confrontations of this kind) will generate the research needed to develop efficient instruction in abstract operations and

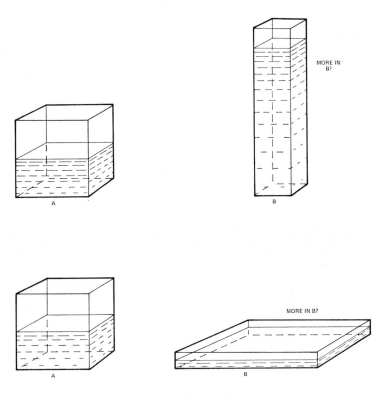

Figure 2.7. Two tasks of 'conservation of liquid' of the sort used by Piaget and other investigators (From Gagné, 1968, Courtesy: American Psychological Association)

problem solving tasks. The conclusion of Gagné's argument is illustrated in *Figure 2.9.*

Suppose the learner ... has acquired all four of the specific conservation principles shown in the bottom row—dealing with conservation of number, conservation of liquid volumes in both rectangular and cylindrical containers, and conservation of solid volumes. Others could be added, such as conservation of weight, but these will do for the present purposes. . . . By *combining* the principles applicable to rectangular containers, and others applicable to cylindrical containers, a learner could easily acquire a capability of estimating volumes of irregularly shaped containers. Other kinds of combinations of previously acquired knowledge are surely possible.... If the external observer assumes that because he can make this classification of such an entity as a principle of conservation, the same entity must therefore exist as a part of the learner's capabilities, he is very likely making a serious mistake. The learner has only the specific principles he has learned, along with their potentialities for transfer.

I believe that many of the principles mentioned by Piaget,

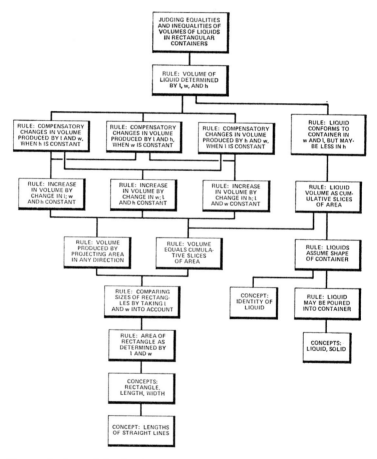

Figure 2.8. A cumulative learning sequence pertaining to the development of nonmetric judgments of liquid volume (From Gagné, 1968, Courtesy: American Psychological Association)

including such things as reversibility, seriation and the groupings of logical operations, are abstractions of this sort. They are useful descriptions of intellectual processes, and they are obviously in Piaget's mind. But they are not in the child's mind.

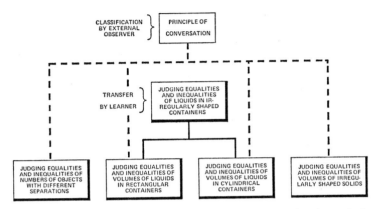

Figure 2.9. The contrast between a principle acquired by the learner through transfer from previously learned principles, and a 'principle of conservation' used as a classificatory aid by an external observer (From Gagné, 1968, Courtesy: American Psychological Association)

This digression does not of course do justice to the work of Piaget. To do so would be beyond the abilities of this writer, who is convinced of the need for a lucid, authoritative statement of the implications of Piaget's work for *instruction,* who is equally convinced that such a text has still to be written, and who, for these reasons, regards the enthusiasm for the Geneva research program, which is current in some educational circles, as uncritical if not retrograde.

But returning to Gagné's earlier (1965a and 1965b) formulations of task analysis—it has been convincingly argued that the organised behaviour which we variously describe as 'experienced', 'expert' or 'skilled' probably is a hierarchy of sub-routines (Miller, Galanter and Pribram, 1960; Fitts, 1964). It seems doubtful, however, that performance categories will be observed in the same hierarchical order in *every* task, as Gagné assumes, e.g. that the organisation of cues and responses called *class concepts* or *generalisation* (i.e. the same response to a *set* of cues) will always be found at a higher level in the structure of a task than the organisation of cues and responses called chains (i.e. an invariant sequence of cues and responses). In the analysis of an industrial task described in the next section, the relative positions of these two categories

E

in the task hierarchy is in fact the reverse of that in Gagné's scheme (1965a and 1965b). The task includes a long chain, the starting up of a distillation column in a chemical plant. Most of the subordinate steps in the chain involve 'multiple discriminations' of control instrument nomenclature and locations, although many require the identification of 'bypass' and 'isolating' valves, classes of plant controls whose appearance and position in the configuration of feed lines vary widely, but whose *function* is the same. Each thus constitutes a set of cues requiring the same response, i.e. by Gagné's definition, a concept. A further point is the relative positions of the chain and multiple discriminations in the hierarchy of this task: these are consistent with Gagné's earlier (1965a) account of his scheme but not with his subsequent (1965b) revised scheme.

The value of the hierarchical notion might be considerably extended if the superordinate/subordinate relations between the categories, i.e. chains, multiple discriminations, concepts, etc. were not assumed to be fixed, but rather that their relative positions might vary from task to task. On this assumption, the major value of a hierarchical model, its sequencing implications, is retained.

A STRATEGY FOR ANALYSING INDUSTRIAL TASKS

On the assumption that a task may be represented as a hierarchy of *operations* and *sub-operations,* a recently advanced strategy proposes that analysis should proceed by successive redescription (Annett and Duncan, 1967 and 1968). Performance is first described in general terms, then redescribed in more detail, i.e. broken down into subordinate operations, to arrive at training requirements.

One of the reasons for this approach has already been mentioned. In practice it is difficult, if not impossible, to determine *a priori* what is an appropriate level of description for the different components of a task. For example, for operations involving an ergonomically satisfactory control panel and flow diagram, 'follow standard shut-down procedure' could be an appropriate level of description. However, other operations in the same task might require more detailed descriptions of procedure, such as 'first stop feed from hopper number three', or 'when both level indicators show bin is empty, switch off vibrator', etc. For some operations successive, increasingly detailed statements may be envisaged, such as 'hold the switch up for at least fifteen seconds', or 'turn the wheel three and a half turns anti-clockwise', or still more detailed statements of limb, hand, or finger positioning. In principle, the process of redescription may cease anywhere between the most general statement of performance and physiological or anatomical details.

Task analysis should, ideally, provide the most concise statement of what operations are entailed in performing the task, where an operation is a statement of performance in just sufficient detail either for it to be trained, or for the decision that training is unnecessary. If this requirement is to be met, then a rule is necessary by which the analyst may decide either that an operation has not been stated in sufficient detail, or that an appropriate level of description has been reached and analysis may cease. The strategy proposed by Annett and Duncan advocates a rule which considers the probability of the man performing an operation inadequately without training—p, and the cost to the system of inadequate performance—c. If the best available estimates of these values are together unacceptable, and if the training required for acceptable performance is not clear, the operation is broken down into subordinate operations. Each of the subordinate operations is then subjected to the same decision rule and so on. In this way flexibility in degree of detail is made possible since analysis may cease at a number of different levels for different sections or sub units of the same task.

It is envisaged that, more often than not, the values of p and c will be judged subjectively. In practice, just how exactly p and c are measured will depend on the importance of the training scheme—'analysis and training should not be pressed beyond the point . . . when they begin to cost more than they save' (Kay, 1968). It is suggested that when deciding whether or not to re-describe, the analyst, if in doubt, should always err on the gross side. For example, there will often be statements of performance with implicit sub-routines which will be clear to the trainee population. Statements beginning with the word 'check' sometimes belong to this category, e.g. 'check the drain valve is closed'. Sub-routines such as 'if the drain valve is *open, then close* it' will not often need spelling out.

In the first instance, then, one should not pursue the analysis into more detail than seems absolutely essential. This is a self-correcting procedure, since it will usually be plain, when training is being designed, if further analysis of a task component is necessary. In the last resort, training will prove impossible to implement. On the other hand, an unnecessarily detailed analysis and unnecessarily detailed and lengthy training will usually be work-

able and will, for that reason, be less easily detected. A further
consideration when deciding whether an operation has been
described in sufficient detail, or that analysis should cease, may be
that a point has been reached where no further *verbal* exposition
is likely to clarify the training problem. Kinaesthetic and tactual
difficulty, for instance, is not adequately described in words.
Indeed, difficulty at any level of description is not necessarily
best stated in words; in some situations, diagrams, sound, or video
records will be both more economical and effective.

An application of hierarchical task analysis

Figure 2.10 illustrates the author's application of this method to a
continuous process control task in a chemical plant. At the first,
most general, level of description, controlling this acid purification process consists of procedural skills, required in starting-up
and shutting-down the plant, and problem solving skills required
for fault location during continuous running of the process. In
addition, operators are responsible for logging instrument readings
at fixed intervals (operation 8).

The procedures by which a unit of the plant is started up or
shut down (operations 5, 6, 7, 11, 12 and 13 in *Figure 2.10*)
are long fixed sequences—between thirty and fifty steps in the
case of the start-up procedures. Mastery of the correct *order* is
thus the training problem in the case of these operations. In
contrast, the problem solving operations of correcting and reporting faults require the operator to *choose* between several alternative actions.

In one of the fault location operations, (operation 140 in *Figure
2.10*), the operator must interpret the various control room console
instrument readings when alarms indicate a plant failure, e.g.
failure of a pump, or an empty feed tank, or failure of a steam
supply, and quickly decide *which* of ten subordinate operations is
appropriate. Plant failures produce readings on pressure,
temperature, level and flow instruments in the control room,
which are markedly higher or lower than normal—i.e. there is no
difficulty in deciding whether a given reading is a symptom or
not. Some control room instruments are linked to alarm panels
which flash when readings move outside preset high or low limits.
The onset of a flashing panel is accompanied by a buzzer which
must be 'acknowledged' by pressing a button (operation 139 in
Figure 2.10). This stops the buzzer and the flashing but the panel
remains lit until the associated temperature, pressure, flow or level
returns to normal. In some cases the operator can restore normal

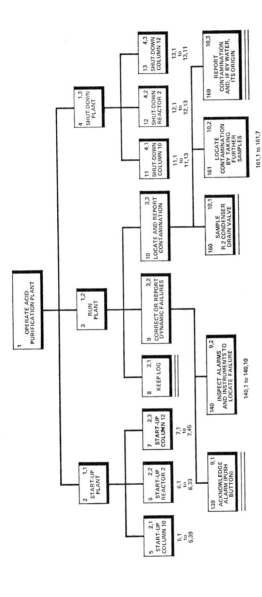

(Operation 140 is expanded in Figure 2.11)

Figure 2.10. Main operations in the acid purification task. Under a box is either a set of numbers indicating subordinated operations, (thus operation 5, start-up Column 10, has 39 sub-operations) or underlining to indicate that analysis has ceased. Double underlining is used to indicate that probability of inadequate performance and attendant costs are acceptable, single underlining to indicate that training required for adequate performance is clear

conditions if he correctly interprets the console symptoms, e.g. by switching the flow from a defective pump to a 'stand-by' pump. However, if the failure is not corrected quickly, the process will either run down or essential conditions such as temperature and flow will move so far out of tolerance that the purification process ceases. A shut-down of continuous process plant is, of course, expensive. The ten dynamic failures may each cause one or more alarms and, initially, as many as seven abnormal instrument readings, though skilled diagnosis will never use more than four indications, and often only one.

The second fault location operation is rather different in character. Periodically the operator sends samples of pure product for laboratory quality control analysis. A common adverse laboratory report is of water contamination. There are various other adverse reports but these the operator *reports* to his supervisor—an activity requiring neither analysis nor training (operation 169 in *Figure 2.10*). In the case of water contamination, the experienced operator will determine its origin by taking further samples of product at different points on the plant. He must decide, taking account of further laboratory reports, an appropriate *sequence* of possible sampling operations. This search problem (operation 161) was described earlier in the chapter.

The major components of the task so far described, the procedures which start up and shut down the plant and the problem solving in locating plant failures, all depend on subordinate operations which the novice must master. Unlike the novice assembly line operator who has only to find his work place and possibly two or three other parts of the factory (e.g. stores, or tool rooms), the process operator must often learn many locations of controls and indicators in multi-storey open plant. In the case of this process there are 128 hand-operated valves on open plant which are not labelled and which must be correctly identified. These valves must be distinguished from an extremely cluttered background.

In the control room, multiple discrimination of some fifty controls and indicators on the instrument console is required. Furthermore, it is essential on two counts that the operator can swiftly locate any indicator or control, i.e. he must literally have learned instrument *locations* and not need to rely on scanning the labels. On the one hand, when dynamic failures occur he should not have to *search* for information in the limited time available for a diagnosis. On the other hand, quick console operations are required for emergency shut-down of one of the columns or the reactor.

With two exceptions, the task calls for no *responses* which would require more than demonstrating to a novice. However, *ordering* responses already 'in the repertory' is often a source of difficulty as in the previous description of start-up and shut-down procedures. At subsequent levels of description also, sub-routines are frequently encountered where the order of responses, rather than the responses themselves, constitutes the training problem.

Examples are switching a control instrument from the automatic to manual mode and the reverse. An incorrect sequence of responses in this case could cause damage to the control mechanism. A further example is the sequence of valve manipulations in 'change-over' to a standby pump, when pump failure is diagnosed (*see Figure 2.11*). One consequence of varying this sequence could be the sudden pumping of acid out of an open drain valve near the operator. These sub-routines, especially the instrument switching routines, are frequently repeated in the task and in view of the contingencies of sequence errors clearly should be over-learned. They are, however, short and for that reason special training conditions beyond sheer practice are probably not indicated.

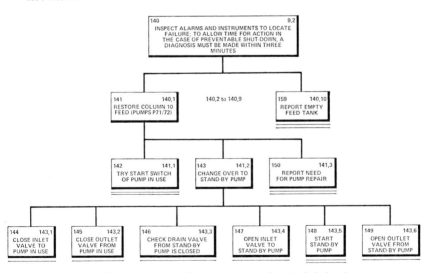

Figure 2.11. Representative subordinate operations in dynamic fault location

Two operations in which the response as such presents a problem are found in the start-up procedures. Both operations involve continuous adjustments of a steam valve to increase temperature at an optimum rate. Temperature is displayed by a continuous pen recorder, thus the skill consists in compensatory tracking of an 'acceptable' slope on the pen record.

Recording technique

Diagrams such as *Figures 2.10* and *2.11* will suffice to illustrate the structure and components of a task. However, diagrams in this form are not recommended as a recording technique in view of the restricted amount of information which can conveniently be entered in the boxes. Rather, a tabular format is preferred, operations in the table are numbered and a box diagram of the operation numbers is drawn up. This preserves the structure of the hierarchy, which is easily lost in any tabular layout, and enables the analyst to locate the position in the task hierarchy of any entry in the table. *Figure 2.12* shows the hierarchical structure of the process control task and *Table 2.7* shows extracts from the corresponding table.

Maximum space is given in the table to a statement of the operation and to training notes. It is envisaged that this entry in some cases may amount to a single phrase, in others to one or more sheets of paper. For this reason, minimum space is allotted to the other columns which, as will be explained, are intended primarily as aides-mémoire.

Difficulty and costs

The operation is first stated and numbered, e.g. 7, start-up water distillation column, C12. Having stated the operation, the analyst decides whether its difficulty for the trainee population and its cost contingencies together constitute a training requirement. Strictly speaking, the decision is based on the *product* of p and c, since if either were zero, analysis would cease regardless of the value of the other. However, as already noted, whether this decision is based on elaborate data collection or on subjective judgment, depends on the circumstances. The point is that this decision, whether or not $p \times c$ is acceptable, is a recurring one which is explicitly recognised. Thus operation 49, position set point control, was judged not to be a problem, the trainee could do this if told to do so. Similarly, $p \times c$ seemed acceptable for turning the switch from manual to auto when temperature and set point coincide (operation 50), for acknowledging an alarm, for reporting the need for pump repair, and for keeping the log (operation 8). Considering this last operation (8), the grounds for the decision were that instruments on the control room console

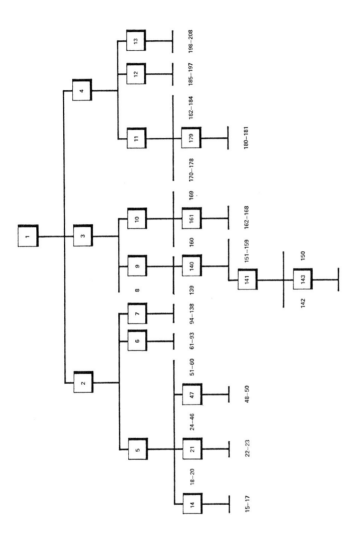

Figure 2.12. Box diagram indicating hierarchy of all operations recorded—see examples of table entries in Table 2.7

Table 2.7 Examples of entries in the Task Analysis Table

No.	Description of Operation and Training Notes	I or F	A	Redescribed
5 / 2,1	Start up vacuum distillation column, C10. **R** Invariant order 5,1 to 5,39. Very long fixed procedure. Use job aid? Group steps under headings and learn order of headings? Few opportunities to practise in a continuous process plant. Delays due to plant response could be avoided and practice speeded on a simulator.	—	X	14 18 to 21 24 to 47 51 to 60
6 / 2,2	Start up hydrogenator reactor, R2. **R** Invariant order 6,1 to 6,33. See 5.	—	X	61 to 93
7 / 2,3	Start up final water distillation column, C12. **R** Invariant order 7,1 to 7,45. See 5.	—	X	94 to 133
8	Keep log.			=
3,1 / 9	Locate and correct or report dynamic failures. **R** Acknowledge first—accept responsibility—then locate.	—	X	139 and 140
3,2 / 10	Locate and report product contamination. **R** Only report contaminants other than water; *report and locate* water contamination.	—	X	160, 161 and 169
3,3 / 11	Shut down C10. **R** Invariant order 11,1 to 11,13. See 5. In emergency, procedure is abbreviated to sub-operations 172, 170, 171, 174 *in that order*. This procedure and locations of console instruments must be overlearned.	—	X	170 to 179 182 to 184
4,1 / 26	Check the isolating valves round LICV 29 are open and the bypass closed. **I** Must find way through plant to slave valve LICV 29—'landmarks' for learning plant geography? Slave valves are labelled but hand-operated *isolating* and *bypass* valves are not. Rote learn which is which, *or* learn generalisation and discrimination of these classes of valve? Sketch to indicate relevant valves and lines against cluttered plant background?	X	—	—
5,8 / 33	Open the correct feed valve on Column 10 feed manifold—the middle one unless otherwise instructed. **I** Must find way through plant to manifold—'landmarks' for learning plant geography? Like most hand operated valves, feed valve is not labelled. Must identify from cues in surrounding vessels, lines, etc., and *overlearn* discrimination from other valves in vicinity. Sketch to indicate relevant valves and lines against cluttered plant background?	X	—	—
5,15 / 47	Slowly increase TRCV 36 from 4 p.s.i.g. to 9 p.s.i.g. (over a period of three hours) until the temperature reaches 125°C, then switch to 'auto'. **R** Must memorise order of switching from 'manual' to 'auto', i.e. valve, set point, switch.	—	X	48 to 50
5,29 / 48	Adjust valve. **A** Compensatory tracking of pen movements to produce an acceptable slope on recorder. Plant control law might be simulated, but expense justifiable? Practice on the job under supervision feasible, but would be infrequent. **F** Examples of 'acceptable' and 'unacceptable' slopes could easily be provided.	X	X	—
47,1 / 49 47,2	Position set point control.			=

Ref	Operation			
50 / 47,3	When temperature and set point coincide, turn switch from 'manual' to 'auto'.	X	—	$=$
60 / 5,39	Open *manifold valve to T.25/26* and shut *valve to T.23*. **I** See 33.	X	—	—
78 / 6,18	Set up a pressure of 1 p.s.i.g. on the gauge after the block valve. Then check that there is a purge through the system by putting a hand over the outlet vent. **F** Must find way through plant to outlet vent. Once pointed out, vent is easily identified.	X	—	—
140 / 9,2	Inspect alarm panels and console instruments to locate failure. To allow sufficient time to take action in the case of preventable plant shut-down, a diagnosis must be made in the control room within three minutes. **I F A** pre-requisite for training is highly practised location of every console instrument to avoid wasting time searching for instruments at the expense of diagnosis. **R** Diagnosis, i.e. selection of *one* of the ten sub-operations, is a major training requirement. Simulation inevitable since opportunities for practice—if acceptable to management—would be infrequent. Three possibilities are: 1. Rote learn associations between sets of indications and faults—a difficulty will be overlapping indications (see attached symptom list). 2. 'Technical story' plus practice in identifying failure consistent with a set of symptoms. A prerequisite: learn conventions for designating the function of an instrument, e.g. LIC (level indicator-controller). 3. Construct decision trees specifying a branching sequence of the minimum instrument readings to reach a diagnosis.	X	X	141, 151 to 159
141 / 149,1	Restore Column 10 feed ($P.71/72$). **I** See 78. **R** First try restarting pump-in-use (it may have been switched off). If pump-in-use fails to start, change over to stand-by as quickly as possible. Then report need for repairs (*both* pumps may fail to start).	X	X	142, 143, 150
142	Try start switch of pump in use.			$=$
141,1 / 143 / 141,2	Change over to stand-by pump. **R** Memorising the fixed sequence 143,1 to 143,6 is vital (acid could be pumped out of an open drain valve).	—	X	144 to 149
161 / 10,2	Locate origin of water contamination by taking further samples from other points on the plant. **R** The number and order of samples taken, i.e. sub-operations, varies. *Given* (a) a relative cost index for each of 7 sampling points *and* (b) for each of 8 plant components, estimated probability of failure (i.e. contaminating product), the operator must apply a search strategy which minimises sampling costs. Need flow diagram showing only relevant information, i.e. (a) and (b). Simulation inevitable (see 140)—in this case instructor might provide 'lab. reports' for a random series of 'faults' (occurring with a frequency proportional to their probabilities). Should trainee 1. be told efficient strategy, e.g. decision tree prescribing branching sequence or samples? or 2. attempt unaided to minimise his sampling costs?	—	X	162 to 168
165 / 161,4	Sample *R2 evaporator sight glass drain valve*. **I** See 33.	X	—	—

were labelled, real time decisions on plant running were not involved, there was plenty of time for log-keeping and errors would not be critical. In each case *two* horizontal lines are entered in the final column of the table, indicating that the estimate of $p \times c$ was acceptable and that no further analysis is necessary.

Examples of operations in this task which, if inadequately performed, would incur unacceptable costs to the system are operations 33 and 60. Each of these operations routes the acids being purified, and mistakes in routing could be very costly indeed; for instance, partly purified acid, or untreated feedstock could be routed to the 'pure product' tank at the end of the line. Clearly, the costs of failing to diagnose and, where possible, remedy a failure which would otherwise cause a shut-down, would be unacceptable. (operation 9). Furthermore, if the operator cannot prevent a shutdown, failure quickly to diagnose a plant fault, when it occurs, could be costly, since the symptom pattern may be rapidly obscured by other failures which the primary failure has induced (operation 140).

Input and feedback

Whenever the analyst decides $p \times c$ is *not* acceptable and that the operation does present a training problem, then the nature of the problem must be recorded, together with any observations as to how it may be overcome. The analyst should first ask—is the difficulty an *input* or *feedback* difficulty? Does this difficulty lie in some signal or information, indicating to the operator what he must do, or indicating to him the results of his performance? If this is not the case, a dash is entered in the column headed I or F, otherwise a cross is entered as has been done for operation 26. The difficulty in this operation is not so much in opening or closing valves, as in finding them in the first place and then distinguishing between them. This difficulty has been recorded immediately after the operation and possible training solutions are noted. These observations are separated from the statement of the operation proper by the prefix I. A similar difficulty is encountered in operation 78 where it is necessary first to find the outlet vent in order to check that the action of setting up a nitrogen pressure is having the desired effect of 'purging' the plant. In this case the prefix F separates the training observation from the statement of the operation. Efficient location of the console instruments in operation 140 is both an input and feedback difficulty, since it is a prerequisite for both speedy diagnosis and checking plant response to emergency operations.

Action

The analyst should next ask himself whether the operation presents an action difficulty. Given that the trainee can handle the input or feedback information, or can be trained to handle it, will the required action present difficulty? If not, the analyst enters a dash in the column headed *A*, otherwise a cross. If he has entered a cross in the action column, the analyst may decide, *either* that the nature of the difficulty and the training required will not be clarified by further analysis, *or* that further analysis into subordinate operations is necessary. Operation 48 is an instance of an action difficulty where further analysis into subordinate operations is not indicated, and the comment on the training problem is separated from the statement of the operation by the prefix *A*.

Subordinate operations

Analysis into subordinate operations, which the analyst will later describe in the table, may be necessary. In that event, the numbers of these subordinate operations must be entered in the final column. Thus if an operation is redescribed, its components can be located by reference to the final column of the table as well as by inspecting the box diagram. Like the *I* or *F* column and the *A* column, the final column is an aide-mémoire. When the analysis is complete the final column must contain, for each operation, *either* two horizontal lines, or a set of numbers, or a single horizontal line. A single horizontal line is used when appropriately prefixed observations of the training requirement have been recorded and no further analysis is needed.

Each operation in the table has a unique number, assigned as may be convenient. No matter how frequently it occurs in a sub-routine, no operation is described more than once. As a further means of preserving the structure of the hierarchy in a tabular format, each operation (apart from the first) may be assigned a sub-routine number specifying the superordinate operation to which it belongs. Thus operation 165 has a sub-routine number 161,4 noting that it is a sub-operation of operation 161, and *the fourth to be recorded so far*. This is all the suffix 4 denotes; it does not, for example, indicate when, or in what order, it must be performed to complete performance of operation 161. The order in which sub-operations are shown in the table, or in the diagram, does not necessarily imply anything about the order of their occurrence. The selection and sequencing of subordinate operations is specified by *rules* incorporated in the record of superordinate operations.

Rules

Whenever he decides that an operation should be redescribed, the analyst must specify, after the prefix R, whether the order of subordinate operations is fixed or varied and whether all sub-operations are always performed to complete the operation, or only a sub-set. The rule specifying that a set of operations must be performed, for example, in an invariant sequence, does not belong to any one operation in the sequence, but rather to the super-ordinate operation. In this case, the superordinate operation would be stated in the form 'carry out fixed sequence X'.

Whenever a precise rule governing the selection and sequencing of sub-operations can be stated, it should be. The fixed sequence, sometimes called 'procedure' or 'chain', is a common rule. Operation 5 is a long procedure; a series of 39 subordinate operations must be performed to start up the distillation column. Shorter fixed sequences are the change-over from manual to automatic control in operation 47, and the change-over to the stand-by pump in operation 143.

An example of a selective rule occurs in operation 10: depending on the laboratory report, either one or three subordinate operations are performed. A much more difficult selective rule occurs in operation 140. One of ten actions is required, selection of the correct one involves interpretation of complex patterns of console indications and on this interpretation may depend the prevention of plant shut-down. This constitutes a major training requirement and various possibilities are noted in the table. In operation 141, one sub-operation is always performed first, i.e. try to re-start the pump in use. If it fails to start, two other operations are required, the change-over operation, and the report of a need for repairs. This, then, is a rule which both sequences and selects sub-operations.

The rules, plans, or strategies encountered when the operations of a skilled man are redescribed may vary in complexity, may not necessarily be explicit, consistent, rational, or optimal. Faced with such problems, the analyst's main responsibility is to record what seem to be the main training possibilities if a novice is to learn how, in different situations, to select a sub-routine which will complete the operation. Operation 161 is a case in point and the problem in this case was described earlier in the chapter. The operator will not necessarily discover the most efficient search strategy, nor even improve with experience. Simply practising this operation will not indicate the optimum strategy to adopt, and there is the danger that he may superstitiously adopt the search strategy which he has invariably found 'successful'.

Rules have been considered separately in this analysis and this will often be convenient. However, rules, strictly speaking, only amount to a shorthand statement of the inputs to a superordinate operation which determine the selection and sequencing of its subordinate operations. Thus the invariant sequence rule summarises a set of inputs of the form 'step 12 completed, therefore perform step 13'. Similarly, the search strategy in operation 161 specifies a set of inputs of the form 'sample from Column 10 reflux pump contains water, therefore take next sample from Column 10 feed pump'.

Assumptions in hierarchial task analysis

This strategy for the analysis of industrial tasks combines economy of data collection with isolation of critical operations requiring training. It also entails adopting an explicit position on fundamental questions such as what criteria must be satisfied by a statement of an operation and what features of behaviour it is essential or useful to consider when identifying training requirements.

First it is assumed that, for practical purposes, the major criterion to be met, when stating the operations in a task, is intelligibility. That is to say, an operation should be stated in language that the operator uses or would understand. It is an *instruction* to do something, which the trainee either can already do, or would be able to do, given the training noted after one or more prefixes. The statement should be as plain and non-technical as possible, but not necessarily without peculiar expressions, if these are current usage among competent operators or supervisors, (e.g. terms such as 'crack the valve' or 'kettle level'). Shop floor dialect, where it is incomprehensible to the trainee population, would be noted by the analyst as input or feedback difficulties indicating training requirements. For some peculiar expressions, sound recordings, diagrams or other visual displays may be essential for successful training.

For practical purposes, then, an action statement is the minimal requirement for recording an operation. It is also assumed that all operations have an input, signal, or cue. Again, for practical purposes, inputs which are generated by the action in question are called feedback, and inputs which determine the selection and sequencing of subordinate operations are called rules, plans, or strategies. Whilst the action component *must* be stated, if the operation is to be stated at all, inputs are only stated when necessary. This may be necessary, either to make the statement an intelligible instruction, or to indicate a difficulty and consequent requirement for training. Notes on possible training methods are separated from statements of operations, although both should be undertaken at the same time.

A single unit of performance, *the operation,* is assumed which, whatever its level in a performance hierarchy,* may be stated in natural language. No attempt is made to define levels of description, nor to specify a list of performance elements. A workable list of performance elements would be one way of achieving a rigorous method of analysis. Gilbreth's list of movement elements was such an attempt in a different context. In the current state of psychology such an approach to the problems of training does not seem to be realisable, foreseeable or even plausible. Rigour must be sought in some other direction. More specifically, task analysis for training may achieve a certain rigour by proceeding from general to detailed statements and by observing an explicit rule as to when analysis must cease.

PROBLEMS OF TRAINING DESIGN

The gulf between task analysis and training design is notorious. In this section some of the principal difficulties and strategies for overcoming them will be discussed. By way of illustration, some of the specific solutions to the problems presented by the chemical process control task will be described.

There will often be more than one possible training solution to the requirements revealed by the analysis. Some may be obvious non-starters, but there will often remain alternatives, such as whether or not to use job aids for long procedures, or decision trees for diagnostic operations. It is suggested that, besides noting the nature of the difficulty, as many feasible training solutions as occur to him should be recorded by the analyst at the same time as he describes the operation—see, for example, operations 5, 26, 140 and 161 (*Table 2.7*).

Spontaneity of comment, whilst in the job situation, is probably important. The analyst should not be over-critical when recording potential training solutions on the spot. Unworkable training proposals can be easily eliminated, whereas the list of possibilities may be less easy to augment away from the job situation. Description of the operation and training required are not recorded in separate columns for this reason and also for economy of statement. A description of the operation and the training requirement will often overlap.

The generality of training

There are a further two reasons for noting several possible training solutions. One is that the analyst encountering a certain kind of difficulty for the first time may not be able to make a sensible choice between training solutions until the analysis is complete and he knows how frequently the difficulty in question will be encountered. The point was illustrated in the comment on operation 26 in *Table 2.7*. It was noted that the novice could rote learn which are the isolating and which .the bypass valves around a particular 'slave' unit. However, when the analysis was complete, it turned out that there were so many isolating and bypass valves that learning generalisation and discrimination of these classes of valves was obviously the better strategy.

Such a decision might be a better strategy for a further reason. If mobility of operators from plant to plant were a feature of a personnel sub-system, then training generalisable skill would often be preferred. In the case of the example cited (operation 26), and the trainee population concerned, training the more generalisable skill would have taken less time. However, for some task components, training a generalisable skill would prove more expensive in training time, training aids and in expertness of instruction required. The two fault location operations (140 and 161) which were described in *Table 2.7*, are cases in point. Both presented major training alternatives, since both could be supported by decision trees. It is possible to construct decision trees specifying branching sequences of the minimum instrument readings needed to reach a diagnosis (operation 140) and specifying the branching sequence of samples which minimise costs in locating sources of water contamination (operation 161).

A general argument for using decision trees, put forward earlier in the chapter, applies in this particular case. Performance supported by a decision tree should be less dependent on intelligence. In that event, appointment and assessment of operators might be based solely on conscientiousness or some other desirable personality characteristic—at least in principle. Another argument was that fault location might be 'time shared' with emergency actions when these were demanded by another process. Under such conditions, performance supported by decision trees should prove less vulnerable to disruption. It also seemed reasonable to predict that use of decision trees might save training time.

The notion of reducing fault location to routines, however, gave rise to some uneasiness on the part of some production and training personnel. It was recognised that decision trees would ensure

F

swift and accurate symptom interpretation and economy of sampling. On the other hand, it was argued that without the decision
trees to hand, the operator might perform little better than an
untrained novice and his efficiency in fault location would be
specific to this plant. As noted earlier, to use decision trees might
simply be to *program performance* rather than *learning*. In short,
the question was whether to trade retention and possibly transfer
for efficient performance.

This kind of question is only ultimately resolvable in terms of
personnel policy. The extent to which operators are required to
master and retain fault locating skill which generalises to several
plants is an objective of the personnel sub-system. It is an objective
which can only be formulated in terms of *how much* retention
and transfer would be gained from training in fault location based
on rules or principles of some generality.

Any adequate training for these fault location operations would
presumably include practice, on the one hand, in identification of
failures consistent with a set of symptoms and, on the other, in
locating sources of water contamination from series of laboratory
reports. If this were not to be rote learning, which would have
been very time consuming, not to say tedious, then the problem
was how to introduce the trainee to the consequences of pumps
stopping, of steam or cooling water supplies failing, and of heat
exchangers leaking steam or coolant into the product.

Just how much instruction in principles or 'theory' is a necessary
prerequisite of fault finding practice in this or many other contexts
is controversial. It does seem likely that the effects on fault finding
performance of instruction in theory may be over-estimated. This
seems to be true at least in electronic equipment servicing, where
the question has been most extensively studied (e.g. Williams and
Whitmore, 1959). Research in that area suggests that a serious
competitor to fault finding by decision trees might be mastery of a
minimum of principles introduced and practised in a 'functional
context' (Brown *et al.*, 1959; Brown and Vineberg, 1960).

Procedural guides

The use of job aids for start-up or shut-down of a plant is less
controversial. It would have been possible, but clearly uneconomic,
to train operators to perform the long procedures of the acid
purification process unaided. Now it will be recalled that an
assumption of the suggested method for recording a hierarchical
task analysis was that the statement of an operation is in fact an

instruction to perform it. The operation should always be stated in language which the trainee will understand, or at least will understand given that the associated training requirements have been met. If then performance supported by *job aids* seems to be the most satisfactory solution for some of the task, the contents of the main column of the table *before* the prefix can be given to the operator as they stand, (e.g. the steps in the long procedure for starting up the vacuum distillation column). This construction of job aids can be achieved with a pair of scissors, leaving the pre-fixed training notes which are the *trainer*'s job aid. These notes may, of course, depart into technical language if this is useful, either as a convenient shorthand, or to identify appropriate conditions of learning.

Thus, for purposes of training design, the proposed table for task analysis has two types of entry which it will be convenient to separate, perhaps physically, when the analysis is complete. On the one hand, it contains a comprehensive set of instructions for performing all the operations in the task, i.e. the entries which are *not* prefixed. They could all, in principle, be put into procedural guides. On the other hand, the prefixed entries in the table define the training which will be necessary if a novice is to carry out the instructions.

Sequencing

Collation of the various training requirements raises questions of sequencing in the training course. Thus, analysis showed that performance of 'start-up' and 'shut-down' procedures entails mastery of many sub-operations, especially discrimination of plant valves and location of console instruments. An implication of hierarchical analysis requiring empirical testing is that practice of an operation should be *preceded* by training in any of its sub-operations not already in the trainee's repertory. Plant valve and console instrument training should on this view, precede practice in following procedural guides.

Similarly, it was found that mastery of sub-operations is also entailed in fault location and, in principle, similar arguments about sequencing could be advanced. However, in a training course there might be advantages in having practice in procedures precede fault location training. Questions about sequencing the fault location sub-operations would not then arise, since many of them—in this particular task, all console instrument locations—would have already been trained. The advantage of placing training in procedures first, rather than fault location, was that difficulties for the trainee in deciding what to do next could be largely avoided, and that experience of success early in training could be more easily arranged and confidence built up before tackling the more difficult fault location operations.

Discrimination training

With regard to discriminating hand-operated valves on the open plant, it seemed reasonable to assume that the skilled operator identifies a valve by using cues in its immediate context, i.e. configuration of lines, vessels and other plant components, so the first training problem was how to establish use of these cues. A

Figure 2.13. A slave valve and sensing device with bypass and isolating configurations. (Photograph by courtesy of B.P. Chemicals (International) Ltd.)

simplified drawing of the relevant context suggested itself as a means of making distinctive the cues for identifying a valve (*see Figures 2.13 and 2.14*).

Of the 128 valves on the plant which the operator had to identify, 82 could be classified as 'inlet', 'drain', 'isolating' or 'bypass' valves, the type or class of valve being defined by its situation in the lines about a pump, slave valve or sensing device (see, for example, operation 26 in *Table 2.7*). Thus, the relevant context for these valves is largely determined, if it is assumed that the novices will be trained to generalise within, and discriminate between, these types or categories.

The remaining 46 valves could not, however, be classified, but had nevertheless to be correctly identified, indeed failure to do so would in some cases have proved extremely expensive. Assum-

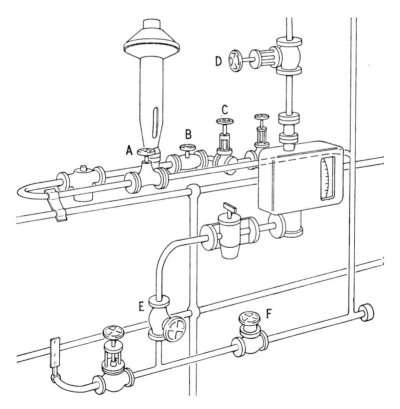

Figure 2.14. A and B are isolating, C bypass, valves about the slave valve (top left). D and E are isolating, F bypass, valves about the sensing device (middle right)

ing that such valves would not be labelled, one could only recommend that discrimination of them be over-learned. For such training any simplified drawing should obviously include 'competing' valves, together with any other distinctive plant features in the immediate vicinity.

Training of the swift location of console instruments, required in the control room, may be regarded as training in *multiple discrimination*, where again the basic problem is making the cues distinctive (Gagné, 1965a and 1965b). Three main ways of achieving this have been noted (Gagné, 1965a; Gilbert, 1962):

(a) By prompts.
(b) By using existing associations as mediators.
(c) By grouping potentially confusable cues or responses.

No obvious existing associations suggest themselves in the case of the console operations (at least, nothing comparable to Gilbert's *'one brown* penny' or *'five* dollar bill is *green'* for resistor colour coding—Gilbert, 1962). However, it seemed that emphasis of position cues could be achieved by having trainees practise labelling outline drawings of the instrument console, and that a plausible application of the grouping principle would be to have trainees practise the locations and functions of all flow instruments together, likewise to group the practice of all temperature, pressure and level instruments. In the event, practice with outline drawings was associated with superior learning of instrument locations and designations, but the proposition that grouping assists multiple discrimination learning was not supported (Duncan, 1969 and 1970).

It is perhaps apposite at this point to note that the practical value of performance categories, which are largely based on laboratory studies, has yet to be established—at least in the case of the learning conditions which have been attributed to *multiple discrimination* and, as was observed in the discussion of Mathetics, in the conditions which were said to favour learning *chains.*

Tracking

Two control room operations were noted which presented a rather different training problem, namely compensatory adjustments of a steam valve to produce an acceptable slope on a temperature pen record. Limits within which a slope is acceptable could probably be defined and demonstrated to a trainee. If not, a refinement would be to determine and provide what Mager has called 'normative feedback' (Mager and Clark, 1963), e.g. 'this slope would be acceptable to 90 per cent of plant supervisors' (or 'on 90 per cent of occasions', or 'by 90 per cent of skilled operators', etc.). The main difficulty, however, would be in learning plant dynamics, specifically in learning to correlate valve movements with consequent temperature changes.

Systematic practice of these two tracking operations on the plant would have been out of the question. Furthermore, simulation of the display-control relationship produced by plant dynamics could be expensive. On the other hand, since they occurred on predictable occasions, a more economic solution seemed to be for the novice to perform just these two operations under the observation

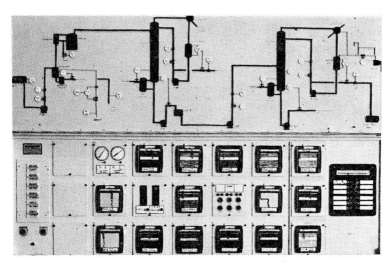

Figure 2.15. The Carmody 'Universal Process Trainer' (Photograph by courtesy of B.P. Chemicals (International) Ltd.)

and, if necessary, guidance of an experienced still-man or plant supervisor.

Simulation

The very nature of the high capital cost of continuous process plant, makes on-the-job training of operators necessarily inefficient, at least for the major procedural and fault locating skills. Scheduled maintenance, excessive stockpiling of pure product and shortage of feedstock aside, management will keep such plants running at all costs. In the specific case of the acid purification process, the novice's first attempts at starting up such a plant would be separated by months and he would be unlikely to experience each of the possible plant faults in less than a year.

Clearly, simulation in some form will be necessary to supplement on-the-job training, otherwise mastery of such tasks will literally take 'years of experience' as is sometimes said it does. The simulation problems encountered in designing training for the acid purification control task are rather general and will, therefore, be briefly described.

Shortly before analysis of this task was undertaken, the factory had purchased a Carmody 'Universal Process Trainer', the main facility of which (see Figure 2.15) is a console on which can be mounted most instruments encountered in a chemical plant control room. With the resources of this simulator, a display of instruments was assembled comprising the various alarms, indicators and controls in the real process control room. The state of the console instruments at each stage of the start-up and shut-down procedures, including changes resulting from control actions by trainees, was then worked out, together with the patterns of alarms and indications which would be produced by each of the dynamic failures (i.e. pumps, steam supplies, etc.) After checking these details with plant supervisors and incorporating several alterations, it was eventually agreed that successful performance on the simulator of the various control room operations in the task would constitute a useful training criterion.

However, the problem remained of a training criterion for *plant* operations, mostly opening and closing hand-operated valves. In view of the distances between the locations of these valves, it was decided that a feasible criterion would be requiring the trainee to indicate, on photographs of the various locations, *which* of several valves should be operated and whether it should be opened or closed (see Figure 2.13). It was recognised that this would not ensure any mastery of 'plant geography', but that it would be a satisfactory criterion of discriminating the valve involved in an operation from others in the immediate vicinity.

Accordingly, photographs of various parts of the plant were displayed next to the control room console simulator. These photographs were shot sufficiently close-up for trainees to practise identifying different valves in a group, whilst preserving a context of plant background against which they must be distinguished. 'Landmarks', e.g. major vessels or distinctive configurations of process lines, were included and all subjects visited the site of each photograph on a tour of the plant before training began.

Human engineering

The engineering of any existing system operated by men necessarily sets some limits on training strategies. Two features of the particular plant which has just been described would, if modified, have considerably reduced the training requirement.

The costs of durable labelling in an open plant are considerable and especially in this case because of the acid purification process. To label all hand-operated valves throughout a factory would have removed the discrimination training problem but might have been prohibitively expensive. The acid purification process alone involved 128 hand-operated valves. However, 90 of these were easily identified, given mastery of four or five functional categories. In such cases training rather than labelling might be more economic. It was the remaining 40 valves which were expensive in terms of training time, since there were no rules to support identification; each had to be separately learned. The cost of labelling these valves, therefore, would probably have been justified.

One of the advantages of systematic task analysis should be that finer distinctions can be made in the possible trade-off between hardware and training costs. In this case the analysis distinguishes (where engineers or accountants may not) between the cost of labelling all hand-operated valves on the plant and the thirty per cent or so, which present disproportionately high training costs.

A second feature of this plant with important consequences for training was its instrumentation. In general, the design of an instrumentation system can drastically augment or diminish the training problem. From the engineering point of view, instrumentation and associated alarm systems may either provide a rather large number of signals of specific failures (e.g. the reflux pump has stopped) or a much smaller number of signals (typically an out-of-tolerance liquid level) indicating that a failure has occurred *somewhere,* in which case the operator must interpret the pattern of console indicators to diagnose the fault. The latter instrumentation policy is, of course, the most costly from the training point of view, but cheaper to install. It is the one which was adopted when the acid purification plant was built.

The writer does not have the resources to assess which of these instrumentation policies, or what compromise between the two, would have minimised joint hardware and training costs in this particular instance. However, the point is raised since it seems to be one which may easily be neglected in the design of instrumentation and alarm systems. Furthermore, it is disturbing to reflect that a considered solution to such design problems as how much specific alarm signalling to build in, or how much to spend on labelling of hand-operated valves, might not in practice minimise joint hardware and training costs, since the latter will often qualify for rebate under the provisions of the Industrial Training Act (1964).

CONCLUSION

Several strategies for task analysis have been described. Any one of these strategies may prove useful, in some contexts as it stands and, hopefully, the teacher or training officer will find it possible to select one to meet his needs. The last approach to be described, a strategy for task analysis in industrial settings, incorporates what the writer takes to be the more useful features of the various strategies which have been proposed. These features will now be reviewed.

The structure of expert performance is assumed to be hierarchical. Analysis begins, as Gagné (1962) proposed, with a general statement of the task and then asks what subordinate operations *need* to be described, based on two considerations: the probability of inadequate performance without education or training, p; and the costs to the system of inadequate performance, c. The specification of entry behaviour, which Skinner emphasised as a prerequisite for programming, is of course entailed in estimating p. The initial capabilities of the target population must be continually considered throughout the analysis. Estimating c recognises that education or training always has a context, i.e. the system of which it is part, and that the general aims of the system must be explicit; c is interpreted widely.

Anything detrimental to the system's aims must be weighed in estimating c. Thus in industrial training, costs in the sense of financial loss are only one consideration. Others are performance contingencies which constitute a threat to safety in the workplace, or which affect the demands made on other people elsewhere in the system. The intrinsic satisfactions of different ways of performing the same task must be reckoned, as indeed must the costs of analysis itself. In the field of education, estimating c will be very difficult because of the difficulty of defining many objectives of education, such as fostering curiosity or encouraging an enquiring critical attitude. However, whilst the questions of what may be achieved and at what costs may not be easy to answer, they should nevertheless be asked. Should the study of science, to take one example, always entail repeating classical experiments, perhaps with inadequate equipment and control and consequent 'cooking' of the data, when these turn out to be less than classical? If one of the aims of science education is to produce scientists, then the cost of somewhat reducing the emphasis on existing subject matter and techniques might be more than offset by an increased emphasis on the many other skills needed by a scientist, such as ability critically to assess research reports, or to distinguish problems which are researchable from those which are not.

An analytic approach to education which made even approximate and subjective estimates of c would seem to be well worthwhile. Assumptions about the content of courses at all levels of education seem to be at best plausible and often questionable, e.g. the extent to which the history of the subject is represented, or, in an experimental science, the amount of time devoted to demonstrating effects which were once crucial. It seems dubious, to say the least, that subject-matter should be selected and structured in accordance with the order in which advances in knowledge and scientific discovery enlarged the field of study. If indeed our knowledge of the universe progresses through a series of misunderstandings and subsequent clarifications, then does this progression necessarily have anything to do with the best instructional sequence when it is the *present* state of the art or science which is to be learned?

Estimating p and c is central to the hierarchical task analysis which has been described and illustrated in this chapter. Several methods of analysis recognise more than one level of description, but levels are exemplified rather than defined and agreement between methods as to the number of levels is far from perfect. It has been argued in this chapter that the level of description appropriate to different task components is not specifiable *a priori* and that both economy of statement and isolation of operations needing training is best achieved by successive redescriptions of an initial general statement of the task. The appropriate level of description may vary considerably throughout the analysis. It is for this reason that a rule requiring estimates of p and c is proposed. Task components, or *operations,* are only further analysed into subordinate operations when the initial probability of inadequate performance and its attendant costs to the system are unacceptable, and when the education or training required for acceptable performance is not clear. When these conditions are satisfied, analysis ceases. Thus arbitrary levels of description are not prescribed beforehand, nor is a fixed number of levels assumed. The extent to which analysis is pursued may vary, within the same task, from very general to very detailed statements.

The writer has reservations as to what extent the expressions 'educational technology' or 'technology of training' are justified at the present stage of development of behavioural science. Minimal assumptions, at least for task analysis, seem desirable. Thus, rather than define levels of description or specify a list of performance elements, a single unit of performance, the *operation* is assumed. Operations, at whatever level in the task hierarchy, are stated in natural language. The minimal requirement is an *action* statement which constitutes an instruction intelligible to a competent operator. Mager's (1962) point about the communicability of instructional objectives is well taken. But actions are *responses*. Identifying the *inputs, signals,* or *cues* to which the operator responds will frequently be crucial, as R. B. Miller (1962a and 1962b) especially has insisted. Inputs are incorporated whenever they are essential to render the statement of the operation intelligible, or when their reception by the novice requires training. For practical purposes, inputs generated by action are distinguished as *feedback* and inputs which determine selection and sequencing of subordinate operations are distinguished as *rules*. Expertise, be it in abstract problem solving or in manipulating a control or work piece, consists of acceptable performance of a set of operations and of selecting and ordering operations as the situation demands. The arbitrary distinction between 'skill' and 'knowledge' is thus avoided.

The task hierarchy will, it is assumed, determine to some extent the sequencing of instruction. The point in training at which particular operations must be mastered will probably not be specified exactly, but practice of a given operation should probably not begin before its subordinate operations have all been learned. Mastery of a subordinate operation will often be a necessary precondition for the practice of several superordinate operations. The analysis will not always specify a unique learning sequence.

Research has still to establish that a learning sequence based on the hierarchy of task components is necessarily the most efficient. Mager's subjects, when allowed to determine their own sequencing of instruction, had a definite preference for proceeding from general functions to the detailed working of electronic equipment. Whether this is an efficient *learning* sequence is questionable, although, from Mager's account of his students' behaviour, it seems to have powerful *motivating* effects (Mager, 1961). The student appears to want to see 'the big picture' at the outset. Even the advocates of what is probably the most thoroughgoing reduction of a problem-solving task to strict procedure-following, would begin training with a 'technical story' (Shriver *et al.,* 1964).

One therefore suspects that, at least in the early stages of learning, the student's interest would be aroused by a description of the structure of what he is to learn.

Attempts to formulate taxonomies are probably premature, nevertheless the observed differences in behaviour, especially outside the laboratory in schools and training centres, are, as Gagné observes, more important than the similarities (Gagné, 1965b). However, the extent to which training methods are optimised rests ultimately on information in the research literature. A method of task analysis should at least ensure that different kinds of skill are identified. The range of different kinds of operation which were isolated in the analysis of the industrial control task includes diagnostic operations, complex procedures, discriminations and manual tracking. This argues the advantage of flexibility in the level of description employed. In particular, proceeding from general to more detailed statements seems more likely to identify the rules, plans and strategies which control and adapt performance to changing circumstances, than working *ab initio* at the more molecular level of, for example the 'therbligs' of time and motion study or the S–R units of the psychological laboratory.

One may conclude that an appropriate strategy of analysis will determine fairly precisely what behaviour must be acquired, and yield a good approximation to the techniques which will prove effective when different task components are learned. Nevertheless, when the usefulness of a well established laboratory paradigm for programmed instruction is cogently criticised (Cook, 1963; Lumsdaine, 1962), and when performance categories apparently lack robustness outside the laboratory, then it must be acknowledged that no strategy of analysis is a substitute for rigorous evaluation.

Finally, it *should* go without saying that techniques of presentation—teaching machines, 'concept loops', closed circuit television, etc.—are essentially secondary considerations in the systematic design of instruction. Before some kind of task analysis has been undertaken the most appropriate presentation styles and devices are unlikely to be selected. This rather trite point is made since it is so frequently ignored. If only task analysis were pursued on the same scale and with the same persistence as the marketing of instructional hardware, then education and training would inherit more genuine *technologists* to replace the present bewildering variety of *technicians*.

3

Presentation Strategies

IVOR K. DAVIES

Once the task analysis has been completed, the instructor has three documents available for his use:

(a) He has a precise specification of measurable objectives, and an associated criterion test.
(b) He has a detailed statement of the behaviours which are involved in mastery. Some of these the student will already possess, others he will have to acquire during the course of instruction—whether it be programmed or not.
(c) He has a detailed specification, item by item, suggesting the sequence to be followed in presenting the topic to the student.

These three documents are used by the instructor as blueprints for the behaviours to be generated in the learner; they suggest strategies of presentation most likely to achieve the objectives of the learning situation.

Educational technology is not sufficiently advanced at the present time to do more than to suggest the differences between successful learning strategies and relatively unsuccessful ones. There is, of course, no lack of ideas, methods, procedures or techniques available to the teacher, but for too long it has been difficult to forecast which is likely to be most effective—or even to explain why one should be more effective than another. However, the research generated by programmed learning is beginning to suggest optimum teaching strategies for realising particular objectives and structures with particular students.

What is beginning to emerge at last is a theory of instruction that will actually predict the conditions under which a particular teaching procedure optimises learning. Bruner (1966) characterises such a theory as one that sets forth rules concerning the most efficient way of achieving knowledge or skill, and he considers that these rules should be derivable from a more general view of learning. Viewed in this way, a theory of instruction is *prescriptive,* in the sense that it prescribes how learning can be improved, whilst a theory of learning is *descriptive,* in the sense that it describes what has happened after the event. It should not be thought, however, that a theory of learning is irrelevant to a theory of instruction; learning and instruction complement each other.

BASIC PRESENTATION STRATEGIES

Today, it is possible to describe two broadly different theoretical approaches to the problem of teaching. These approaches represent significant but conflicting views of the nature of the learning process, and are theoretically almost impossible to reconcile. One approach is concerned with 'connectionist' theories of learning, and the other with 'configurationist' theories (*see* Hilgard and Bower, 1966). Many of the different, and often controversial views which have evolved in the design of programmed learning material reflect these two basically different teaching/learning positions. Whilst it is unlikely that their differences will be resolved at this particular stage, the two approaches have much in common when it comes to actually writing a program. Indeed, many programs today contain a mixture or blending of the different styles and formats, so that the two schools are tending, in practice at least, to become less and less exclusive as far as actual teaching is concerned (*see* Rowntree, 1969). However, despite this amalgam of approach, it is worthwhile first to discuss the two positions separately, in terms of the strategies which they employ. Viewed in this way, the strategies can be classified in the following manner:

(a) Configurationist or stimulus-centred strategies which are commonly found in branching and adjunct programs, and are largely based on the work of Dr. S. L. Pressey and N. Crowder, as well as that of Dr. R. F. Mager.

(b) Connectionist or response-centred strategies which are commonly found in linear and mathetics programs, and result from the work of Dr. B. F. Skinner and Dr. T. F. Gilbert.

A final style of programming, with a limited range of objectives, involving the use of algorithms, will be discussed later in this chapter.

Adjunct programs

In the early 1920s Sidney L. Pressey of Ohio State University became aware of the inefficiencies of question and answer sessions in the classroom. Only one student could answer a question at a time, and other students became bored and listless whilst this was going on. As a result, Pressey decided to use mechanical devices in order to administer and score the test questions. In this way every student in the class could be asked questions at the same time, could actively respond, and then receive immediate confirmation of whether or not these responses were correct. Since the primary purpose of these materials was to indicate to the student whether or not he was learning, multiple-choice responding was inevitably used. This type of testing also greatly simplified the mechanical problem of presenting the questions and their correct answers.

Pressey subsequently discovered that not only did the question and answer sessions test the students, but that students also learnt from the experience. In effect, the objective style tests were implementing several of E. L Thorndike's so-called Laws of Learning (Thorndike, 1913). Whilst Skinner later developed and made a more precise use of Thorndike's Law of Effect (which deals with the tendency for behaviour to be 'stamped in' when followed by certain satisfying consequences), Pressey utilised the Law of Frequency (the more frequently a response is made the more likely it will be repeated) and the Law of Recency (the more recent a response, the more likely it will be made again). In other words, Pressey found that the test materials drilled and rehearsed the student in his newly acquired skills, and—at the same time— informed him of the correctness or incorrectness of his responses.

The impact of these early ideas and findings, however, was limited until the surge of interest in programmed learning in the late 1950s. Since then, Pressey has developed this technique into a type of program which he calls 'adjunct auto-instruction' (Pressey, 1963). In essence, Pressey argues that response centred programs tend to destroy meaningful structure by fragmenting the material into a set of serially presented frames, whereas adjunct programs keep and enhance subject-matter by extending its meaningfulness. What happens is this: the student first undergoes a short learning experience by reading a brief chapter or section of a chapter in a book, watching a film or attending a field excursion. He then reviews the experience selectively for major or difficult points, before he turns to a series of questions designed to 'enhance the clarity and stability of cognitive structures by correcting misconceptions and deferring the instruction of new matter until there has been such clarification and elucidation' (Pressey, 1962). A typical extract from an adjunct program is shown in *Table 3.1*.

The questions need not necessarily cover all the points dealt with by the chapter or film. Adjunct programmers are not interested in developing an intricate and self-sufficient set of items so well cued that the student falls into little or no error. The purpose of the program is to help the student to determine whether or not he has mastered the material, whether he needs to review the topic again, or whether he needs to seek additional help from a teacher. Learning has been initiated before ever the student comes to the adjunct program; the program only deals with those items that may need extra clarification or emphasis. An advantage of this method over other forms of programming lies in the fact that it can be prepared relatively easily and quickly, and it can make use of textbooks and manuals already available to student and teacher. Successful applications of this method in an industrial context have been described by Bensen (1968) and Harper (1969).

Branching programs

The approach of Norman Crowder, formerly of U.S. Industries Inc., was also essentially stimulus-centred. For Crowder, 'The essential problem is that of controlling a communication process by the use of feedback. The student's response serves primarily as a means of determining whether the communication process has been effective and at the same time allows appropriate corrective action to be taken when the communication has become ineffective' (Crowder, 1960). Crowder's approach is thus based essentially on a psychology of individual differences. Indeed, he is very little concerned or interested with the nature of the learning process itself.

Thus, the identifying feature of a Crowderian program is the way in which material is presented to the student on the basis of

G

Table 3.1 An extract from an Undergraduate Adjunct Program to accompany a chapter on psychological testing in a standard textbook

36. Identical twins are used as subjects in studies of the role of environment in the development of ability because such persons have the same ....

    A. environment   C. development   B
    B. heredity   D. discernment

37. Newman *et al*, 1937, found that measures of height for identical twins reared together had a correlation coefficient of ·98, and identical twins reared separately had a correlation coefficient of ·97. Hence the effect on height of being reared apart is ....

    A. inverse   C. significant   B
    B. meaningless   D. slight

38. Newman also found that the achievement test scores for identical twins reared together showed a correlation of ·96: for identical twins reared apart it was ·51. The difference is ....

    A. inverse   C. significant   C
    B. meaningless   D. slight

39. Intelligence test score correlations were found by Newman to be ·96 for identical twins reared together, ·67 for those reared apart. This tends to emphasise the importance of............ in the development of intelligence.

    A. weight   C. heredity   D
    B. height   D. environment

From Bell, Feldhusen and Starks (1964).

his performance. In order to permit this type of control over the material seen by the student, a multiple-choice type of format is used for the student responses (*see Figure 3.1*). The multiple-choice question is asked in order to decide what piece of information the student should see next; it is not necessarily regarded as playing an important part in the learning process. Whilst this view of learning may well be regarded as naturalistic or even as naive, it has proved to be the basis of a most powerful teaching medium.

In many ways the technique of branching programming is particularly suitable for dealing with material that involves complex problem solving strategies. Preferably, the subject matter should have a logical basis or structure which can be systematically developed frame by frame. At the same time the technique can, with advantage, be employed for groups of students amongst whom there is a wide range of individual differences, since the material automatically adapts to different learners' needs. A fuller description of this approach may be found in Rowntree (1967): approaches combining the contributions of Crowder and Skinner are described by Kay and Sime (1963).

Learner controlled programs

Finally, in this section on stimulus-centred programs perhaps we should note that Mager (1961) has put forward the novel thesis that the learner rather than the teacher should control the sequencing of topics to be learned. Such a position is, of course, in direct contrast to that which allows the logic of the subject matter itself to determine the arrangement of the material. Mager and his associates have also shown that student-generated sequences have considerable commonality in their ordering of subject material, and are very different indeed from the sequences generated for them by their own teachers. Further work has demonstrated that when the learner is provided only with behaviourally stated objectives and is permitted to instruct himself in any way and in any order that he chooses, then he will considerably reduce the conventional time taken (in some cases by as much as 65 per cent) to realise those objectives by dovetailing what he needs to know with what he already knows (Mager and McCann, 1961).

In essence, such student generated sequences tend to differ from traditional teaching sequences in a number of important ways:

(a) Initial student interest tends to be in the concrete rather than in the abstract, in things rather than in theory, in how rather than in why. For instance, whilst instructor generated

YOUR ANSWER: 5 amperes.

Correct. With a voltage of 100 and a resistance of 20 ohms we apply Ohm's Law, $I = E/R$, to get a current of $100/20 = 5$ amps.

This is a simple circuit and it can be shown as the diagram at left:

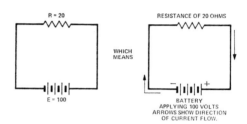

And this should look familiar by now. Remember the formula for calculating watts, $P = EI$? Given any two quantities, you can solve for the unknown.

The same is true for Ohm's Law. If you know voltage and current, you can find resistance. If you know resistance and current, you can find voltage. If you know voltage and resistance, you can find current. How?

If $I = E/R$, then $E = I/R$ and $R = EI$.   **page 49**

If $I = E/R$, then $E = IR$ and $R = E/I$.   **page 52**

If $I = E/R$, then $E = IR$ and $R = I/E$.   **page 55**

If $I = E/R$, then I don't know what comes next.   **page 61**

Figure 3.1. A typical frame from a branching program on electronics (From, Introduction to Electronics, Tutortext, HUGHES, R. J. *and* PIPE, P. *Copyright 1961. Reproduced by permission of The English Universities Press Ltd., and Doubleday & Co.)*

sequences in electronics usually begin with magnetism or electron theory, student generated sequences typically begin with the vacuum tube.

(b) Students tend to show interest in function before structure. In electronics, they tend to want explanations of what *happens* to generate a picture on a TV screen before they tackle the question of what *causes* the electron beam to be moved back and forth.

(c) Students tend to proceed from a simple *whole* to a more complex whole. For instance, they will ask questions about how radio works before asking questions specifically about what makes it work; teachers, on the other hand, tend to proceed from the simple part to the more complex whole.

These findings are in accord with Ausubel's (1967) principle of subsumption, since new ideas can only be meaningfully learned and retained if more inclusive and appropriately relevant concepts are already available to serve a subsuming role or to provide ideational anchorage.

A short guide to sequencing instructional units will be found in Mager and Beach's *Developing Vocational Instruction* (1967), and it is interesting to note that whilst there is nothing in these findings to upset the well-known order of presentation set up in 'old-fashioned' textbooks on teaching method (e.g. Pinsent, 1941), they do tend to run counter to a good deal of actual classroom practice. Mager concludes his study by suggesting that 'student motivation increases as a function of the amount of control, or apparent control, he is allowed to exercise over the learning experience, probably because a set of greater participation is achieved'.

Associated with learner controlled programs has been the growing interest in independent study. Teachers have long bemoaned the practice of spoon-feeding students, and particularly the assumption that learning bears a close relationship to the frequency with which a student sits in front of an instructor in the classroom. Recent developments in education, however, are beginning to do more than challenge 'the packaging theory of education'. Accordingly, a large number of schools, colleges and universities have been successfully experimenting with independent study programs as part of their regular teaching procedure, with a view to developing students' initiative, responsibility and understanding for what they study, so as to fashion an educational system that provides for its own continuous renewal.

Independent study has been defined by Baskin in his now classic booklet *Quest for Quality* (1961) as 'independent work or reading, sometimes on one's own, sometimes in small groups, but with such work taking place in the absence of the teacher and in lieu of certain regularly scheduled class meetings.' In all instances, however, the program is characterised by precisely defined objectives, and the successful accomplishment of an associated criterion test. Until now such programs usually have been held to be the special prerogative of the superior student. What is new is the use of independent study as part of a teacher's regular repertoire, and its employment with *all* students within a particular class or course.

The results of such programs, of course, have been varied: whilst they do not support the contention that independent study is significantly superior to more conventional classroom methods, the data do demonstrate that students perform just as well on conventional tests of achievement. In addition, there is evidence that students who have undergone independent programs are more interested and enthusiastic in their attitude to the subject, more independent and less restricted in their thinking, and significantly more resourceful in their overall approach to learning. Teachers, on the other hand, who have employed the strategy have found that whilst their work is significantly different from that under conventional programs, it is no less difficult or exacting. They have an essential and critical role to play in so selecting and structuring student experiences that maximum learning is achieved and the student's resources used to the fullest extent. The fundamental question underlying both learner controlled and independent study programs is not whether teacher-teaching should be replaced or eliminated, but rather when and to what combinations of learning experience should a student be exposed?

Linear programs

Linear programs, which are essentially response-centred, are based upon a stimulating yet controversial analysis of learning made by B. F. Skinner, as a result of his studies in the experimental laboratory (Skinner, 1953). Essentially, Skinner's work centres around the effect of reinforcement, which includes what the layman refers to as 'rewards'. Complex, overt and observable behaviour is broken down into sets of responses called operants. Conditions are then brought into play with the effect that a particular set of responses are made by the subject. Every response that contributes towards the desired behaviour is reinforced; responses that do not contribute are ignored. In this way the behaviour of the subject is gradually shaped. As Skinner (1953) reports: 'The original probability of the response in its final form is very low; in some cases it may even be zero. In this way we can build complicated operants which would never appear in the repertoire of the organism otherwise. By reinforcing a series of successive approximations, we bring a rare response to a very high probability in a short time.' Whilst food or water is the normal reinforcing agent with animals, human beings can be reinforced with success—provided that the success achieved is valued by the student. The instructional problem is to set up conditions which will ensure that the student is always right, without, at the same time, debasing the currency that is being used.

Once the problem is conceived in these terms, some sort of mechanisation or even automation is necessary for this type of teaching. Skinner saw that such a device would need to attract and hold the student's attention, present him with subject material, cause him to respond, guarantee him success, check his progress, reinforce him for the response made, and finally demonstrate to the student that real and meaningful learning had indeed been taking place. The simple linear teaching machine is meant to be such a device.

In the linear program, the student progresses at his own rate through a series of small steps, each step leading logically through the subject matter. Since it is important that the student should make as few errors as possible, the increments of information which he is expected to absorb are necessarily small. The student begins with frame one, and then proceeds to frame two in the manner indicated in *Table 3.2*. Some programs contain many thousands of frames and take several hours work, but although the student takes only a small step between frames, by the end of the program considerable progress has been made. For instance, one vast two-volume program by Klaus covers the whole of the conventional High School physics syllabus (Klaus, 1961). Whilst individual differences amongst learners are not denied by linear programmers, they are largely ignored; instead, attention is focused on learning and teaching mechanisms that are assumed to be more or less universal. For this reason, linear programs often make little or no adjustment to individual differences once the target population for the program has been defined and the program successfully validated in the field.

Since operant conditioning places its primary emphasis on the observable or overt response of the learner, frames normally demand a constructed type of response such as filling in a missing word or phrase, answering a question, or solving a problem.

Table 3.2 An extract from an Undergraduate Linear Program on the Analysis of Behaviour

	Correct Response
7.1 Performing animals are sometimes trained with 'rewards'. The behaviour of a hungry animal can be 'rewarded' with	food
7.2 A technical term for 'reward' is reinforcement. To 'reward' an organism with food is to .... it with food.	reinforce
7.3 *Technically* speaking, a thirsty organism can be .... with water.	reinforced (NOT rewarded)
7.4 The trainer reinforces the animal by giving it food .... it has performed correctly.	when (if, after)
7.5 Reinforcement and behaviour occur in the temporal order: (1)........... (2)...........	(1) behaviour (2) reinforcement
7.6 Food given to a hungry animal does not reinforce a particular response unless it is given almost immediately .... the response.	after
7.7 Unlike a stimulus in a reflex, a reinforcing stimulus .... act to elicit the responses it reinforces.	does not (will not)
7.8 A reinforcement does not elicit a response; it simply makes it more .... that an animal will respond in the same way again.	probable (likely)
7.9 Food is probably not reinforcing if the animal is not	deprived of food (hungry)
7.10 If an animal's response is not followed by reinforcement, similar responses will occur .... frequently in the future.	less (in–)
7.11 To make sure an animal will perform, the trainer provides .... for the response frequently.	reinforcement(s)

(By permission from, *The Analysis of Behaviour*, HOLLAND, J. and SKINNER, B.F., Copyright 1961. McGraw Hill Ltd)

Clearly, too small an overlap will result in the program being too difficult, whilst too large an overlap will result in redundancy; the result is that a balance has to be struck by the programmer in order to ensure that the frames are not too overly dependent upon each other. (A fuller description of the linear program and its theoretical basis may be found in Skinner, 1959.)

Mathetics programs

Traditionally, linear programs are regarded as direct applications of Professor B. F. Skinner's technique of instrumental conditioning. However, an examination of them will demonstrate that few follow the Skinnerian model. Their emphasis on learner responses, their preoccupation with cues and prompts, and their regard for fading are all hallmarks of Guthrie's position of contiguous conditioning (*see* Guthrie, 1952). Skinner, on the other hand, stresses the importance of successive approximations towards mastery, differential reinforcement and precise shaping behaviour. Mathetics is a distinguished attempt to capitalise upon these techniques, something that it has accomplished with considerable success. Viewed in this way, Mathetics can be regarded as the only 'pure' example of a Skinnerian approach in educational or training philosophy today.

For Gilbert himself, Mathetics is nothing more than a highly formalised application of existing scientific principles taken literally from the science of animal behaviour. It is not just another point of view about teaching and learning; it is an authoritative scientific technology based upon 'the systematic application of reinforcement theory to the analysis and reconstruction of those complex behaviour repertoires usually known as "subject-matter mastery", "knowledge" and "skill"' (Gilbert, 1962). To a very large extent, the whole approach is based upon the operation of 'prescribing a mastery repertory', a phrase which can be considered as adding greater precision to the more widely used technique of stating instructional objectives. Indeed, Gilbert would probably argue that there are no 'instructional objectives' as such, there are only operating objectives—some of which can be accomplished, in whole or part, by training.

In essence, Mathetics systematises the succession of acts, duties and responsibilities, the presentation of which adds up to the routine of programming. As in any technology, its principles are derivative rather than novel; indeed, its principles are few in number, and are taken almost literally from the study of behaviour in the experimental laboratory. What is new, however, is the way these principles have been formalised and systematised into a series of procedures useful to the analysis and solution of particular instructional problems. A matheticist sees the basic problem of program writing as:

(a) Determining what steps a student must take in order to master a subject (i.e. how to control the stimulus configurations).
(b) Arranging conditions so as to ensure that he will take these steps (i.e. how to motivate or reinforce him).

Since most acts of mastery will already exist in the initial repertoire of behaviours in an adult, learning usually involves rearranging these so that 'acts will occur in a different sequence and on different occasions than they do in the initial repertoire' (Gilbert, 1962). John Dewey's definition of education as the reconstruction of experience is a simple statement of this same principle.

In the education of children, the repertoire of appropriate behaviours has to be established *before* the constituent behaviours can be rearranged or restructured. Thus, the education of children involves an additional strategy to that of adults: the establishment of a repertoire of behaviour, as well as the restructuring of it into a new behaviour pattern. In this way, Gilbert distinguishes the twin concepts of 'acquirement' and 'accomplishment' in terms of performance deficiencies, and points out that a small change in acquirement can often produce an enormous change in accomplishment.

This precept, of course, is basic to all reinforcement theory, since —if an operant is to be strengthened or reinforced by its consequences—the response must already be present in the repertoire in order to produce that consequence. As a corollary to this, individual differences amongst students entering a course of study will often be small, compared with the communalities that exist; however, the *effects* of these differences can be very large indeed. Once this has been grasped, Gilbert holds that it is easier to deal with problems of student motivation. If a student is to learn, then consequences of mastery must already be, or be made to be, reinforcing to him. Indeed, the main purpose of any well-designed program is to motivate the student, otherwise he will not invest the minimum effort that mastery requires. Gilbert believes that the idea that progress through a program is inherently self-reinforcing is a gross over-simplification of the truth: it confuses homage to education with the desire to learn. In well-designed programs on the mathetics model, the aim of the lesson or frame is to arrange conditions so as to ensure that the desire to learn will be cultivated and controlled.

Gilbert's approach to the progress of 'shaping-up' behaviour is essentially different from Skinner's in technique rather than in philosophy. For Skinner the technique of shaping, which is essentially a process of building new responses on the basis of preceding ones, leads to the notion of small steps and thus to small frames. Gilbert, like Mager, has suggested that the programmer ought to allow the student to write the program, or—if this cannot be done —to define an optimum route for him to take on the basis of the skills that he already possesses. Inevitably, such an optimum route involves forcing the student to take as great a step as he can manage, leading to the notion of large steps and so to large frames.

Mathetics is both analytic and synthetic in approach. It provides not only guidelines but also a notational system for breaking a selected skill into its component parts, and suggests a method for putting these components back together again in the form of an appropriate teaching sequence. The successive stages of analysis carried out by a matheticist produce a series of 'exercises', which should in no way be confused with frames. The matheticist views the exercise as a functional unit of behaviour, the size and scope of which are determined by the amount of material required to establish and maintain the greatest possible behavioural change by a standard effort.

The procedure for writing a mathetics lesson begins with a *task analysis* to determine what behaviours are necessary to mastery, and what behaviours are already in the students' repertoire. Following the task analysis, a *learning prescription* is written. This consists of a provisional course of remedial action (hence the term prescription) likely to bring about the desired behavioural change as quickly and as efficiently as possible. The basic unit of the prescription is the operant, consisting of a single act of behaviour (R) together with its associated stimulus condition (S), arranged in such a way as to indicate the actual structure of the task. Once the prescription has been completed, it is examined so as to discover the basic theoretical schematic or 'domain' which can be used as a model for the lesson. The purpose of the domain is to foster generalisation by helping the student to see through the detail of the situation, and to increase reinforcement by shortening the route to mastery.

The final stage of Mathetics, before exercise writing, consists of what Gilbert calls *characterisation*. This identifies responses or stimulus situations which are likely to facilitate or compete with mastery, and goes on to specify ways in which these might be

Table 3.3 An example of a mathetics sequence for learning the colour code of resistors. (From Gilbert, 1962, Courtesy: Praxeonomy Institute)

1. Each of the *first three colour bands* can have only one of 10 colours. Read through this list twice. Learn the *number* for which each *colour* stands.

a *five* dollar bill is *green*

one brown penny

a *white* cat has *nine* lives

seven purple seas

a *blue* tail fly has *six* legs

zero: black nothingness

a *red* heart has *two* parts

three oranges

a *four* legged *yellow* dog

an *eighty* year old man has *grey* hair

(No answer required)

2. List the number for which each *colour* stands:

red...... *white*...... *purple*...... *brown*...... *black*......
(heart)   (cat)   (seas)   (penny)   (nothingness)

green...... *grey*...... *blue*...... *orange*...... *yellow*......
(bill)   (hair)   (tail fly)   (oranges)   (dog)

(Learn any you miss before going on to the next exercise).

3. List the *number* for which each colour stands:

black...... *brown*...... *yellow*...... *grey*...... *green*......

white...... *purple*...... *red*...... *orange*...... *blue*......

dealt with in the exercise. In essence, the characterisation determines appropriate teaching strategies, and from it exercises are written. A typical mathetics program will consist of three different types of exercise: every response is first demonstrated to the student by means of text and special illustrations; it is then *prompted* by getting the student to perform the actual act of mastery with assistance, and then every response is *released* so that the student performs the behaviour entirely on his own. An example from a typical mathetics sequence is illustrated in *Table 3.3.*

It will be appreciated that the writing of a mathetics program is a very complex task, confounded by a remarkably difficult terminology and associated mystique. However, the technique is boldly original and contains a number of novel features. Whenever doubt exists as to the amount of material a student can be expected to assimilate, the basic rule of the matheticist is to make the step as large as possible—since the error will be discovered when the lessons are first tried out. Another basic rule is to teach only that theory of a subject that is pedagogically applicable to the behaviours prescribed by the curriculum. Again, procedures are sometimes taught backwards or retrogressively, in the belief that reinforcement for the final act is end-product mastery and so each act will have obvious validity to the student. Finally, whenever possible, tasks are taught under conditions which are characteristic of the environment under which mastery is to be displayed. If such conditions are not possible, the matheticist attempts to simulate the conditions and equipment as part of the program package.

Recently, Gilbert (1967; 1970) has developed and extended his mathetics approach into a philosophy called Praxeonomy for systematically identifying real training needs by performance analysis. The philosophy highlights the essential difference—often overlooked by teachers and programmers—between *accomplishment* and *acquirement,* and introduces the concept of performance deficiency. A distinction is then made between performance deficiencies arising from deficiency of knowledge, for which training or guidance might be considered, and performance deficiencies arising from a deficiency of execution on which training will have little or no impact.

Achievement has two main aspects: it can refer to what a person has learned (acquirement), or to the value of what has been learned (accomplishment). Praxeonomy places great importance on the student's level of accomplishment. Indeed, a student's level of acquirement—in terms of the knowledge he already possesses— may be very high indeed, but this knowledge is of little value if his level of accomplishment is low. A young child may be able to carry out separately every action involved in tying his shoelace, but still be unable to accomplish the task because he doesn't know the correct sequence of actions. Thus a small deficiency in acquirement (the correct sequence) can make a very high difference in accomplishment (the tying of the shoelace):

> Let us examine ... the confusion between acquirement and accomplishment. You say that you know nothing about bank tellering, but this is not true. If you examine all the operations a bank teller uses to balance his books, you will find that you have already acquired most of them. Nevertheless, the few operations you have not acquired prevent you from accomplishing the objectives of the bank teller's job. In terms of what the teller and you know about his job, there is very little difference between you; in terms of the value of what you know, you are worlds apart (Gilbert, 1967).

Once this essential difference is realised, it can be readily appreciated that a test of accomplishment can be used when we are concerned with promotion or job placement, whereas a test of acquirement must be used in order to determine what deficiencies are present in the student's repertoire.

The differences between these two tests is an essential one in terms of a theory of teaching, not because of the semantic value of the discussion but because of the consequences that are involved. Analysis of a problem may well reveal that minimal training (to bring about a small change in acquirement) will result in doubling or even tripling the effectiveness and value of an individual's performance capability; for this reason Praxeonomy is particularly concerned with overcoming such performance deficiencies. If the discrepancy between the student's behaviour and that of the master is due to deficiencies in execution, then strategies involving better information systems, or management changes or incentive systems would be considered depending on the actual cause of the difficulty. If the discrepancy is due to deficiencies in skill or knowledge then strategies involving training or guidance would be considered. Whatever decision is taken will depend upon the economics of the situation. Up to now, as Gilbert has pointed out, the unspoken rule is that people who aren't performing up to par need to be trained. But there is more than one way of overcoming human deficiencies and training is seldom the best, a point that courses in instructional technology tend to ignore with resulting financial penalties!

TEACHING STRUCTURES

The selection of an appropriate presentation strategy for a sequence of frames is dependent upon the objectives to be realised, and the structure of the behaviours involved. Both of these are detailed in the task analysis, whilst the detail and limits of the actual structures may be visually illustrated in the matrix—if this technique of analysis has been employed (*see* Davies, 1965b; 1967a). Generally speaking, five broad structures of behaviour are discernible, as summarised in *Table 3.4*. (The reader is also referred here to *Figure 2.6* in Chapter 2).

The structures shown in this figure must be carefully sought for in the task analysis, since it appears that each requires a different kind of teaching strategy if it is to be acquired by the student in as efficient a way as possible (Gagné, 1965b). Furthermore, as a general rule, there is a striking contrast between the different structures in terms of retention; chains and multiple discriminations are subject to rapid forgetting, whilst concepts and principles seem to show marked resistance, probably due to their highly organised nature.

In teaching *the chain* several different strategies are available to the programmer:

(a) The chain can be taught progressively, linking each element to the previous one, and using prompts which serve to cue in the individual links.

(b) The chain can be taught by a 'progressive part' method. Students learn first A, followed by A + B, then A + B + C, and so on.

(c) The chain can be taught retrogressively; the student may be taught the final or terminal act of mastery first, then the next-to-last act, and so on through the chain. The advantages of this backward or retrogressive teaching strategy, which might at first sight seem highly illogical, are said to lie in the fact that reinforcement for the final act completed by the student is end-product mastery, that each act is self-completing (so that revision and consolidation problems are overcome) and, in addition, that the technique is novel for the student. A good example of a program using this technique is Ferster's (1965) 'Programmed College Composition'.

(d) The chain can be taught by mnemonics, or by worked examples. Flow charts and decision trees (see below) can be used as 'copy'.

It is difficult at this stage to indicate which of these strategies

Table 3.4 Common stimulus–response patterns

Structure	Notation	Definition	Examples
Signal or Stimulus response learning	$S \xrightarrow{\hspace{1cm}} R$	The subject acquires a precise response to a discriminated stimulus. What is learned is a connection or discriminated operant, sometimes called an instrumental response, and the student is reinforced for responses that are correct.	(a) Learning a new vocabulary in science or in a foreign language.
Chain	$S \rightarrow R.\ S \rightarrow R.\ S \rightarrow R$	An initial stimulus triggers the first response, which then becomes the stimulus for the second response, and so on, until the final response. In the chain the sequence of stimuli and responses is fixed. One situation causes an event which creates conditions leading to another, and so on, to the final event.	A fixed sequence of acts that one has to go through, e.g. (a) in solving a mathematical problem (e.g. simultaneous equations); (b) writing an essay; (c) tying a shoelace.
Multiple Discrimination	$\begin{aligned} S &\rightarrow R \\ S &\rightarrow R \\ S &\rightarrow R \\ &\vdots \\ S &\rightarrow R \end{aligned}$	A situation produces two or more stimuli, each leading to a different response. Each response is related to a common theme, and the discrimination exists in the ability to distinguish one category of phenomena from another.	Learning the difference between, e.g. (a) latitude and longitude; (b) different wave forms displayed on an oscilloscope; (c) triangles and quadrilaterals.
Concept	$\begin{aligned} S &\uparrow \\ S &\uparrow \\ S &\uparrow \rightarrow R \\ &\vdots \\ S &\uparrow \end{aligned}$	A situation or event produces two or more stimuli whose combined effect produces a response. One stimulus may be more influential than the others, but all stimuli converge or generalise to one result. The ability to generalise is closely related to the ability to discriminate.	(a) Responding in terms of abstract properties, such as colour, shape, position, number. (b) The meaning of terms such as 'good' and 'evil', or 'electromotive force' and 'potential difference'.
Principle	$\begin{aligned} Ss_1 &\rightarrow r \sim s \\ Ss_2 &\rightarrow r \sim s \\ Ss_3 &\rightarrow r \sim s \rightarrow r \sim s \rightarrow R \\ Ss_4 &\rightarrow r \sim s \\ Ss_5 &\rightarrow r \sim s \end{aligned}$	A situation or event produces the chaining of two or more concepts. It functions to control behaviour in the manner of a verbalised rule like 'If A, then B', where A and B are concepts which the subject already knows in the sense that he can identify any member of the class that they name.	(a) Metals expand when heated. (b) Latitude is angular distance north or south of the equator. (c) Potential difference is a measure of the rate at which energy is used between two points.

is the most effective, as they seem appropriate to different subject matters. Some pilot studies suggest that under certain conditions the retrogressive strategy results in faster learning (*see* Lewis *et al.*, 1967), but as Duncan notes in Chapter 2, several investigators have failed to substantiate this claim.

Multiple discriminations involve an interesting technique. Most teachers and programmers tend to teach two or more conditions separately: for example, they teach 'latitude' step by step, and then they teach 'longitude'. Inevitably, this results in a long program spread over a large number of frames, so that time and effort are wasted. A more efficient strategy seems to teach each of the conditions at one and the same time, so that the student is forced to see not only the associations between each individual S and R, but also to observe the discriminations, between the different S–Rs, which have to be made. This type of presentation allows the student to make different, but highly competing, responses to different but closely associated stimuli. Since each of the conditions involved in the discrimination is often a chain, the links can be taught in parallel, retrogressively; an example of this is to be seen in the sample program illustrated in the latter part of this chapter.

Practice plays a different and more limited part in establishing multiple discriminations than it does in signal and chain learning, since it does not appear to strengthen any of the discriminations involved. Indeed, it does not seem to make any logical sense in thinking that it should, unless the chains making up the multiple discrimination have not been previously fully acquired. The one function that practice does have in the overall strategy, however, is to widen the universe of each of the conditions so that better generalisation can be established as a prelude to more precise and subtle discriminations.

Concepts can be obtained, and often are, as a result of trial and error, as indeed can multiple discriminations; however, this is not a particularly efficient teaching strategy unless one's objective is to set up conditions for discovery—with unlimited time available. Furthermore, the learning of a concept is not necessarily a verbal matter, although verbal strategies make learning relatively easier if they can be used. For this reason, diagrams, pictures, tapes, films, film strips, etc. are all useful and worthwhile presentation techniques—as long as they do not interfere with the primary purpose of concept formation. In essence, to establish a concept the student must be taught to generalise within a class of stimuli, and then he must be taught to discriminate between this class and all other classes with which it is likely to become confused.

H

Whilst this overall strategy is taking place, a number of subsidiary strategies are involved. Discriminations between classes should not be pointed out to the student by instruction. Instead, the student should be asked directly to state the difference himself. Once a major discrimination has been acquired, the student should then be asked to identify additional and more subtle instances. Contiguity is obviously an essential characteristic of the strategy, and it may well be that it is the absence of contiguity in the trial and error situation that makes that strategy so laborious for concept learning. Research (Davies, 1969a) has demonstrated that repetition, rehearsal and practice contribute little or nothing to either the establishment of a concept or its retention—although they substantially increase the learning time and so make for a less efficient learning situation. The same investigator has also shown that the classic mathetics sequence of demonstration, prompt and release exercises, appears to be an unnecessary elaboration as far as the acquirement of concepts are concerned (Davies, 1969a).

Principles, in simplest terms, consist of chains of two or more concepts. An example of such a principle would be the simple proposition that 'metals expand when heated', where 'metal', 'expansion' and 'heat' are the three concepts that are linked together in a precise and predetermined way. The chain, therefore, represents *relationships* between concepts rather than the simple S–Rs we have studied earlier. Insight can be regarded, in limited terms, as nothing more than the acquiring of such relationships.

The prerequisite for learning a principle is an obvious one, although often forgotten in practice by many teachers. Students must already know the concepts involved, in the sense that they can identify any members of the class that the concepts name. Once this has been accomplished, the instructional strategy involves chaining these concepts together. Great care, however, needs to be taken so as to ensure that conceptual, rather than the more limited verbal chains are acquired. Many students can *say* a principle without being able to *do* it.

Once the prerequisites are fulfilled, the conditions for learning a principle follow a particular instructional sequence. This consists of five steps (Gagné, 1963):

(a) Inform the student about the nature of the task and the performance to be expected of him.
(b) Get him to recall the component concepts.
(c) Cue him to chain these concepts into the required order, so that contiguity is established and the principle derived.
(d) Ask him to demonstrate or give examples of the principle.

(e) Lead him to make a verbal statement of the principle for himself.

It must be remembered that few principles are learnt in isolation, since organised knowledge involves a hierarchy of them. Learning such a hierarchy of principles involved the organisation of these principles into a structure, and an appreciation of their organisational pattern.

THE FUNCTION OF THE FRAME

So far we have been concerned with the different overall strategies that programmers may decide to use in shaping the behaviour of their students, so as to realise precisely defined objectives. The concept of a technology of education, however, introduces the idea of the frame as a behavioural unit, rather than a simple unit of presentation. As a consequence, the frame has a very definite function to perform, and in carrying out this function it must perforce fulfil a number of behavioural requirements. Seen in this way, each frame must involve a predetermined and predicted *change* in the behaviour of the student working through the sequence, and this change must also be relevant and meaningful to the establishment of that complex repertoire of behaviours envisaged by the objectives of the program. In other words, the frame does something much more than merely present material, it helps to shape the student's behaviour.

In order to bring about this required change in behaviour, the student must be motivated in some way as an essential precondition for learning (Gagné and Bolles, 1959). Gagné has pointed out, however, that it is probably a mistake to think of this necessary state as a 'motivation for learning'. He argues that it is more meaningful to think of motivation as involving two interacting states which compete with other possible alternatives:

(a) A willingness to enter into the learning situation. As Bruner (1965) has demonstrated, this involves *activation* (i.e. the learner must be willing to start the actual task), *maintenance* (i.e. he must be willing to keep going once he has started it), and *direction* (i.e. he must have a sense of goal and a knowledge of the relevance of the task). If any of these essential components are missing, then it is unlikely that the task can be accomplished.

(b) Alertness to the actual stimuli of the task. Research by

Lindsley (1957) has suggested that stimuli will only reach the higher levels of the central nervous system if the 'alerting' system in the brain is functioning in an appropriate manner. If the alerting system is functioning inappropriately (i.e. not attending to the stimuli of the task) then instruction cannot take place.

Since learning depends upon the exploration of all the alternatives in a situation, the goal of instruction via the medium of a frame or lesson must be to facilitate and regularise this exploration by controlling the appropriate behaviour.

To bring about such a high degree of control, the behavioural frame must realise a number of specific requirements:

(a) It must so interest and stimulate the student that he will engage in the required behaviour.

(b) It must present material (or stimuli) so that the student is forced (overtly or covertly) to make the desired response.

(c) It may present stimuli in such a way that the student is forced to respond in a novel way. (Familiar stimuli might be presented together so that the more usual responses they would normally call forth, when given separately, are combined to produce an entirely new response, i.e. a discovery is made.)

(d) It should either confirm that the response given is the desired one, and/or reinforce the novel response so that the same behaviour will occur more easily in the future. (Often the most effective reinforcement is the exhilaration of being able to do things that were previously considered too difficult or even impossible. Individual frames supply the necessary confirmation that the responses are correct: sequences of frames reinforce the student by demonstrating that real skills are actually being acquired.)

(e) It may contain auxiliary material not essential to the desired behaviour. (This material may be introduced because of its interest value, or because it may help to enrich the experience as a whole. Auxiliary material is often used by programmers for its continuity value, or because it helps to relate newly learnt material with behaviour already acquired or enjoyed. Such material can also help the programmer to establish rapport with the student, and maintain motivation.)

Using programming terminology, it can be seen that every frame must present—at the very least—a stimulus (S^D) which will elicit or cue the student to make the desired discriminative response (R). Some frames will also contain a stimulus complex ($\bar{S}^D$) which will elicit a single novel response not formerly in the repertoire of the student. However, S^D type frames will almost always precede $\bar{S}^D$ frames, since the latter will usually appear at the end of a subsequence which has deliberately led up to their creation. These two types of frame must be carefully distinguished, since their functions are different. Indeed, the difference between early and modern programs can often be seen in the increasing skill with which the $\bar{S}^D$ frames are created, and programs thereby are often considerably shorter in length, as well as more challenging and interesting to the student.

Unfortunately, in writing frames many teachers and programmers have tended to make certain assumptions about motivation, either to assume a motivated student or else assume that success is intrinsically motivating. Recently Premack (1959; 1965) has offered a useful principle of motivation for frame writers by increasing the generality of the law of effect. Premack points out that the law of effect as generally stated implicity assumes that those behaviours which are to be reinforced are neutral or are of no intrinsic value to the student. He argues that it is more useful to consider that all activities are likely to have some value, and that these activities can be classified from the most to the least preferred. This means that the law of effect can now be restated in such a way as to tie together the twin concepts of reinforcement and order of preference; in other words, a given activity can be used to reinforce all those of lesser value, but none of those of higher value. In this way a given response can be used to reinforce some responses but not others, a useful point to remember.

Stated in full, the Premack Principle states that 'If behaviour B is of higher probability than behaviour A, then behaviour A can be made more probable by making behaviour B contingent upon it' (Premack, 1959). Suppose, for instance, that for a particular child it is possible to rank order four activities from the most preferred to the least preferred in the following way:

(a) Watching a Walt Disney film on television.
(b) Playing ball in the garden.
(c) Eating a bar of chocolate.
(d) Hammering on a wooden pegboard.

If this order is real then it is possible to predict that watching television can be used to reinforce the other three activities. Premack

(1959; 1963; 1965) and Homme *et al.* (1963; 1964) have presented data that indicate that predictions of this sort are accurate, and can be used with great effect for controlling and motivating the behaviour of both school children and young adults. Unfortunately, the principle has, as yet, been little used by other workers, although there are echoes of it in the frames of some of the more modern programs that are beginning to appear. An example of the technique is seen in retrogressive chaining (where the final step in the sequence can be ranked as having a higher preference than the first step), and a further example is to be found in Moore's automated responsive environment where young children are taught to read and write by utilising the child's natural and preferred exploratory activity (Moore, 1960; 1962).

Since the publication in 1960 by Evans, Homme and Glaser of their ruleg system, one of the more pervasive issues of frame writing has been the relative advantages of the ruleg strategy over the egrule strategy. In either case the basic assumption is that all verbal material can be classified into one of two types of statement: first, rules (ru) or statements of generality like 'Most metals expand when heated', or secondly, examples (eg's) or statements of specificity like 'Copper expands when heated'. In the ruleg system, it is considered that there is a learning advantage in teaching the rule and then either giving or getting the student to give examples (i.e. an inductive approach), whereas in the egrule system it is considered preferable to teach a whole series of examples before getting the student to derive the rule for himself (a deductive approach).

Whilst it is certainly not possible to be dogmatic about the best order to be employed, research does suggest a number of guidelines (Hendrix, 1947; Haslerund and Meyers, 1958; Ausubel, 1961, 1963; Mechner, 1967). The ruleg or inductive approach is to be preferred when the concept is an easy one for the target population for whom the program is being written, whereas the egrule or deductive approach should be used when the concept is likely to be a difficult one. Furthermore, the evidence strongly suggests that the deductive approach undoubtedly enhances the learning, retention and transferability of meaningful material, although students generally prefer the inductive approach—probably because they are more accustomed to this method of teaching. The problem which the program writer has to resolve, however, is whether the advantages of the deductive approach are sufficient for students who can still acquire the concept via the inductive method, to warrant the greatly increased expenditure of time that is necessarily involved.

TYPES OF FRAME

Once the teaching structure and the actual presentation strategies have been decided, the programmer is ready to begin writing the program. All frames have in common a limited but specific aim, their objective is to produce:

(a) A new behaviour combination in the student.
(b) To relate new behaviours to all other components of mastery.

Students do not usually fail to complete a frame because they cannot make the correct response: they fail because they cannot make the mastery responses on the right occasions. All mastery responses are normally present in the adult student's repertoire, the problem which faces the frame writer is how to force the student to display them in the proper order and at the proper time in response to the proper stimuli. For this reason the initial draft is usually prepared on 'oversize' paper; successive refinements and drafts can then be made as the actual materials are developed, often with a student from the target population physically present.

Criterion frames, which release the behaviour after it has been finally established and rehearsed, are often the first frames to be written. Normally, there will be one criterion frame for each of the structures or sub-structures that the programmer has recognised. The criterion frame will always use the language of the domain theory and will usually ask a direct question or instruction. No explicit prompts are given. Instead the student's behaviour is 'released' (S^L) to complete the sequence, although he may of course prompt himself (r.sP) to make the correct mastery response (R^M). (Since the prompt in this case is covert rather than overt, lower case letters are used in the symbolic notation of the programmer. A typical criterion frame would look like this:

Write down the three principles of hydraulics:

1. ....

2. ....

3. ....

If less help is required, the programmer will forgo the prompt and simply instruct the student 'Write down the principles of hydraulics'. Obviously, if the student is unable to respond to the criterion frames correctly, the frame sequence leading up to it has failed to work, and requires revision.

Once the criterion frame for a structure has been written, the *teaching frames* can then be constructed. These frames will introduce and demonstrate all the essential behaviours of mastery. Students follow the example or examples given, and a description is usually presented of the domain in the order or sequence required by mastery. Whilst the language employed may be that of the domain theory, this is not essential at this particular stage. The operant is initially introduced to the student in such a way as to force him to look at and identify the stimulus (i.e. observe), and then it will instruct him to make the mastery response (*see Figure 3.2*). In this frame, behaviour is gradually shaped by using a variety of 'non-items' (S^Δ) to establish the actual observing stimulus (S^O).

Proper stimulus control is the primary objective of the teaching frame. For this reason, several aspects of the stimulus are treated in a routine way, and are always present in the frame:

(a) S^D or discriminative stimulus is the actual stimulus which produces the required mastery response. As this S^D cannot always be presented *per se,* some verbal representation is sometimes necessary.

(b) S^O or observing stimulus leads the student to make the response of looking at and identifying (R^O) the critical elements in the situation or stimulus. In accomplishing this, the S^O has two critical functions:
S^O locates the S^D for the student so that he does not overlook it. This is referred to as the S^a function of the S^O. S^O identifies the essential characteristics of the S^D so that he can make a generalisation about it. This is the S^c function. Both the S^a and the S^c functions must be fulfilled if the S^O is to be successful, since observation requires both attention and direction.

(c) An instruction stimulus S^I forces the student to make the correct mastery response R^M to the discriminative stimulus S^D without error in the presence of the observing stimulus S^O.

The reader may well like to locate for himself these three aspects of the stimulus conditions in the Ifkov sequence.

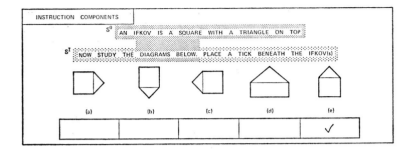

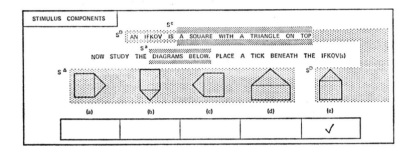

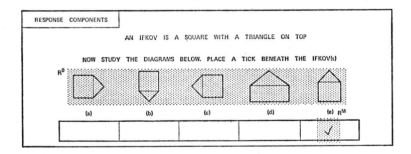

Figure 3.2. A typical frame teaching a concept. A behavioural notation is overprinted to illustrate the structure of the unit. Note the gradual shaping from the S^Δ to S^D

After the behaviour has been acquired, practice and rehearsal are necessary if the structure involves signals or chains before the behaviour is finally released in the criterion frames. A *practice frame*, if it is necessary, repeats the performance established by the teaching frame, however the language and vocabulary employed are taken as far as possible from the domain theory. Students are helped or prompted to make the correct mastery response (R^M) in the presence of the most distinguishing characteristic of the S^D. The prompt is thus a modified and more general version of the S^I: an instruction is detailed and specific, whereas a prompt (which in theory would be unnecessary were there no competition or interference with what the student has learned) is a short, simple and generalised verbal statement that the student can learn to cue himself. (For a discussion of different types of prompts, *see* Fry, 1963).

In thinking of these three types of frame—teaching, practice and criterion—it is useful to think of a single operant in the chain. The response to this operant is evoked in a different way, depending on the type of frame involved:

Frame 1. (Teaching frame)

$$S^O \rightarrow R^O.S^D \ (S^I) \rightarrow R^M$$

Frame 2. (Rehearsal frame)

$$S^O \rightarrow R^O.S^D \rightarrow (S^P) \rightarrow R^M$$

Frame 3. (Criterion frame)

$$S^O \rightarrow R^O.S^D + (S^L) \rightarrow (r.sP) \rightarrow R^M$$

In drafting actual frames, it seems good practice to begin by designing and drafting the form or topography of the S^D itself. It is seldom efficient to try and draft the whole frame at once; it is better to start with the most critical element as the foundation block and then build the surrounding superstructure. As the S^D will eventually form the mental focus of the frame, it should be placed in a dominant position—often in the centre of the page. Whilst this procedure seems contrary to normal teaching practice, since it is unusual to begin by talking about the S^D, it has two great practical advantages: it constantly reminds the writer of what has to be accomplished, and it enables him to see how much of its own story the S^D tells.

Once the S^D has been located, the position and form of the response (R^M) can be determined. Responses should consist of either the act of mastery, or acts that will help to maintain this mastery behaviour. The basic rule, however, is to try to minimise, as far as possible, the effort the student must make, so that—provided other things are equal—it is preferable to have him checking or ticking choices or pushing buttons rather than to have him copying out responses. Normally, the space for the response should be positioned below the S^D.

The observing and instruction stimuli (S^O and S^I) can sometimes be simultaneously effected in one single sentence; the important rule is to keep them as simple as possible. Normally, they are located to the left and above the S^D, so that they are the first thing the student's eyes will light upon.

The frame is now complete except for making the stimuli more distinctive and memorable. Three main methods are generally employed:

(a) The use of prompts or cues (S^p) which are later 'faded' and then finally 'vanish'.

(b) The use of induction or stimulus generalisation ($S^{abc} \longrightarrow R^{abc}$), by which similar stimuli whose responses possess elements in common are grouped together in the presentation.

(c) The use of specialised mediators (r.s.) which can best be viewed as a fraction of some overt response (Osgood, 1953), which aids the learner to make the correct mastering response by either simplifying the situation or by supplying an analogy.

Simplicity and precision are here as important as elsewhere, but it is important to recognise that prompts, cues, and specialised mediators may not be necessary if competition is unlikely. Care should be taken to ensure that the student is not caused to repeat any acts of mediation overtly after he has first made them: but he may perform them covertly, so long as he feels they are necessary. *Figure 3.2* shows a typical frame with each item labelled in accordance with this discussion.

Most conventional programmers stress the importance of a student immediately checking his responses against some model. All too often it is assumed that these answer checks provide the only form of reinforcement. Theory alone, however, does not require such independent checks; the more usual source of information about the adequacy of the response lies in the product of that response. If the student can see the adequacy of what he has done directly he performs it, then the checking need not be essential. However, there are three other justifications for using such checks:

(a) They increase the student's confidence.
(b) They compete with any careless study habits that he may have developed.
(c) They serve as a check against possible errors in the lesson.

THE LANGUAGE OF FRAMES

For many students, language, the prime means of communication, is a barrier. Industrial trainees, for example, often lack the verbal and intellectual skills necessary to understand technical prose. Yet, instructors feel that they have communicated to their students if they present information in the form of words.

This problem is most often seen in Government publications. The sheer density of their prose style is often enough to make comprehension extremely difficult. *Table 3.5* illustrates the problem with an example from a Ministry of Pensions and National Insurance leaflet which sets out the qualifications for a small grant payable on death. In attempting to read and understand this paragraph it should be remembered that this is not an extract from a legal document; rather it is taken from a leaflet designed to help the layman to understand an Act of Parliament.

Table 3.5   Section taken from Leaflet N.I.48. 'Late paid or unpaid contributions'. (M.P.N.I. 1963)

'Contributions paid late cannot normally count for death grant (other than towards yearly average) unless they were paid before the death on which the grant is claimed and before the death of the insured person if that was earlier. But if the insured person died before the person on whose death the grant is claimed, contributions which, although paid late, have already been taken into account for the purpose of a claim for widow's benefit or retired pension, will count towards death grant.'

Programmers, faced with the problem of programming such subject material, often go to considerable lengths to choose the right words and to arrange the sentences in such a way so as to make their meaning clear. Although clarity is a virtue, sorely needed in technical writing, this approach may result in programs which are over-long, boring to read, and seemingly infantile in approach. The basic question which programmers must ask is whether continuous prose really is the best vehicle for expressing complex interrelated rules. The difficulty in understanding prose is not solely concerned with the choice of words, nor with the meaning of individual clauses. A good deal of the difficulty lies in the order in which the clauses are presented, the way in which they are related to each other, and in their grammar.

A number of research findings have suggested that the time taken to understand a sentence varies according to the grammatical structure employed. These results (*see* Davies, 1967b; Miller and McKean, 1964, for references) can be summarised as follows, and the reader is advised to compare each research finding with the prose section given in *Table 3.5.*

(a) Simple sentences—which are affirmative, active and declarative—are more rapidly identified and processed than are more complex sentences built upon the simple ones.

(b) Each grammatical complication (e.g. negatives, passives, and queries) when added to the simple sentence, creates an increment of difficulty which delays correct identification and processing.

(c) Semantic and pragmatic factors in language, relating to the way in which logical connectives are ordinarily used, interact with syntactic factors so as to inhibit or facilitate understanding.

(d) Negative qualifiers, except in simple instructions, can appreciably affect the efficiency of understanding.

(e) In the absence of context, it takes longer to respond to negative statements than to affirmative ones, even when the amounts of information conveyed by the statements are equal.

(f) It takes longer to match sentences expressed in the active voice with correlative sentences in the passive voice.

(g) Connectives, such as 'except', 'or', 'if', and 'unless'—which are difficult to avoid in continuous prose—can appreciably affect the efficiency of performance.

A final point of particular relevance to those concerned with writing multiple-choice alternatives is:

(h) The time taken to evaluate the truth of a sentence is affected more by its syntax (affirmative or negative) than by its truth value (true or false).

As a result of these research findings it will be seen that continuous prose is not the best vehicle for dealing with complex verbal instructions. Algorithms (dealt with in the next section) present a far more effective strategy.

Special stimulus effects of audio-visual media

Media decisions are normally of two kinds (Heinich, 1965): the enrichment and optional media under the control of the teacher or programmer, and the basic, required media specified at the curriculum development level. It is with the latter, however, that the most critical and important decisions have to be made, since this involves special stimuli effects demanded by the characteristics of the task.

Often in writing a sequence of frames, for instance, the programmer considers the possibility of using audio-visual techniques in order to strengthen and increase the impressiveness of his stimulus materials. Unfortunately, research into the effectiveness of such techniques in a form that would allow them to be incorporated into programmed sequences is confused, but a number of trends are discernible.

Black (1962) has found that simple line drawings, containing a minimum of detail, are more effective for teaching visual discriminations than pictures containing a great amount of detail. Dwyer (1967, 1968), using a medical program, compared presentation by means of simple line drawings, detailed shaded drawings and realistic photographs, with presentations containing no illustrations. He found that simple line drawings were more successful at prompting total student understanding of the concepts presented in the instruction; that the more detailed shaded drawings were better at prompting the learning of location, structure and position; but that oral presentations, with an absence of any kind of illustration, were more effective in promoting the learning of information about terms and the development of new views or reorganisations.

Leith (1968b) found that lower ability children profited more from concrete illustrations (as opposed to abstract) in a geography program, whereas there was no difference between these two kinds of illustration for higher ability children. It appears that the important variables to consider in the design of illustrations are therefore the age, ability and experience of the students who are to use them (Vernon, 1962), and the function of the learning task that the illustrations are designed to complement (Dwyer, 1969).

In a number of experiments which compared the relative effectiveness of different presentations involving three-dimensional mock-ups, symbolic diagrams and realistic pictorial charts, no significant differences were discovered, although there were suggestions that mock-ups might be superior on a parts-recognition test, and symbolic diagrams on a test of functional interconnection (Lumsdaine, 1961). Job aids, such as check-lists, however, are effective for aiding performance in procedural tasks containing such a large number of steps that it is highly unlikely that they could be remembered.

In an incisive review of the research that has been carried out on learning from films Hoban (1960) arrived at three broad conclusions.

(a) People do learn from films.
(b) The amount learned varies with individual differences such as age and formal education.
(c) Learning can be directly increased by repetition, student participation, and the use of such attention-directing devices as the inclusion of arrows, etc. Of particular importance is the use of 'implosion' techniques for assembly sequences, whereby the different parts of a component 'jump' into their proper place in the correct sequence (Sheffield, Margolius and Hoehn, 1961). Other than in the occasional instance, there is no real experimental evidence that cartoon embellishments (designed to add 'interest' or help clarify the spoken or written word), either add or detract from learner performance (Popham, 1969).

At the same time, research into learning from films brings into relief the importance of proper task analysis, and the integration of such an analysis with the pertinent learning variables.

Many film theorists have asserted that the unique formal property of film is motion, and that such movement is capable, *by itself*, of producing a response in students. Furthermore, it is frequently held that much of this specific response to the motion component of a film is affective or emotional or ineffective. Little experimental evidence, however, has been found for any of these assertions, although motion films are generally preferred by students (Miller, 1969).

Studies have also been carried out involving animation techniques. In most of them the results indicate that animation can materially aid learning by directing student attention to relevant cues (Lumsdaine *et al.*, 1961). However, Lumsdaine and Gladstone (1958) have shown that fancy versions of a film containing pictorial and auditory embellishments, intended to stimulate interest, were actually less effective than a simple, straightforward presentation. Later studies suggested that a crude, pencil-sketch version of a film on elementary science did not significantly affect learning as compared with a polished colour version of the same film costing ten times as much to make. More recent work by Kanner (1968) has indicated that colour, whether on TV or film, does not provide a learning advantage over black and white presentations provided appropriate verbal cues are employed. The aesthetic effects of colour were not, of course, considered in this study.

Gropper (1961) found that science demonstrations performed by children on film were more effective in stimulating children of the same age group in the viewing class, than were the same demonstrations performed on film by an adult teacher. Further research by Gropper (1967), working with educational television, has indicated that conventional television lessons, involving no active responding on the part of the students, 'may be adequate with lesser goals in mind'. Active, overt responding, however, is necessary when the student is required to acquire, retain and transfer large amounts of information.

It is important, when considering the effectiveness of instructional television or film, not to forget the contribution made by the verbal commentary. Vernon (1962) points out that people infer meaning from pictures, and that this inference may be more or less correct. Providing a verbal commentary ensures that the correct interpretation is directly stated. Indeed, at one point, Vernon remarks that it may be more instructive to show still pictures or diagrams with a good verbal commentary than to show a film without one. Laner (1954, 1955) demonstrated that the commentary to a film was of the greatest importance to the understanding of its meaning, and the gaining of knowledge from it.

In selecting the presentation most likely to realise their objectives, teachers and programmers are increasingly tempted to employ multi-media approaches. However, in a most interesting study into the connotative meanings that students associate with single and multi-media presentations, Anderson (1969) found that:

1. *Single-media presentations*
   (a) The pictorial mode was seen as abstract, feminine, beautiful and active.

(b) The written mode was seen as confused and complex.

(c) The spoken word was seen as unexciting, mature, and precise.

2. *Multi-media presentations*

(a) The pictorial-spoken combination was seen as clear, easy and complete

(b) The pictorial-written combination was seen as blunt and artless.

(c) The written-spoken combination was seen as imperfect and small.

(d) The pictorial-written-spoken combination was seen as bland, boring and warm.

On average, however, single-media presentations elicited more high intensity connotative meanings than multi-media presentations. Whilst it is not easy to generalise from these results, the difficulties associated with the written mode suggests that particular care needs to be taken when it is not possible to introduce pictures, diagrams, tables and other illustrative materials. The connotative meanings associated with the pictorial-spoken combination are of particular interest, particularly in the area of language teaching.

Gagné (1962b) has reviewed the successful use of simulators in all types of training. He points out that it is not necessarily the device itself that is simulated, but the operations or tasks performed on the equipment. The use of simulators has been shown to be particularly effective in those areas where task analysis suggests that difficulties may well exist in acquiring chains and multiple discriminations—both of which can present difficulties in terms of retention (Davies, 1969b).

Annett (1968) has pointed out that there is no reason why a programmed course should not include a simulator, but to have a simulator does not necessarily imply that the course has been programmed. Annett considers that many simulators are in fact used in an unprogrammed way (i.e. without sufficient attention being paid to analysis of what should be simulated, or to revision of the program on the basis of self-correcting procedures). Annett's views here are pertinent to a special type of simulator—the language laboratory—which is playing an increasingly important part in modern language teaching.

Carroll (1963) in reviewing the research on language teaching concluded that next to nothing was known concerning the effectiveness of many of the procedures that were employed in language laboratories, and this conclusion still seems true today. Some

I

worthwhile comparisons have been carried out between conventional methods and language laboratory teaching (Antioch, 1960), but no significant differences in achievement were established between the two methods: student attitudes were more favourable towards the laboratory situation, and teacher time was also saved. Present-day research on language teaching is surveyed in reports issued by the Committee on Research and Development in Modern Languages. New techniques of presentation demand changes in the structure of class grouping and timetabling, and the architectural implications of different language teaching systems have been interestingly compared in the Department of Education and Science's *Building Bulletin* (1968).

It has been argued that auditory and audio-visual materials will play an increasing part in programmed instruction in the future. Apter (1968) has presented an effective summary of research carried out in this field. The evidence suggests an advantage for audio programs in certain specific areas (e.g. with subnormal and blind children) and there is certainly a future for audio-visual programs which could be presented by the mass media of radio and television. Work in this area (summarised in several papers in Dunn and Holroyd, 1969) links up with another—that of group as opposed to individual programmed instruction. Experiments carried out successfully demonstrating the viability of this approach have been summarised by Hartley (1968).

One stimulus effect that is often overlooked in educational materials, apart from general overall attractiveness, is that of print type and size. Several investigators have made psychological studies of typography, examining the effects of such variables as length of line, style, and size of type in terms of speed of assimilation and retention. As early as 1928 Tinker and Paterson, for instance, found that material printed in capitals took 12 per cent longer to read and understand than the same material printed in a mixture of upper and lower case type. While it is difficult to generalise from this and other studies without regard to the nature of the students, the task and the material used in the experiments, differences were found. A summary of the somewhat confusing research findings is shown in *Table 3.6*. It has been demonstrated that whilst the manipulation of one variable may make little difference, the simultaneous manipulation of a number of variables does have an effect upon speed of assimilation and upon retention.

Of particular interest to program writers are the findings concerning the use of italics (often employed as a prompt), the length of line, and colour of the print and paper. Italics are not

Table 3.6 Recommendations for Optimal Printing

	Burt (1955, 1959)	Tinker and Paterson (1949)	Luckiesh and Moss (1942)
Type style	Old style best, except possibly for scientists	Only American Typewriter and Cloister Black not recommended	Modern better than Old Style
Type form	—	Roman better than all Capitals or Italics	Italics insufficiently bold
Boldness	Only if eye defects	Unnecessary	Medium Bold recommended
Size	10 point	10 point	At least 12 point
Leading between lines	1 or 2 point	2 point	3 points or more
Length of line	3½–5½ inches	3 inches	2 inches or less
Colour of print and paper	—	Dark letters on light paper best. Contrast alone matters	Ditto; nonglossy paper and ink recommended

From Poulton (1960), Courtesy: Taylor and Francis Ltd

to be recommended as a means of drawing special attention to a word or phrase, they take longer to read and sometimes they are regarded as too difficult even to read.

In an experiment carried out at the suggestion of the Cambridge University printer, Poulton (1959) found that rate of reading was not related to age. However, faster readers tended to score more highly on tests of comprehension, and age was also found to be a determinant of understanding. Larger type and longer lines were found to be read more quickly than smaller type and shorter lines, so that the double column format often found in many scientific journals is not to be recommended. Poulton (1967) also demonstrated that 9 point Times Roman type face was scanned 7 per cent faster than 8 point Times, so that differences as small as one point (0·0138in.) can significantly affect the rate of skim reading. He also found that the minimal size of print for rate of reading and comprehension is about 4 points for students and 6 points for older people.

Poulton and Brown (1968), using 367 adults, investigated the comprehension problems of reading different typewriter typefaces. They found that pica, élite and Siemens typefaces were about equally effective, although text typed in the usual combination of upper and lower case letters was comprehended on average about 13 per cent more rapidly than text typed only in upper case. Lower case letters have more distinctive shapes, with their ascenders and descenders, as well as more distinctive lengths, whilst the occasional use of an upper case letter cues such important features as the beginning of a new sentence or a proper noun. A similar experiment (Poulton, 1967) measured the legibility of printers' typeface, and concluded that for men and women between 21 and 66 years of age large lower case titles and headlines were superior to capital ones of the same height. Furthermore, if subsidiary headlines or titles are used, it is preferable to print these in capitals, although subsidiary titles always tended to distract attention away from the main heading. A general survey of these results is given in an article by Poulton (1969), who concludes that the present trend in typography 'to eliminate overcrowding by refusing to use small print and demanding a more spacious layout' is not opposed by the experimental evidence.

THE USE OF ALGORITHMS*

In the last section we saw that continuous prose seemed to express rather inadequately the complex logical structures necessary to follow procedures or to make decisions. This section describes a different programming strategy which has been devised for this kind of material. One way of making learning easier is to present the information in the form of a 'logical tree'. This is nothing more than a simple flow-chart designed to *lead* the reader to a correct decision. In the logical tree a series of situations—beginning with the most general and ending with the most specific—are presented to the student in such a way that the response to the first statement leads him to the next relevant statement, and so on until the problem is solved. Any consistent set of rules can theoretically be presented in this way, although three formats are generally employed in programming:

* An algorithm is an exact prescription or recipe leading to the achievement of a specific outcome.

(a) *Linked statements* consist of a series of numbered questions, the answers to which instruct students to consult relevant conditions. An example of a linked statement for the previously quoted Death Grant Regulations is shown in *Table 3.7*. The linked statement approach is particularly useful for tasks which are small and self-contained, and for situations in which a solution to a problem is the main objective to be realised.

(b) *A decision tree* consists of a 'family tree' diagram, where the lines show the relations between conditions. An example of such a decision tree is shown in *Figure 2.2*, and further examples may be found in Lewis *et al.* (1967). Decision tree algorithms are ideally suited to tasks involving classifications, such as regulations, rules and instructions, although they can be used for diagnosis problems, as in medicine or law.

(c) *Visual diagrams or 'Whifs'* (when or if), are used to illustrate a causal chain of events (again, Lewis *et al.* provide examples). The visual diagram approach is particularly useful for people who have difficulty with words, and for this reason it is especially appropriate for tasks involving psycho-motor skills. In addition, visual diagrams may emphasise the functional structure of equipment. It is possible to redraw diagrams so that they are simpler to use

Table 3.7 Qualifications for Death Grant: Decision Tree in the form of linked statements

Question 1.	Were the contributions paid late?	*Yes* Read Question 2. *No* Contributions count towards death grant
Question 2.	Were the contributions paid before the death of the subject of the claim?	*Yes* Read Question 3 *No* Contributions don't count
Question 3.	Is the insured person alive?	*Yes* Contributions count *No* Read Question 4
Question 4.	Were the contributions paid before the insured person died?	*Yes* Contributions count *No* Read Question 5
Question 5.	Have the contributions already been taken into account in a claim for a widow's or retirement pension?	*Yes* Contributions count *No* Contributions don't count

Late contributions *always* count towards yearly average

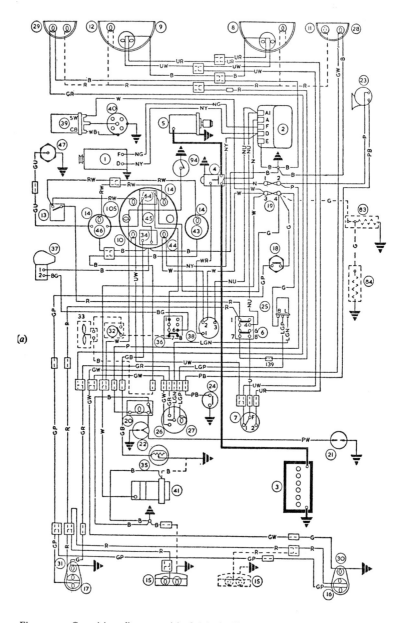

(a)

Figure 3.3. Car-wiring diagrams: (a) Original, (b) Functional (From Stainer, 1967, Courtesy: Institution of Electrical Engineers)

STARTER MOTOR
INTERIOR LIGHT
DOOR SWITCHES
HORN
LH TAIL LAMP
RH TAIL LAMP
NUMBER-PLATE LAMP
LH PANEL LAMP
RH PANEL LAMP
TEMP-GAUGE LAMP
OIL-GAUGE LAMP
SIDELAMPS
HEADLAMPS MAIN BEAM
MAIN-BEAM WARNING LAMP
HEADLAMPS DIPPED
OIL-FILTER WARNING LAMP AND SWITCH
FUEL PUMP
COIL AND DISTRIBUTOR
TEMP GAUGE
FUEL-GAUGE AND TANK UNIT
WINDSCREEN-WIPER MOTOR
STOP LAMPS
FLASHER WARNING LAMP
LH FRONT
LH REAR
RH FRONT
RH REAR

STARTER SOLENOID
35A
CONTROL BOX
DYNAMO
IGNITION WARNING LAMP
LAMP SWITCH
IGNITION AND STARTER SWITCH
VOLTAGE STABILISER
FLASHER UNIT

WIRES CAN BE COLOUR CODED
B = BLACK, U = BLUE ETC.
CONNECTORS CAN ALSO BE SHOWN

(b)

and considerably more job-oriented than those currently in use. *Figure 3.3* shows an example of such a functional flow diagram for the wiring of a mini compared with the conventional car wiring diagram (*see* Stainer, 1967). Its effectiveness as a job aid in a fault finding program is self-evident.

Although linked statements use less space, decision trees and visual diagrams have greater impact on trainees and, seemingly, greater job relevance.

More recently Davies and Packer (1970) have applied decision tables, increasingly employed in systems analysis and computer programming, to the communication of complex rules and procedures. This form has a number of advantages over the more usual algorithmic forms of presentation, since the decision table is not just an aid to the decision making process. It is a means of writing the original regulation and of subsequently revising it so as to expand or limit the number of cases or conditions leading to a particular course of action. At the same time, the format is sufficiently flexible as to be amenable to both serial search strategies, such as that found in the logical tree approach developed by Wason and Jones (1965), or parallel processing such as that involved in checking a football coupon. Information already available in the form of an algorithm can be readily transcribed into a decision table format.

The use of algorithms, including decision tables, gives rise to a new approach to instruction. The basic problem is seen as involving the redundancy of pre-task instruction, since algorithms are produced so as to be sufficiently intelligible to the trainee that they can be used straight away on the job itself. This method of presenting information, either in frames or exercises, has three main advantages over the continuous prose method usually employed. The student is called upon first to make a sequence of explicit decisions (often of a binary kind) about a limited series of simple facts. Each decision is about a *specific* issue, and the problems of relevancy and outcome are kept to a minimum. Finally, in working through the logical tree, the student need not necessarily remember his previous decisions, often essential in continuous prose, with consequent memory strain and confusion when trying to arrive at an answer. A program entitled *Algorithms and Logical Trees: A Self-Instructional Course* by Lewis and Woolfenden (1969) teaches the sequence of procedures necessary to the construction of a well defined algorithm.

Student attitudes are generally extremely favourable to this type of presentation: comments such as 'well set out', 'concise', 'unambiguous' are fairly commonplace. In two experiments (Wason and Jones, 1965) the time taken to process verbal information was reduced by 26 per cent for the linked statement group, and by 36 per cent for the decision tree group. In the first experiment 78 per cent of the trainees arrived at the correct solutions to the problems set (compared with 66 per cent in the continuous prose group) and in the second experiment the figures were 86 per cent as opposed to 79 per cent respectively. Experiments by Knight (1961) and by Shriver *et al.* (1961) also support the superiority of this algorithmic approach over conventional instruction, but when considering this approach, Duncan's distinction (Chapter 2) between programming performance and programming learning needs to be borne in mind.

A MODERN APPROACH

One of the most difficult problems facing a physician is that of keeping up with new advances and techniques in medicine. Accordingly, Pfizer Laboratories Inc. of New York commissioned Basic Systems to write a special ten minute program for practising physicians, on how to read an electrocardiogram of myocardial infarction for publication in the medical journal *Spectrum*. Over 50 000 people wrote to the journal saying how enthusiastic they were about the program, an unprecedented response which both startled and worried the editor. Since the program was written something like one in every three physicians in America has written to Pfizer requesting a copy of the program.

A sample sequence from the program is illustrated in the following pages in order to demonstrate a typical example of a modern program (*see Figure 3.4*). One obvious characteristic is the greater complexity and larger step size of this program compared with the more typical linear or branching program that we have seen so far. The approach used is reasonably characteristic of that employed today for teaching diagnostic skills, and it owes a great deal to Gilbert's mathetical approach. Whilst the sequence shown only teaches a physician the limited skill of determining whether a Lead 1 tracing shows myocardial ischemia, injury, infarction or some combination of these, it does illustrate presentation strategies that are being used by programmers today.

Figure 3.4. An extract from a program concerned with interpreting an electrocardiographic pattern (From Mechner, 1964, by permission of Warner-Chilcott, New Jersey)

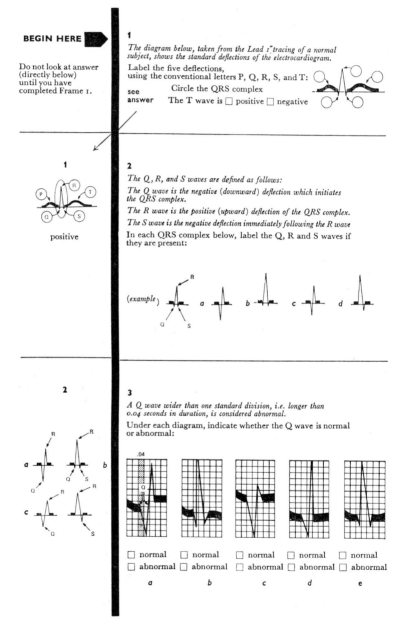

BEGIN HERE ▶

Do not look at answer (directly below) until you have completed Frame 1.

1

The diagram below, taken from the Lead 1 tracing of a normal subject, shows the standard deflections of the electrocardiogram.

Label the five deflections, using the conventional letters P, Q, R, S, and T:

see answer

Circle the QRS complex

The T wave is ☐ positive ☐ negative

1

positive

2

The Q, R, and S waves are defined as follows:

The Q wave is the negative (downward) deflection which initiates the QRS complex.

The R wave is the positive (upward) deflection of the QRS complex.

The S wave is the negative deflection immediately following the R wave

In each QRS complex below, label the Q, R and S waves if they are present:

(example)   a   b   c   d

2

3

A Q wave wider than one standard division, i.e. longer than 0.04 seconds in duration, is considered abnormal.

Under each diagram, indicate whether the Q wave is normal or abnormal:

☐ normal   ☐ normal   ☐ normal   ☐ normal   ☐ normal
☐ abnormal   ☐ abnormal   ☐ abnormal   ☐ abnormal   ☐ abnormal

a   b   c   d   e

4
The S-T segment begins at the end of the QRS complex and ends at the beginning of the T wave. An elevated S-T segment is abnormal.

For each diagram below, indicate whether the S-T segment is normal or abnormal.

a   S-T segment elevated
 □ normal
 □ abnormal

b   S-T segment isoelectric
 □ normal
 □ abnormal

S-T segment   □ elevated   □ isoelectric
 □ normal
 □ abnormal

d   S-T segment   □ elevated   □ isoelectric
 □ normal
 □ abnormal

e   S-T segment   □ elevated   □ isoelectric
 □ normal
 □ abnormal

5 Referring to the diagrams in the panel below, check the correct box:

a. An elevated S-T segment suggests. . .
 □ ischemia   □ injury   □ infarction
b. A negative T wave suggests. . .
 □ ischemia   □ injury   □ infarction
c. An abnormally wide Q wave suggests. . .
 □ ischemia   □ injury   □ infarction
These diagrams show the ECG changes which, in various combinations may be observed in myocardial infarction

Normal   Pattern of   Pattern of   Pattern of
Pattern   Ischemia   Injury   Infarction

6 Again referring to the above diagrams, check the correct box:
a. The difference between the pattern of infarction and the normal pattern is the
 □ negative T wave   □ elevated S-T segment
 □ abnormally wide Q wave
b. The difference between the pattern of injury and the normal pattern is the
 □ negative T wave   □ elevated S-T segment
 □ abnormally wide Q wave
c. The difference between the pattern of ischemia and the normal pattern is the
 □ negative T wave   □ elevated S-T segment
 □ abnormally wide Q wave

6

a abnormally wide
   Q wave

b elevated
   S-T segment

c negative T-wave

7

The difference between this diagram and the normal pattern
is the ☐ negative T wave   ☐ elevated S-T segment
        ☐ abnormally wide Q wave
It suggests ☐ ischemia   ☐ injury
            ☐ infarction

7

elevated
S-T segment

injury

8

The difference between this diagram and the normal pattern
is the ☐ negative T wave
        ☐ elevated S-T segment
        ☐ abnormally wide Q wave

It suggests ☐ ischemia   ☐ injury   ☐ infarction

8

abnormally wide
Q wave

infarction

9

The difference between this diagram and the normal pattern
is the ☐ negative T wave   ☐ elevated S-T segment
        ☐ abnormally wide Q wave

It suggests————————
          (write in the answer)

9

negative T wave

ischemia

10

Check the myocardial state suggested by each diagram:

a	b	c	d	e
☐ ischemia	☐ ischemia	☐ ischemia	☐ ischemia	☐ ischemia
☐ injury	☐ injury	☑ injury	☐ injury	☐ injury
☐ infarction	☐ infarction	☐ infarction	☐ infarction	☐ infarction

---

10

a infarction

b injury

c injury

d ischemia

e infarction

11

Check the myocardial state suggested by each diagram:

a	b	c	d	e
☐ ischemia	☐ ischemia	☐ ischemia	☐ ischemia	☐ ischemia
☐ injury	☐ injury	☐ injury	☐ injury	☐ injury
☐ infarction	☐ infarction	☐ infarction	☐ infarction	☐ infarction

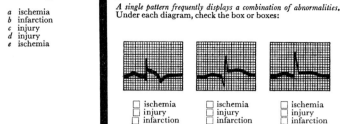

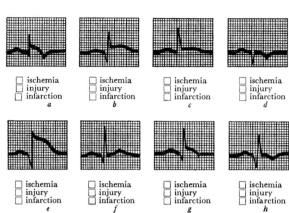

In the frame sequence shown, the programmer is attempting
to teach three different chains in a reasoning process:

Tracing
{
Find Q wave —— { Q wave – 0·04 sec – abnormally wide – infarction
                 Q wave – 0·04 sec – normal ————no infarction

Find S-T segment { ST elevated ———— abnormal ———— injury
                   ST isoelectric ———— normal ———— no injury

Find T wave { T negative ———— ischemia
              T positive ———— not ischemia
}

It will be seen that three major chains are involved; the student
must make a major discrimination between each of them in
terms of the different parts of the wave. Finally, each of the three
main chains involves two other chains dealing with the consequences of different widths of the wave or segment; since each
of these result in a different diagnosis, further discriminations have
to be made between them.

In Frame 1 the programmer (Mechner, 1964) forces the student to discriminate the QRS complex from the other portions of the Lead 1 tracing. At the same time, the T wave is discriminated from the other portions of the tracing, and the positive nature of the T wave is discriminated from its negative form. Frame 2 has one specific purpose. It sets out to give the student a clear concept of Q, R and S waves by adopting two different teaching strategies; it then teaches the student to generalise amongst different types of Q, R and S waves, and then teaches the student to discriminate between the different forms of these three waves. Frame 3 strengthens the concept of the Q wave by continuing the discrimination of it from other portions of the tracing. The frame also teaches the student to discriminate between Q waves which are wider or narrower than 0·04 secs. and links width to normal or abnormal states.

In Frame 4 the student is taught to discriminate the S–T segment of the wave from the other parts of the tracing, and this skill is strengthened by means of practice. At the same time, the student is taught to generalise amongst different kinds of S–T segments, and to discriminate between the range of elevated and isoelectric S–T segments. Frame 5 teaches the discrimination between an elevated and a normal S–T segment, and the link to abnormality of the width of the Q wave and to injury is established. The student is also taught to discriminate between a negative and a normal T wave, and the link of the former to ischemia is strengthened. Finally, the discrimination between an abnormally wide Q wave and a normal Q wave is made, and the relationship of the former with infarction established. The purpose of Frame 6 is to establish three important links in the chain: the relationship between an infarction pattern and an abnormally wide Q wave; the relationship between an injury pattern and an elevated S–T segment; and finally, the relationship between an ischemia pattern and a negative T wave. In Frames 7, 8 and 9 these three relationships are strengthened by further practice.

Frame 10 is the last major teaching frame. In it the student discriminates a negative T wave from a normal one, and generalises amongst different kinds of negative T waves. At the same time, he discriminates an elevated S–T segment from a normal one, and generalises amongst different kinds of elevated S–T segments so as to strengthen the overall concept. Finally, the student discriminates between abnormally wide Q waves and normal ones, and generalises amongst the different kinds of abnormality so as to strengthen this concept too. Frame 11 simply provides further practice of Frame 10 so as to strengthen the three concepts and chains established by it. The last frame of the sequence goes over the same material as Frames 10 and 11, except that each pattern is examined three times—for ischemia, injury and infarction —because more than one of the three abnormalities may be present at the same time.

When the program is examined in this detailed form, the complexity of the strategies employed is clearly discernible. In the matheticist's terminology, Frames 1, 2, 3, 4, 5, 6 and 10 are typical demonstration exercises, whereas Frames 7, 8, 9, 11 and 12 are typical release exercises. No purely prompting exercises are used, since competition is thought to be unlikely. It would have been easier to teach the sequence by rote, but this would not have given the physician a concept or enabled him to discriminate between the whole universe of forms he may well meet with on a Lead 1 tracing. The important part that visuals play in the program should be carefully noted. Furthermore, the programmer has not set out to teach the physician to talk about the consequences of various patterns, but to recognise them on an actual Lead 1 trace. For this reason the appropriate student responses are to label waves and to indicate states by placing a tick in the appropriate square: responses that require as little time as possible to complete. Because at no time in diagnosis would a student be called upon to draw a tracing, such a response would be inappropriate.

One particularly noteworthy feature of the program lies in the language employed. Grammatical constructions are simple and straightforward. The sentences are expressed in simple, grammatical forms, and there is an absence of negative statements, whilst qualifications—which can appreciably diminish comprehension—have been avoided. Yet at the same time, the vocabulary used and the structures employed are relevant and meaningful to the level of students for whom the program was written.

CONCLUSIONS

As with other presentation techniques, such as film making and television producing, frame writing is an art, but like all arts it is dependent upon advances in science and technology. Indeed, so skilled is the work that often it is conceived as a team task, beyond the capabilities of any one man. The frame writer must be a subject-matter expert, he must be able to determine the optimum amount of information to put in each frame, able to select and use appropriate shaping strategies, and able to analyse and determine what response must be elicited from the student. The frame writer must also be able to work with other media specialists so as to present the stimuli in their most effective and attractive form. In other words, the frame writer must be a skilled and gifted teacher.

4

Evaluation

JAMES HARTLEY

Three main procedures are covered under the general heading 'evaluation', as shown in *Figure 1.4*, 'the process of programmed instruction' (p. 13). These are:

(a) The development and validation of measures of proficiency.
(b) Empirical testing.
(c) Revision.

This chapter examines each of these areas, and discusses, in a final section, some wider implications.

THE DEVELOPMENT AND VALIDATION OF MEASURES OF PROFICIENCY

One of the first procedures in the preparation of programmed material is to state the objectives of a program in a precise and measurable way. It was argued in Chapter 1 that different objectives lead to different teaching strategies, different methods of learning, and demand different methods of evaluation. To measure the achievement of objectives thus necessitates the development of appropriate measuring instruments. A program that teaches an industrial motor skill should be tested on the job. A program that teaches recognition (e.g. of medical symptoms, aircraft or traffic signs) will demand a test which measures achievement in this respect: it should present material for the student to

K

recognise, rather than ask him to recall the material. Programs which aim to change a student's social behaviour (e.g. his smoking or his study habits) should be tested by behavioural measures rather than by questionnaires. Tests, then, must be appropriate to objectives. The logic of this argument may be strained, especially, for example, in the field of sex education, although even here objective measures are not impossible. Krishnamurty (1968) and Thiagarajan (1969) have demonstrated with group programs on family planning, that written records of discussions over time indicate a knowledge of contraceptive techniques and a desensitisation in the use of emotional words.

Tests must also be appropriate to the teaching method employed. It has been argued elsewhere, for example, that recall tests are not appropriate measures to use when evaluating lecture systems (Hartley and Cameron, 1967), and similarly, it has been suggested that it may not be appropriate to use verbal tests to evaluate the success of visual presentation (Smith and Smith, 1966; Duncan and Hartley, 1969). Comprehensive lists of measures which can be used to evaluate the attainment of cognitive, affective and per-formance skills have been provided by Angell et al. (1964), and Metfessel and Michael (1967).

The discussion so far may seem obvious enough, but there seems to be an assumption—when preparing to test programmed instruc-tion—that all that is required is the writing down of a set of problems based upon the instructional content. Yet it is upon scores obtained on such a test that the effectiveness of the instruc-tion is likely to be judged. In view of this it is essential that the tests used should be carefully, rather than hastily, constructed.

Several standard textbooks describe in detail the principles of test-construction, and it is the purpose of this chapter to comment briefly on them only insofar as they do or do not apply to pro-grammed materials. (Recommended textbooks are, for example, those by Anastasi (1968), Cronbach (1960), Guilford (1956) or Magnusson (1967). For details of construction of test items see, for example, Gronund (1965), Katz (1961) or Lindvall (1967).) It seems clear that the components of a 'good' test—such as validity, reliability and objectivity—are all relevant to tests for programmed materials, and this viewpoint has been strongly developed by Jacobs (1962) and others. However, as will be argued below, not all of these ideas now seem equally applicable to programmed materials.

In a sense, the topics under discussion above were concerned with the *validity* of the test being used, and validity is a key concept in the production of tests. Essentially, a test is 'valid' if it measures what it purports to measure. A final test to be used in a program is valid, therefore, if it discriminates between those learners who achieve each and every objective of the program and those who do not. Validity can be assessed in two ways:

(a) The test can be judged independently by subject-matter experts (they can indicate how far they agree that the test is a good test of what it is testing; that the items are, for example, representative of the total information taught).
(b) The test can be given to students who are known to have already achieved the objectives (independently of the program), and to similar students who are known not to have achieved these objectives. If the test measures what it is supposed to measure, then the first group should pass with high marks, and the second group should not. (An example of where these kinds of methods were used, in a programmed instructional setting, was provided by Davies (1969a).)

Naturally, it may be possible to achieve a valid test with some topics and some objectives more easily than with others, but attempts to establish the validity of the test should be made by programmers. An implication here is that, as shown in *Figure 1.4,* tests should be tested before they are used to assess the effectiveness of an instructional method.

A test is said to be *reliable* if, like a ruler, it measures in the same way each time it is used: thus we would expect that the results obtained from a student on one testing should be the same, or very similar, on a second testing. A test would have little usefulness if people scored differently every time they took it.

Tests might be unreliable for a variety of reasons. Sime and Dodd (1964) outlined the following:

(a) Because the student misinterprets the meaning of the question.
(b) Because the quantity of information, or amount of detail required, is not specified.
(c) Because the question can be answered correctly by a student who still has a deficiency in the criterion behaviour.
(d) Because the student who is not deficient gets less than full marks.
(e) Because a test item looks more difficult than it really is to some students, and may be neglected for this reason.
(f) Because some acceptable answers are not listed in the marking scheme.

If, however, each of the test items can be shown to be reliable, and if they can be related back to a specific section of the teaching sequence, then failure on these items will be a powerful indicator of the location of weaknesses in the program.

There are a number of strategies for measuring the reliability of a test, which centre basically on the correlation coefficient. A correlation coefficient expresses the degree to which two sets of scores vary together. If the relationship is direct, if there is a one-to-one agreement between two sets of test scores, then the correlation cofficient is expressed as $+1 \cdot 0$. If the relationship is directly inverse, then the correlation cofficient is expressed as $-1 \cdot 0$. Correlation coefficients thus vary between $+1 \cdot 0$ and $-1 \cdot 0$, and a correlation of $0 \cdot 0$ would indicate no relationship between scores.

Table 4.1 Reliability coefficients and sources of error (From Anastasi, 1968, Courtesy: Macmillan Ltd)

Procedure	Conventional Designation	Error Variance
Retest with same test on different occasion	Coefficient of stability	Time sampling
Retest with alternate test on same occasion	Coefficient of equivalence	Content sampling
Retest with alternative test on different occasion	Coefficient of stability and equivalence	Time sampling and content sampling
Split-half (odd-even or other parallel splits)	Coefficient of internal consistency	Content sampling
Kuder-Richardson (and other measures of internal consistency)	Coefficient of internal consistency	Content sampling and content heterogeneity

In practice, of course, correlations like $+1 \cdot 0$ and $-1 \cdot 0$ are extremely rare, and values such as $+0 \cdot 87$—meaning a high degree of positive relation—or $-0 \cdot 32$—meaning a slight degree of negative relation—are more common. Various methods of calculating correlation coefficients can be found in standard statistical textbooks.

A test is therefore said to be reliable if there is a high degree of agreement between the first and second testing, and this agreement is expressed in the form of a correlation coefficient (usually of the order of $+0 \cdot 80$ or more). The *test-retest* method is one way of assessing reliability. Another way is to create alternate or parallel forms of the same test to see if there is an agreement between the scores of each student on the different forms of the test. If this can be shown, using correlation coefficients, then alternate forms of the same test can be used for before, after and retention tests. A third measure of reliability is to examine the test's 'internal consistency', that is when scores on different questions closely agree with each other. (This is an appropriate measure to use if the different items of the test are of equal difficulty.) *Table 4.1* summarises different procedures for measuring reliability and their main sources of error.

These different types of reliability indicate that there are different ways of looking at this particular problem. In programmed instruction all these ways may be relevant, and programmers should make some attempt to establish the reliability of their tests. This implies, again, that the tests themselves should be tested prior to their use. Few programs known to the writer give any indication of attempts made by the programmer to establish the validity and reliability of the tests provided, and few investigators have given these details in the reports of their experiments (Wheatley, 1969), although the situation does seem to be improving in this respect.

Sime and Dodd's final point criticising the marking scheme for the test introduces the remaining quality of a 'good' test to be discussed: that is, that the test should be objectively, easily and reliably scored. This means that a clear and easy marking system should be devised so that different investigators can score the answers to the test in the same way. Different types of test and different marking schemes can produce slightly different results (*see* Fry, 1960; Gagné and Dick, 1962). It is important, therefore, in successive usage of the program that the same marking scheme and tests should be applied so that valid comparisons can be made between test results obtained under different conditions. Again, it may be noted, few programmers provide marking schemes to accompany the tests they provide with their programs.

The principles of test construction described in standard textbooks have been derived from experience gained in creating standardised psychological tests (e.g. measures of intelligence and personality). It is debatable, however, whether one of the most important ideas of these tests is applicable to tests used for programmed materials. Psychological tests aim to grade and position respondents along a broad continuum, to differentiate between them, and to indicate a respondent's position relative to others in his group. Most tests used with programmed materials, however, aim to indicate whether or not the student has learned, and not to separate out students. If the aim of a program is, as it is sometimes stated, to achieve 90–90 (i.e. 90 per cent of the students should obtain 90 per cent on the test of the program's objectives), then it is clear that results on such tests (if the program 'works') will be narrowly distributed at the top end of the scale. Such results, as will become apparent in the next section, have certain statistical properties which have implications for evaluation strategies.

There is here, therefore, a problem. Tests are required which are valid, reliable and objective, and yet it is expected that learners will successfully complete them. Conventional measures of validity and reliability are difficult to obtain in this kind of situation. These difficulties can partly be resolved by testing the tests prior to their use (thus assuming that spreads of scores will be obtained from a non-programmed situation), but it may be as Green (1967) remarks, that 'Evaluation will not be achieved through a classical approach to measurement, but rather, that it will be made in terms of some essential economic facts. A program must be assessed in terms of (a) what it purports to teach, (b) whether, in fact, it does teach, and (c) how much it costs to teach.' It is to areas (b) and (c) that the discussion now turns.

THE EMPIRICAL TESTING OF PROGRAMS

The procedures adopted by programmers to assess whether or not they have produced an effective teaching instrument have often been described under the general heading of 'evaluation'. Evaluation in this sense refers to the testing of the program during its development, and to the strategies adopted to improve its effectiveness. This *internal* evaluation may be contrasted with *external* evaluation, the process of comparing the 'finished' product with other teaching media in order to make a comparative assessment of their effectiveness.

Developmental testing

The internal evaluation of programs usually takes place in two distinct stages—called 'developmental testing' and 'field testing' respectively. Developmental testing, as its name implies, takes place during the development of the program. It is characterised by the fact that it is usually carried out informally with individual learners, one at a time. The purpose of the developmental test is to check how far the first version of the program produced (which is essentially still only a guess about how the material should be taught) is, in fact, suitable for those for whom it is written. If there are any serious defects in the program, these become apparent as the program is tried out with individuals. Several investigators have outlined strategies for developmental testing, and the following is close to that proposed by Becker (1963). (This paradigm, of course, would have to be amended for the developmental testing of a multi-media program, but the principles would remain the same.)

1. *The preparation of tests.* As discussed above, tests should be prepared before the instruction, but test questions designed to cover the information and skills taught may also, in a sense, be tested themselves by trying them out informally in the developmental testing situation.

2. *The preparation of material.* The instructional items are prepared on separate pieces of paper, or cards, with the correct responses on the reverse, or separate, as desired.

3. *The preparation of the learner.* A student is selected who is typical of the students for whom the program is being written. He must have the desired 'pre-entry requisites', but he should not know the material which is to be taught. It is usual to select a student from the middle, or just below the middle range of the abilities of the specified students. The student is informed that he is not being tested, but that he is, in fact, helping the programmer, and every effort is made to put him at his ease. It is pointed out to him that his comments, especially on his difficulties, will be welcomed.

4. *The try-out of the program, and subsequent discussion.* The programmer presents the program, one item at a time, to the learner, thus making the situation cheatproof. He observes and notes down whether the learner answers correctly or not. If the learner makes a mistake, then the programmer either notes this, and says nothing, observing whether the feedback in the program is sufficient to correct the error, or he discusses the error there and then with the learner to see just why that particular response was made. In this latter case the programmer must, of course, note that he has provided additional material at this point for the learner—and he should also note what the material was. When the learner has completed the section of program being tested, and attempted the test questions, then the programmer discusses with him in more detail the specific points outlined above, as well as more general points. These may include the learner's opinion of the program—whether he found it interestiig or boring, too easy or too difficult, or whether he thought that there were some parts which were in some way worse than

others ('worse' generally meaning, in this case, difficult, boring or badly explained). The programmer at this stage has to be careful not to be hostile to any criticism, but to accept it, and to note it down. These sessions could profitably be tape-recorded, for at this stage in program writing the learner is teaching the programmer.

5. *Revision of the program.* When the programmer reaches this stage there are two strategies open to him. He can either make adjustments to the program (on the basis of comments given by the learner) or he can try it out in its original form with another student, to see whether or not the same difficulties recur. It may well be that the first difficulties resulted from individual idiosyncracies of the first learner. Usually a middle way is taken. Items that have proved ambiguous or badly worded, or have employed words above the first student's level, are revised before the second test is done.

6. *Further try-outs and revision.* A repeated individual try-out situation provides the programmer with considerable information about his program. If errors are consistently repeated then this indicates weaknesses in individual items or in teaching sequences, or in test questions. Thus, all of these need scrutiny. Gilbert (1960) has suggested that if individual try-outs were repeated 'fewer than ten times', then the program would be extremely efficient and suitably adapted for a much larger group of similar students.

Perhaps, however, what is important to note at this stage is that although the procedures listed above seem systematic, the actual implementation of them is far less so. As Markle (1967) says in an important article on evaluation, 'There are no firm rules. Each programmer is on his own.' Thus variations in strategies for developmental testing may be observed. Kay *et al.* (1968), for example, argued that developmental testing in the presence of the programmer might be stressful for the learner: they preferred to allow students to work on their own, using cheat-proof machines with facilities for reversing. They reported, 'What surprised us was how much students did reverse when working with a program in its first version...' and 'We gained a lot of information about what was wrong with our programming by studying the points where students had reversed.'

The author feels, following his work with children learning in pairs (*see* Hartley and Hogarth, 1971), that it may be profitable to record the discussion of pupils learning together from the first version of the program. Sometimes, especially if the program is lengthy or the conditions difficult, it may not be practical or possible to carry out developmental testing: some workers have been forced to make an immediate field test of their program. Others, such as Blake (1966), Griffiths and Edwards (1967) and Roebuck (1968), have used an intermediate system: frames are first presented to classroom groups by means of an overhead-projector; they are revised (on the basis of results obtained from before and after tests) and then duplicated for field testing.

It is not possible to suggest what differences might result in programs from using such different, or indeed, other strategies: no comparison studies known to the writer have been made between those programs developmentally tested and those not, or between different techniques of developmental testing. Program writers generally consider developmental testing to be time consuming, but to be of considerable value. In terms of procedure, however, developmental testing may be judged at present to be more of an art than a science. It is a technique, nevertheless, that could be profitably applied to many forms of teaching.

Field testing

When a program has been developmentally tested, and the programmer is satisfied with his revisions, then the next stage in the production of a program is to prepare it for a trial using a larger number of learners 'in the field', that is, in the actual situation in which the program is going to be used. Field testing is characterised by a larger number of students (say, any number above fifteen) and by the fact that it need not necessarily be carried out by the programmer. Indeed, some writers would argue that the programmer's presence might create an 'experimenter bias' in the results, and that more natural results might be obtained if the normal instructor carried out the field test. Often, however, the instructor is also the programmer, so this problem is usually ignored.

Field testing is more formal than developmental testing, and the procedure thus more systematic. Nevertheless, as will be shown, a great deal of 'art' intrudes even here. 'Evaluating programs in the tropical rain forest'—the title of an article by Roebuck (1968)—makes the point.

The purpose of field testing is to assess whether the program satisfactorily achieves its stated objectives when it is used with those for whom it was written under the conditions in which it is likely to be used in practice. If the program fails to achieve these objectives satisfactorily—which, of course, can and at first usually does happen—then the data obtained on the field test can be used to identify where the program has failed, and to suggest strategies for overcoming these failures.

A number of measures are usually made on a large-scale field test in order to assess the effectiveness of a program. Apart from measures taken to confirm that the learners have the prerequisite abilities, the main measures made are:

(a) *Test* scores (before, after and retention).
(b) *Errors* made (on the tests and on the actual frames).
(c) *Time* taken.
(d) Student *attitudes.*

It is proposed to discuss each of these measures to point out how they—both separately and together—can indicate where weaknesses occur in a program, and how they can suggest remedies for these weaknesses. Whilst discussing these measures it will be indicated how better use might be made of them than is the current practice.

Tests. As noted above, the scores on the final test of a program are usually taken to provide the most powerful evidence of a program's effectiveness. If 90 per cent of the learners score 90 per cent or more on the final test, then the program is said to have 'worked'. Unfortunately, such a result may be the product of several undesirable factors, for example:

(a) The test might be invalid, and unreliable.
(b) The learners might have known 80 per cent of the material before they began, and indeed.
(c) They might have spent far longer working on the program than was commensurate with the amount they learned.

The first of these factors has been discussed above, the last will be discussed further below. The second factor involves a discussion of two related topics, (a) the initial knowledge and skills of the learners, and (b) the relationship of this initial knowledge to their final knowledge. Initial knowledge is usually measured by a *pretest,* that is, one given before the instruction commences. In fact, pretests may be of two main kinds—they may either measure the learner's knowledge of what it is that he should know before he begins the instruction (so, in this case, he should score highly), or they may measure the learner's knowledge of what he is about to be taught (so in this case he should score badly). Some programs suggest that the final test may be used as a pretest of the second kind, whereas other programs provide tests of both kinds. All tests, of course, should be valid, reliable and objective. Precise pretesting with programmed instruction has been rather neglected up to the present day, but with the advent of computer-assisted instruction pretesting becomes more important. There would seem to be more scope (whether computerised or not for 'diagnostic' pretesting, that is, pretesting in order to discover either (a) weaknesses in learners which must be remedied before they start on the program, or (b) to indicate sections of the program which a learner is advised to use. A strategy for devising diagnostic test items has been described by Dodd (1967a). Experiments have now been successfully carried out to demonstrate that pre-test scores can be used to indicate appropriate teaching strategies and sequences required by learners (e.g. Stolurow and Davis, 1965; Melaragno, 1967; Dodd, 1967a; Hilton, 1969; Eraut, 1969), although in the first two of these studies the term 'pretest' has been widened to include aptitude and achievement scores on a variety of measures.

One related further aspect of testing which requires more attention in programmed learning, particularly with long programs, is the development of tests to be given as the instruction is proceeding. These *interim* tests can have several functions: they can serve as diagnostic tests given during the instruction to indicate appropriate teaching strategies or sequences (e.g. the learner might skip material, or receive remedial work); they can assess the effectiveness of specific sections of the program; and they can assess the effectiveness of the program as far as it has proceeded. The results of Melaragno's experiment suggested that sequences based on diagnostic interim tests were more successful than were sequences based on pretest measures. Furthermore, it appears that interim tests may have unsuspected teaching and motivating functions (Hartley *et al.* 1971). Work in other contexts, e.g. on the positioning of questions in prose passages (Frase, 1968) also suggests that interim tests and test questions may have unsuspected functions that need to be explored further.

To return, however, to the main discussion. In order to assess the effectiveness of programmed instruction, it is important to relate test scores obtained after using the program (the *post-test* scores) to the learner's initial level of knowledge and skills as determined by the pretest(s). McGuigan and Peters (1965) suggest that the best measure of a program's efficiency is the ratio between the amount learned and the amount that could possibly be learned. This 'gain ratio' is found by dividing the mean gain between the pretest and the post-test scores by the mean possible gain (defined as the difference between the mean pretest scores and full marks on the post-test, the tests being the same or parallel). This concept has been widely used and extended in the field of programmed instruction (see Blake, 1966; Davies, 1969a), and indeed McGuigan (1967) argues that the gain ratio can be used as a measure for assessing all educational methods, whether they be programmed or not.

The 'gain ratio' has, however, not been without its critics. McGuigan and Peters themselves observed that it was distorted by the presence of easy items in the post-test. Blake (1966) suggested that its value was distorted by learners with high pre-test scores, and proposed an amended formula. Dubois (1965) and Wheatley (1969) raise perhaps the most critical objection. They argue that gain scores obtained from a lengthy program are quite meaningless because—as noted earlier—the achievement measuring instruments do not generally have the scale properties which permit a comparison of gains. For example, it is not statistically legitimate to say that students who score 10 out of 20 on a test of traffic sign knowledge are equally deficient, nor is it legitimate to conclude that they know 50 per cent of the traffic signs. Furthermore, it is not legitimate to say after instruction when they score full marks, that they have all learned the same amount, for many of the signs vary in difficulty. These criticisms may seem rather esoteric, but they serve to point out methodological weaknesses in our evaluating instruments. Much difficulty stems from the nature of measurements taken and the selection of appropriate test statistics for use in any subsequent analysis (for a wider discussion of these problems *see* Davies, (1971)).

The concept of 'gain ratio' has been applied to *retention* as well as to post-test measures (Davies, 1969a). In most circumstances it is not necessary to measure retention, for the materials being taught are to be put into immediate use. However, it would seem important to measure retention when (as discussed later in the section on evaluating instructional methods) different methods of instruction are being compared. If it is decided to measure retention, the problems become *when* and *how* to measure it, and how to *interpret* the results. American investigators have measured retention following programmed instruction after as little as two days, or as much as one year, but there have been few systematic studies of this problem. If it is desired to measure retention after regular periods of time, then, in order to avoid contamination from repeated testing, this alters quite dramatically the complexity of the study.

Other problems raise themselves, especially if rates of forgetting differ following different instructional methods (*see Figures 4.1a and 4.1b*). Several experiments in programmed learning have been carried out which show results like those schematically depicted in *Figure 4.1a*, that is, where retention measures have indicated significant differences between methods that were not

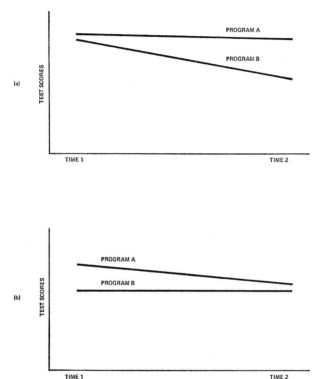

Figure 4.1. Schematic representation of results following two methods of instruction

apparent on immediate testing. Similarly, results like those shown schematically in *Figure 4.1b* have also been obtained. Here the conclusions often drawn are that one program initially teaches more effectively than the other, but that the differences disappear over time. An equally valid conclusion, however, is that one method results in less forgetting than the other. *Figures 4.1a and 4.1b* thus illustrate the argument for making retention measures, for although results must always be relative, the efficiency of a method cannot be assessed properly without taking into account

Table 4.2 Errors obtained on a test before using the program

Pupils	1 (i)	1 (ii)	1 (iii)	2	3 (i)	3 (ii)	4	5	6	7	8	9	10	11 (i)	11 (ii)	Individual Totals
1		X	X		X			X						X	X	6
2	X	X		X	X		X		X	X		X	X	X	X	11
3	X	X			X		X							X	X	6
4	X	X				X	X	X	X			X	X	X		9
5	X	X			X		X		X					X	X	7
6												X	X	X	X	4
7	X	X						X	X			X	X	X	X	8
8	X	X			X		X		X		X	X	X	X		9
9														X		1
10					X					X		X	X	X	X	6
11	X	X	X	X	X	X	X	X	X	X	X	X	X	X	X	15
12	X		X		X		X	X	X	X		X	X	X	X	11
13							X	X	X			X	X	X	X	7
14				X	X		X	X	X			X	X	X	X	9
15					X		X	X	X			X	X	X	X	8
16	X	X			X	X	X	X					X	X	X	9
17							X	X	X		X	X	X	X	X	8
18					X		X	X	X	X		X	X	X	X	9
19		X	X	X	X		X		X	X		X	X	X	X	11
20	X	X	X	X	X	X			X		X	X	X	X	X	12
21	X		X		X				X			X	X	X	X	8
22					X		X			X		X	X	X	X	7
23	X	X			X	X	X	X	X		X	X	X	X	X	12
24	X		X		X		X	X	X	X		X	X	X	X	11
25							X	X			X	X	X	X	X	7
26	X		X				X	X	X			X	X	X	X	9
27												X				1
28				X			X	X	X		X	X	X	X	X	9
29									X			X	X	X	X	5
30							X	X	X	X		X	X	X	X	8
31					X											1
32					X			X			X	X	X	X	X	7
Totals	14	12	8	6	20	5	21	17	22	9	9	25	26	30	27	251

Pretest Errors — *Question Nos.*

the amount retained at a later time. Furthermore, it could be argued, research is needed to isolate these factors which increase retention scores, and some work along these lines has been carried out (Hamilton, 1965, 1967).

Again, it may be noted in passing, that in *Figures 4.1a and 4.1b* there is an assumption that equal interval scales are being

Table 4.3 Errors obtained on the same test after using the program. (Unpublished data reproduced with permission from McGregor).

Pupils	Post-test Errors															Individual Totals
	Question Nos.															
	1 (i)	(ii)	(iii)	2	3 (i)	(ii)	4	5	6	7	8	9	10	11 (i)	(ii)	
1																0
2																0
3																0
4														X		1
5																0
6														X	X	2
7										X				X	X	3
8																0
9																0
10							X	X	X					X	X	5
11										X		X			X	3
12											X					1
13															X	1
14													X			1
15					X											1
16							X							X	X	3
17								X								1
18							X						X	X	X	4
19								X								1
20																0
21				X									X	X	X	4
22																0
23							X	X						X	X	4
24		X	X								X					3
25																0
26																0
27																0
28																0
29									X							1
30																0
31																0
32												X		X		2
Totals	0	1	1	1	1	0	4	4	2	2	2	2	3	9	9	41

employed, that 'ceiling effects' are not present in the measuring instruments, that both methods of instruction take equal time and have the same objectives, and that the learning in question is somehow 'in vaccuo' between test and retest—all assumptions that are often unwarranted in the field of programmed instruction. (For a more detailed analysis of results more complex than those shown in *Figures 4.1a and 4.1b,* and a survey of appropriate statistical techniques for use in dealing with them (*see* Wodtke, 1967).

Finally, it may be noted that some investigators prefer to use *transfer* tests rather than, or as well as, direct tests of the material taught (*see* Leith, 1969). Transfer tests measure the ability of the learners to apply what they have been taught to new situations. The results of an investigation by Duncan (1969) suggested that retention test scores declined over a period of time, whereas transfer test scores remained constant. It may be agreed with Duncan that if this is the case then 'further studies of transfer, and in particular, of how programmed instruction may maximise the components which do not deteriorate with time, seem to be overdue'. Levy (1969) too, has pointed out that 'our measurements should be infinitely more subtle, particularly in the direction of tracking the longitudinal development of concepts'.

Errors. After the final test scores, errors made on the test provide the next best indication of a program's effectiveness. More specifically, they point out weaknesses that need revision. Actual quantitative measures and mean scores are not very useful, for what is really required is knowledge of what the errors are, and where it is that they occur. *Tables 4.2 and 4.3* show the results observed on the same test before and after the first field test of a program. Such results, apart from demonstrating the success of programmed instruction, also point out by implication where there are weaknesses in the program which need to be remedied. If, as in this case, the test questions can be related back to the original teaching sequence, then the results give a clearer indication of where revision is needed. Indeed, the users of commercially available programs might be well advised to make such analyses for themselves in order to ascertain whether there are sections of the program which could be profitably augmented by 'conventional' instruction.

Errors that are made on the actual frames provide a second source of indication of a program's weaknesses. Matrices of errors, for students and for frames, can be drawn up, and *Table 4.4* shows a typical example taken from a program being developed by the G.P.O. (Hall and Fletcher, 1967). In this table x indicates an error, R indicates an unexpected but reasonable response, and a dash indicates failure to respond.

From the table it is apparent that trainee number eleven is in considerable difficulty: if there were several trainees in this condition and they all had the desired pre-knowledge, then this would indicate that the program was too difficult. Here there is

Table 4.4 Error analysis for frames and students.
(Reproduced from Hall and Fletcher, 1967, Courtesy: Pergamon Press Ltd)

Trainee Reference numbers	Frame 1	2	3	4	5	6	7	8	16	17	18	19	20	21	22	23	24	25	26	27	28	29	30	31	32	33	34	35	36	37	38	Time taken minutes	Number of errors
1									X	X	X								R	X									R			48	4
2																												R				57	—
3																				X	X				X		R	R				37	2
4																								X								41	3
5					X																											25	—
6																				—		R						R			X	35	2
7																												R				38	—
8										R	R							R						X				R				38	1
10																				—	X		X	X								37	2
11				X	X	X	X	X		X	X		X					R	—	—	X		—	X	X	R	R	—	X		—	48	20
12																		R		—	X				X		R	R				50	1
13													X							—					X		R	R				51	1
14																X																38	5
15																		R												R		46	2
16																		R										R	X			37	1
17																		R		—	X				X			R	R			35	—
18													X					R	—	—								R				40	1
20																		R	—									R				66	3
21																		R		R								R				56	—
22																		X		—												38	1
23																																74	1
24																									X		R					51	3
25																																43	2
26																												R	R			42	—

Average time: 46 minutes.

only one such student, and assistance given in the early stages of the program might have overcome his difficulties. Looking at the actual frames, it can be seen that Frames 27, 28 and 32 have a large number of incorrect responses, and thus require attention. It may be, for example, that Frame 27 is ambiguous, or badly worded, and that this is leading to unexpected responses. If, for example, Frames 32–35 were test items, then it is clear from inspection that the teaching sequence leading up to them must be in some way inadequate. An analysis of the actual errors made on Frame 32 would probably reveal the nature of this inadequacy. Again, however, sheer quantitative measures of errors are not as useful as qualitative ones. *Table 4.4* suggests that the trainees are only making one response per frame. Usually, however, frames often demand several responses, not just one, and these responses may vary in difficulty. Just plotting an error does not indicate the type of error made—whether it is serious or trivial, whether it is unique or repetitive, whether it is on an introductory or a test frame, or whether or not it is related to what has been taught in the program. The successful answering of test frames may involve the use of several intervening processes before the solution is reached, and a single error made here may be a simple slip or a complex misunderstanding.

It should be clear by now that to write about a program having a mean error rate of 5 per cent is almost useless for the programmer—and, indeed, for the user too. Essentially, what the programmer needs to know is what each student did on each frame, why he did it, how long it took him, and what he feels about it. Field testing, unfortunately, rarely yields all these data. Nevertheless, techniques have recently been developed that make error-data more useful. Instead of just providing means, the distributions of error rates have been plotted (*see* Cook, 1962). Graphs, such as shown in *Figure 4.2* can indicate that some sections of a program are more difficult (in this case, especially, for the poorer students on lesson 8), and the implication of this is that such a section needs the programmer's further attention. Attempts have been made to overcome the difficulty of labelling all varieties of errors simply as 'error' by categorising the types of errors that occur (Austwick, 1965; Mills, 1969). These analyses, although useful, tend to become extremely tedious for lengthy or complicated programs.

How the learner perceives an error adds yet another complication. Data reported by Hartley (1966a) showed that some school-children perceived a simple error—in fact, not really an error at all—as important: they judged an answer of 609·3 to be incorrect, when the correct answer was, in fact, 609·1. Other children judged an important error as trivial: they marked as correct 6·091, when the answer should again have been 609·1. As Bjerstedt (1965) has argued, 'there is no one-to-one correspondence between

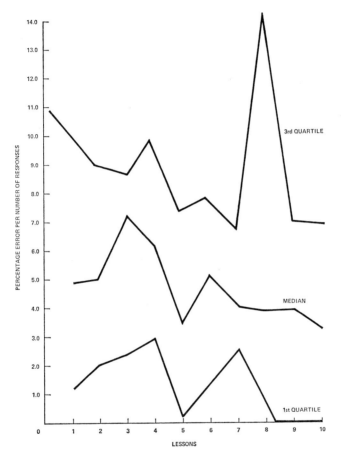

Figure 4.2. Profile of difficulty: The distribution of errors for 'separate' lessons (After Hartley, 1964)

the dichotomy "correct versus incorrect" on the one hand, and the dichotomy "understanding versus lack of understanding" on the other hand', and he suggests that students in both developmental and field testing correct their answers with symbols equivalent to one of the following:

(a) Error with remaining doubt (i.e. 'I got it wrong, and still don't really understand your explanation').
(b) Error without remaining doubt (i.e. 'I got it wrong, but now I understand').
(c) No error but doubt.
(d) Neither error nor doubt.

The discussion so far has centred on linear programs where responses are recorded for almost every frame. However, many modern programs are not linear, and thus techniques for evaluating branch points and subsequences dependent upon them are important. Here programmers are primarily interested in knowing:

(a) What sort of mistakes are made on the main sequence frames.
(b) Whether or not the subsequences which they have provided are, in fact, used.
(c) Whether or not the subsequences used effectively remedy the errors made.

Investigators (e.g. Markle, 1963; Bjerstedt, 1965; Greenway, 1965) have put forward models for analysing the relationship between errors made on main sequence frames, and performance after using appropriate subsequences. (These models have been compared elsewhere, Hartley, 1966a.)

As a consequence of trying to evaluate programs with branches, new techniques for recording responses have developed. An efficient evaluation of a branching program cannot be made unless steps are taken to record the decisions of each learner. This usually means that the machine or student is required to record the number of the frames (or pages) studied. In order to expedite the process of evaluation, it would be helpful if this recording could also indicate whether the learner was working on a main or a subsequence frame. A simple cheat-proof technique for recording these data has been described by Annett (1964).

For programs to work effectively, each component in the system must act reliably. The learner is an essential element in a programmed intructional system, but the assumption, often made, that he always acts in a reliable manner may in fact be a little naive (*see* Hartley, 1968). With multiple-choice branching programs students have been known to devise an ingenious variety of games and strategies to make their 'learning' more enjoyable (*see* Cavanagh, 1967); indeed, some of these 'games' have been malicious (Noble, 1968); Hill and Cavanagh (1969) reported that some of the verbal responses made by adults to a 'talking typewriter' were unprintable! If systematic evaluation procedures are to be developed, it is important, therefore, that the teaching system is made as reliable as possible.

To take another but related issue, it is important to prevent 'cheating'—whatever form it takes. Some investigators have stated that cheating is not important in programmed learning, for if a pupil can successfully complete the post-test then it does not matter if he has cheated. The argument developed here, however, is that cheating should be prevented: if students cheat then, as Reid (1963) pointed out, information about their difficulties is lost to the programmer, and thus any error analysis made represents an under-estimate of the true position. Evidence from programmed text versus machine presentation of programmed instruction (Holz and Robinson, 1963) supports this contention in that higher error rates are recorded in more cheat-proof situations, and Barlow (1967) showed that students who cheated (by copying misprints in the text) scored significantly less than students who did not cheat. One point of interest here is the observation by Dolejsi (1969) that (with a branching program) pupils worked honestly at first, but then tried out what he called 'purposeful wrong manipulation'. After this period (during which pupils found out that it wasn't as satisfactory as they had expected), they then returned to using the program correctly. The amount of cheating observed may therefore depend upon the time of measurement. It is for these reasons—to prevent loss of information that may be useful in program revision—that research workers argue that cheat-proof formats should be devised when evaluating programs.

The writer would like to stress, following his experience (Hartley 1966b), that if there are branches in the program, then the entrances to these branches should be controlled by the teaching system and not left to the learner's own option, although this view is contrary to that held by Silberman et al. (1961) and Kapel (1966). It is arguable that exits from branches may be machine or student controlled (see Wendt, 1967), although more research is needed here. What seems to be important in studies of optional branching is the amount of control it is thought necessary to exercise over the learner, and clearly this is relative to the subject matter being taught and the abilities of the student. Further studies are required in order to find the minimum control needed to achieve maximum scores on tests of objectives. Work on learner-centred instruction—where the learner determines the instructional sequence—is of great interest here.

In concluding this section on error analyses, one point must be observed, and that is that an error analysis will not reveal all the weaknesses of a program. It is possible for a student to work through a program without making errors, but this does not necessarily indicate that the program is a good one. Horn (1964) has presented an effective discussion of what programming errors can be made which will not necessarily be detected by making an error analysis. His main points are that testing does not reveal

(a) Faults in subject matter, or in organisation.
(b) Faults in frames—for example, over-prompting, over-reviewing, using too small a step-size.
(c) More general faults—such as boring presentation and lack of illustrative material.

Indeed, as Austwick (1965) has pointed out, it is extremely difficult to revise a program that has a low error rate. Perhaps, in writing programs, programmers should not err too much on the side of caution: programs with a high error rate may be easier to revise than those with a low one—although this point is perhaps more relevant for developmental than field testing.

Time taken. It is useful to record the time taken to work through a program when assessing its effectiveness. The mean overall time taken to complete a program can be measured and compared with that taken by conventional instruction (either by making a direct comparison study, or by making inferences from previous experience). In the direct comparison situation the efficiency of the two systems can be determined by dividing the amount learned by the time taken. The resulting 'efficiency indices' have, however, limitations :

(a) They imply a direct relationship between time taken and amount learned.
(b) They assume equal units in the test.
(c) To be useful for comparison purposes one condition of learning must be equal or superior to the other both in the amount learned and in the time taken (Goldbeck and Campbell, 1962).

Again, retention scores which may be a further contributing factor to measuring program efficiency are often not taken into account (and nor is the cost).

Thus, once again, a general measure is only of limited usefulness, especially if it is not related to other measures. If a program takes longer than a conventional instructor to achieve the same objectives, then the implication is, once again, that the program needs amending in some way. An extreme example of this—where the time taken was not commensurate with the amount learned—has recently been provided: Gilbert's program which uses a set of associative devices to teach the colour code of resistors does so almost as successfully in four frames as do other programs (not using this device) which take many more frames to teach the same associations (*see* extract in *Table 3.3*). In this case it is probably correct to assume that the shorter program is more efficient, although this may not be true in all cases: associative devices and mnemonic systems may prevent learning with understanding, or even further learning from occurring (Hunter, 1964). This example does serve, however, to illustrate a more important point: it is not legitimate to assume, because a program has been tested and revised (and perhaps reaches 90–90) that it is a 'good' one: a more efficient program could possibly be developed. (This argument has been further considered by Knight, 1965.)

The overall time taken, unless it is much longer than that normally taken, does not really indicate where weaknesses in programs occur. However, an examination of the distribution of time, particularly on separate lessons, might (as does an examination of errors) indicate where difficulties in a program lie, and again, where revision might be necessary. It might be expected, for instance, that a parallel graph for time taken might be drawn from the results of the program shown in *Figure 4.2*.

This leads to the suggestion that an analysis of time taken per individual frame would perhaps be the most useful time measure to record, but this measure (which would require mechanical recording) has not often been made. Speed of responding has, however, been shown to be related to error rate (Brooks, 1967), and Silberman *et al.* (1961) considered it to be a more appropriate criterion than error rate for directing a student into a branching sequence. The time taken to do tests might well be another important indication of the difficulty of the material, even when full marks are obtained (*see Table 6.3*).

Obviously, time data might be distorted by unknowns (such as the student losing his pencil) but in general it ought to be possible to pick out items that students take longer to complete than others. Again, what would be important to compare here would be items where students take longer but are still correct—with items where students take a long time and then make errors. As Brooks (1967) points out, 'while the general relation between response time and errors suggests the validity of response time as a measure of task difficulty, instances of the discrepancy between the two indicators are potentially instructive. Unusually long times for a correctly answered item may indicate confusion. Errors resulting from this confusion may occur on a later item concerning the confusing topic, but not show precisely where revision is needed.'

The time taken to learn something is a potent measure of its difficulty. The realisation of this with respect to programmed instruction is perhaps reflected in the recent increase in the number of experiments which have investigated the limitations and advantages of group and external pacing in programmed instruction.

Student attitudes. One final measure which is often made to help in assessing the effectiveness of a program is to measure student attitudes towards it. Few workers have gone to the trouble

Table 4.5 A sample response sheet for collecting comments
and suggestions

Frame No.	Response	Comments	Suggestions
32	no cycling	—	—
33	cyclists only	misleading layout	Split into two
34	keep left	—	—

of constructing properly validated attitude scales for use with programmed instruction, although Neidt and Sjogren (1968) and Ellams (1969) have reported work in this direction. With such a scale it should be possible to make more valid comparisons between the attitudes of students to different programs. Most investigators, however, have contented themselves by using informal questionnaires, which although generally useful, do not provide much specific information which can be used for revision purposes.

Opinion on each lesson, or better, on each frame (e.g. 'Do you have to sound like "Listen with Mother" '), with constructive suggestions for improvement would, from a class of, say, 30 students, provide a wealth of data which the programmer could take into account when revising his program. In one of the writer's investigations (Hartley, 1966a) students were asked to grade what they thought were 'good' frames with a 'G', and to query frames they did not fully understand, but few students in fact did this, and the results were equivocal and not very helpful. Perhaps a better designed response sheet, such as the one suggested by Hanson (1963), which could incorporate Bjerstedt's suggestion mentioned earlier, would provide more useful information (*see Table 4.5*).

Certainly, without this sort of response sheet much information may be lost, although possibly the greatest controlling effect of

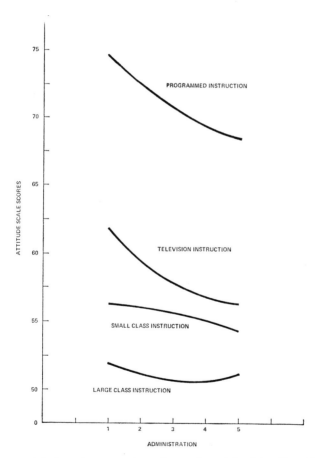

Figure 4.3. Attitudes to four presentation media over five periods of time (From Neidt and Sjogren, 1968, Courtesy: Audio-Visual Communication Review)

Table 4.6 Learner attitudes to programmed learning

'I found the course a great help. None of the material was new to me, but I have never really understood it before, and I have not been able to assimilate it at my own speed'.

—female undergraduate (Hartley, 1964).

'Programmed instruction gives you something to do.

—backward child (Wanless, 1969).

'I enjoyed working with the program at the start, but towards the middle I found it considerably harder, if not a little boring . . . . The idea of working from a book such as this came as a surprise, but I found it profitable in the way that I could go at my own pace; the thing that I thought was good, was the summary: by writing down various things it helped me to learn more easily.'

—blind girl (Freedman, 1968).

'I liked the test at the end because it wasn't too hard and it wasn't too easy: it was just about right for me.'

—8 year old girl (unpublished).

'Perhaps in the future there won't be any teachers and you could learn from books, or you could have computers in the room to tell you what to do, and then on a card you could punch it out and then just slip it in the computer. If it doesn't think you're right the card will come out with the writing on.'
(Do you think that would be a good way to learn?)
'Yes'.

—8 year old boy (unpublished).

'I think that this programmed work is O.K. I also think that it should be continued. Programmed work I think is a lot better than having books to read. I think you get more out of programmed work than books. You can work at your own rate.'

—maladjusted student (Chittick et al., 1966).

'The inmates expressed a desire to have more courses made available in programmed form. Among those mentioned most frequently were mathematics, auto-mechanics and electrical courses.'

—prisoners (Bertrand, 1966).

'On the whole the patients took to the situation surprisingly well. Many of them obviously enjoyed the experience, which they regarded as a game, and some were reluctant to leave the testing room and return to the ward afterwards.'

—elderly hospital patients (Gedye, 1967).

'I'm putting some of this (the program) into practice and it's having an effect already.'

—manager (Cavanagh and Jones, 1968).

student opinion is found in developmental rather than field testing. Attitude questionnaires may be used in two other ways. First, they can be used to sample the student's opinion of the program after different sections have been used, and after different periods of time, in order to assess novelty effects. For example, the writer found in one experiment (Hartley, 1965) that the extremely favourable attitudes towards his program expressed after four weeks were significantly reduced in fervour after nine weeks; the attitudes became much more neutral and the programmed lesson was treated the same as any other. Similar results have been found by several other investigators, but the relationship of attitude to final performance is not clear-cut (*see* Frey *et al.*, 1967; Noble, 1968; Noble and Gray, 1968).

Secondly, attitude questionnaires can be used in comparison studies to assess students' reactions to different kinds of presentation. Neidt and Sjogren (1968), for example, compared attitudes to four presentation media—programmed instruction, televised instruction, small class and large class. Attitudes scales were administered to over three hundred students in each condition at equally spaced intervals. A consistent decline in the mean scores was found over five testing periods, but the means were always consistently ordered as follows: programmed instruction (most favoured); televised instruction; small class; large class. These results are shown graphically in *Figure 4.3*.

In short, student attitudes may not be very helpful for revision, although they may be encouraging in many other respects. It is indeed remarkable how spontaneous statements made in open-ended questionnaires and interviews reflect so faithfully the principles of programmed learning (*see Table 4.6*).

REVISION

Techniques for locating sources of difficulty in programmed instruction have developed steadily in the last few years: there has, however, been little corresponding increase in statements of what programmers should do about these difficulties, other than 'revise the program'. Some investigators have, however, put forward decision rules concerning revision. Thomas (1966) used the gain ratio as a basis for decision making (*see Figure 4.4*), although the validity of this procedure, as noted above, may be questioned especially if students have high pretest scores. This decision chart, however, could still be used with whatever figure one cared to introduce at the first decision level.

Sime and Dodd (1964) suggest rather different strategies. They argue that if the final test is reliable, and if the learners have the necessary prerequisite entry behaviour, then errors made on the final test are either the result of a failing to retain what has been taught, or of a misunderstanding of it. If, by reference to the teaching sequence, it is found that there is no evidence of misunderstanding, then failure to retain the material long enough to successfully complete the final test may be the fault. If several students are in this position, then extra review, revision and 'drill' frames are indicated. If students made mistakes on items of the test, and on appropriate prior teaching sequences, then these errors must be examined in order to see what responses were given, so that the causes of these responses may then be deduced. If a large proportion of the students is making the same mistake, the sequence may need to be re-written: if the mistakes are more varied but clear-cut, specific remedial sequences for each mistake may be added: if the mistakes are few but very varied, then it would seem more advisable to add a single general remedial sequence.

It may be important to note at this stage that revision generally leads to an increase in program length, and that this is often considered undesirable. Strategies have, however, been devised to prevent this. Editorial strategies (Taber *et al.*, 1965) and flow-diagram analyses, such as those discussed by Hartley and Franklin (1965), attempt to help novice programmers keep their programs precise. A comprehensive list of such procedures had been provided by Bjerstedt (1964). What is important to note about these strategies is that they can all be applied to programs without reference to student performance, and, indeed, they all have been advocated for use *before* developmental or field testing. As noted earlier, in the preparation of programs, program writers perhaps should not err too much on the side of caution: programs should be 'brisk and vigorous' (Kay *et al.*, 1968). If evaluation does, in fact, show the initial (short) brisk and vigorous program to be too difficult, then the final revised product may still be acceptable in terms of length.

The internal evaluation of programs described above is not difficult to do, but it is time-consuming to do it properly. This is especially so because revised versions of programs need to be retested in order to assess the improvements brought about by the revision. It seems that present-day programs usually undergo— following the first tryout—a major revision, and then, following subsequent tryouts (usually *one* only), minor modifications. This is regarded by some as a serious criticism of present-day published programs (e.g. Komoski, 1966).

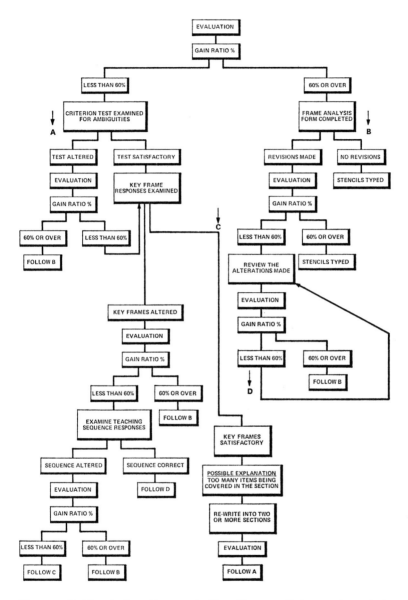

Figure 4.4. Decision rules for revision strategies (From Thomas, 1966, Courtesy: Pitman Ltd)

The strategies for revision described in this section are helpful, but they are still rather vague. Perhaps the best way to study revision is to examine the specific analyses made by people who have actually done it (*see* Austwick, 1963; Hartley, 1964). To some extent this vagueness is inevitable for, as already noted, programmers have different objectives and different subject matters, data are often obtained in poorly controlled conditions, and thus dealing with the results becomes less objective than is desirable. As Markle (1967) observes, between evaluation and implementation 'It is a rare programmer indeed who can resist the tendency to further "improve" the program'. Revision at these later stages involves a subjective tinkering rather than an application of a systematic methodology.

The discussion on empirical testing of programs earlier in this chapter, was organised as though each measure was made independently of the other. In fact, as was suggested, combinations of measures may lead to more powerful indicators for revision. Indeed, many investigators have made correlational analyses between these measures and test results—usually, however, with little success, largely because of the narrowness of the distributions obtained.

The strategies described above for collecting all these data involve, after field testing, 'the tedious tabulation of student written responses obtained under poorly controlled conditions', and it may be that we should look to computers for more precision in this respect, for 'computer systems make possible the collecting of responses under well controlled conditions' (Zinn, 1967). Interesting possibilities arise when one considers the idea of measures being made in combination, and decisions based upon them made *as the instruction proceeds*. For example, the computer-assisted program developed by Smallwood (1962) 'honed down', as it were, from trying many strategies to using one or two effective teaching sequences: in effect, it 'learned' from its teaching of the first students through the course. Computer-assisted instruction (CAI) offers much in this respect: computers can determine the strategies and tactics of the presentation of material dependent upon combinations of measures such as response times, the history of errors made, the students' pre-knowledge, the paths taken by other similar students, and indeed, student personality measures. Furthermore, computers can be programmed to take into account the certainty the student feels about the correctness of his response as he makes it (*see* Baker, 1969).

These researches highlight a basic problem in this area: this is how to make an appropriate decision about what information should be presented next to the learner, given all these data. As Baker (1969) laconically remarks, 'Given a response technique which produces a distribution (of certainty about the correctness) over the response, the branching structure becomes considerably more complex.' The strategies described in this chapter may be of considerable value for the initial programming of such decision rules, but it would seem that more will be learned from the pragmatic application of decision rules in a CAI setting.

Techniques of computer-assisted evaluation are now being rapidly developed. The state of the art in the U.S.A. and the United Kingdom is summarised in papers edited by Dunn and Holroyd (1969) and Mann and Brunstrom (1969). Much discussion centres on strategies of approach: whether or not the computer should monitor key areas of a teaching-learning system and diagnose where improvements could be made (an argument advanced by Sime (1968) with especial reference to the United Kingdom), or whether whole educational systems should be linked to a 'computer-grid'. Some would suggest that a monitoring system would represent a 'consolidation of ignorance' which, whilst admittedly making more efficient what little we know, would not lead to a full realisation of the potentials involved. Needless to say, much discussion centres on costs, and some attempts to consider cost effectiveness will be made when concluding the next section.

EVALUATING INSTRUCTIONAL METHODS

Comparison studies

In view of the often heard claims that programmed instruction can teach as effectively as teachers, and in less time, there is naturally great interest in comparison studies between programmed and 'conventional instruction', and a large number of such studies has now been made. To carry out a comparison study between different educational methods is not in principle difficult, but it is difficult to do it precisely, and it may not be possible to generalise from the results. In order to support this statement it is necessary to examine the procedures generally adopted in such experiments. (A fuller treatment of these problems can be found in Lumsdaine (1963) and Jacobs et al. (1966).)

Generally speaking, two groups are formed, and if the numbers are small (e.g. less than 25 in each), they are usually matched on the basis of items which may be relevant to the particular experiment: such items may include pretest scores, age, sex, IQ, verbal, mathematical, and spatial ability, socio-economic status, and so on. It may be desirable in fact to match on the basis of one score rather than another (e.g. pretest score rather than age). This can be done, and the other variables then examined in the two groups to see if there are any differences which might be statistically significant. If the numbers are large (e.g. above 30 in each group), then members may be randomly allocated into their respective groups.

Both groups first receive a pretest, then their respective instruction, and at the end of this a final test. Mean scores and variability on this test can be calculated and the results tested for significant differences. In addition, by using the appropriate statistical techniques, relationships—e.g. between time taken, test scores, attitudes, final test, errors, etc., and the matching criteria—can be established for the groups and thus compared.

But there are a number of limitations to these comparison experiments. They are difficult to carry out precisely because the number of variables interacting in the two groups can never be fully itemised or controlled. Despite the matching procedures some particular variables cannot be adequately balanced out between the groups—a machine-taught group is almost certain to be affected by the novelty of the situation: members of different groups may communicate with each other: and the effects of group pressures may influence speed of work, attitudes towards it, and towards cheating. Furthermore, an assumption being made is that the objectives of the methods being compared are the same, and that these can be measured by the same test. Such an assumption is often invalid. As Dodd (1967b) remarks, 'For conventional instruction there is no such thing as a criterion test with its own marking scheme which can be used by anyone.' Giving pre- and post-tests may alter student expectations about what they are required to do, and giving the same test to both conditions is perhaps tipping the balance in favour of the experimental method: indeed, some researches have shown this to be the case (for example Pikas, 1967).

Finally, the results of any single comparison study must remain specific to the study carried out: it is not possible to generalise about the effectiveness of a method of instruction from one single study. Thus, despite the fact that, for example, Holt (1963) carried out a study which was exemplary as far as research design was concerned, his findings—that programmed instruction was superior to conventional instruction in terms of test and retest results—were restricted to:

(a) The population used (64 technicians).
(b) The program used (a 2 500 frame linear program providing between 30 and 60 hours of instruction).
(c) The presentation used (programmed text).
(d) The presentation used by the conventional lecturer (matched closely with the programmed presentation).
(e) The test used.
(f) The amount of delay between test and retest (six months).

It is important to note that in single comparison studies neither the method used nor the teacher involved can be representative of all examples of the method, or all teachers. (Indeed, if it was the teacher who prepared the experimental material then it may well be that his 'conventional' instruction will have much improved.) So, despite the fact that it is not in principle difficult to do a comparison experiment, it is difficult to do it precisely; and clearly it is not legitimate to generalise from the results of a single study. Indeed, individual studies should be replicated before firm conclusions—specific only to them—can be made.

A different approach for writers wishing to generalise about the efficiency of methods of instruction has been for them to collect together instances of single experiments, to pool them, and to consider generalisations that emerge. This is difficult to do when there are only a few reported studies, such as is the case with language laboratories, but it is easier with programmed instruction

Table 4.7 The results of 112 studies comparing programmed with conventional instructions (Hartley, 1966c)

Measures recorded	Number of Studies recording these measures	Programmed Instruction Group		
		Significantly superior	Not significantly different	Significantly worse
Time taken	90	47	37	6
Test results	110	41	54	15
Retest results	33	6	24	3

Note: Figures in the first column differ because not all three measures are recorded for every one of the 112 studies.

M

and with educational television. The reader can make his own generalisations about the efficiency of programmed instruction by inspecting *Table 4.7* which combines together the results of over 112 studies comparing teachers and programmed instruction. *Table 4.7* seems to present a clear-cut picture: programmed instruction can teach some things as effectively, or more so, than can conventional instruction, and quite often it can do this in less time. This combination of factors suggests that programmed instruction is a more efficient teaching method than is conventional instruction. Such a conclusion is typical of the popular article on programmed instruction. It is one purpose of this chapter to suggest, because of the difficulty of doing such studies, that this conclusion is not as well supported as it might initially appear to be.

In collecting instances of experiments on programmed versus conventional instruction, few writers have evaluated their research design. Clearly, there are a number of decisions to be made, and investigators have put forward criteria for designing such experiments (*see* Gilbert, 1966, for references). Cheris (1964) suggested that the content taught should be identical, that both presentations should be optimum, and that the effectiveness of the instructive technique should be measured by accurate measures of the learning time, and by an unbiased criterion test. Hartley (1966c) added further criteria: that the experimental report should include a statement about the length and type of program used (and how it was presented), the number of students involved in each condition, and—as a further measure of efficiency—the results of a retention test. Hartley then showed that the conclusions drawn from *Table 4.7* could, in fact, be questioned because nearly all of the experiments whose findings were included either lacked one or more of these criteria. Thus, the limitations of *Table 4.7* are that:

(a) Some of the experiments have a very small number of students.
(b) Some use a very short program.
(c) Long-term retention has been overlooked.
(d) Some of the data are reported second-hand. (This usually means that not enough details are reported, so it is impossible to evaluate the original research design.)

It is also important to note that experiments where the programmed group did not do so well as the conventionally taught group may not have been reported.

The studies reported in *Table 4.7* are studies where a direct comparison between conventional and programmed instruction is made: a number of studies have now shown that 'integrated' programmed instruction—that is, where instructor and program work together—provides a more efficient teaching system than either taken separately. Again, most of these studies can be criticised on technical grounds, but the encouraging thing here is the virtual unanimity of their conclusions. (For further studies the reader is referred to: Goldbeck *et al.*, 1962; Baldwin, 1964; Wallis, 1964; Lankford, 1965; Bartz and Darby, 1965; Wriggle, 1965; Ripple, 1966; Noble, 1967a, Blount *et al.*, 1967; Leith and Webb, 1968; Ryan, 1968; Ives and Wallis, 1969.) Taking them overall, it seems that the most effective instructor activities, when using programmed materials, are to ensure (by reviews and overviews) that adequate learning is taking place, and to maintain motivation. It may be argued that further research is needed into discovering the social and administrative factors that lead to effective learning from programmed instruction. Neale *et al.* (1968) have indicated the importance of such factors with respect to adult training.

The comparison study has been the most popular experiment in the history of programmed instruction. This section of this chapter has indicated that any individual study is limited, and that the overall picture shows a sorry state in terms of scientific rigour.

In the writer's view, the comparison study is a strategy which is wasteful in terms of effort and resources. As Levy (1969) put it, 'If two or more educational systems can be evaluated on the same scales and judged by the same criteria, then the systems are not sufficiently distinct to be worthy of (a comparison) study.' Experiments are required to determine what factors make a method effective, and how these methods can be improved. Given different but effective methods of achieving more or less the same objectives, then we are left with a further set of complex questions—how much do they cost, and which one is the cheapest?

Costs

Costing a method of instruction is difficult, but not impossible. In this section three areas will be discussed, 'cost estimates', 'comparative cost studies', and 'cost benefits', although these terms are not used with the precision given to them by economists. In each area problems soon become apparent.

Cost estimates. The estimates put forward by some investigators of the costs that they have incurred in the production of programmed materials are many and varied. The disparity of the figures revealed indicates the difficulty of the task, and indeed, many investigators have found the exercise somewhat futile. As Dodd (1967b) remarks, 'Commercial programming companies will quote widely different prices because each offers a different service. Some companies will simply quote the cost of converting the client's material into programmed form. Others will expect to carry out a thorough investigation of the job for which training is intended.' The estimates given depend upon several interacting factors, the most important of which appear to be as follows:

(a) The cost of production (which may or may not include evaluation time).
(b) Trainee, instructor, and program writers' salaries during construction and instruction, plus general overheads.
(c) The cost of use (e.g. hiring, or purchasing machines and programs).
(d) The number of students involved.
(e) The stability of the subject matter.
(f) The amortisation of costs over a specified period of time.

It is important to consider these different kinds of costs, and their relationships when comparing alternative systems of training. For example, a system which costs a lot to develop and to install may be cheap to run, and thus, if the number of students to be trained is large, it could prove cheaper in the long run.

As all programs differ in length, format and purpose, it becomes clear that generalising about costs becomes unwise. Bearing this in mind, some of the costs of programming calculated in terms of student hours, are listed in *Table 4.8*. (Readers interested in the more factual details of how given figures are arrived at are referred to the studies reported in this table, and also to papers published in Margulies and Eigen, 1962.)

Table 4.8 Reported cost estimates for programmed materials

Investigators	*Cost per Student Hour*
Kopstein and Cave (1962)	$0·013–$0·422
Aerojet General Corporation (Ofiesh, 1965)	$0·50
Taylor (1967)	£0·06–£0·32
Barry (1967)	£0·20–£6·90
Jeffels (1969)	£0·09½

Comparative cost studies. The difficulties of estimating the costs of instruction have already been indicated. The difficulties increase when one wishes to compare two (or more) estimates for two (or more) methods. The first problem is that two *estimates* are being compared (and thus the bases for the estimates must be known). Next, there are certain assumptions involved. Do, for example, the different methods have the same objectives, and the same side-effects—both short and long-term? If (as one might

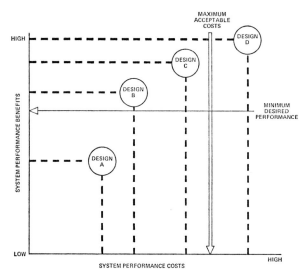

Figure 4.5. A schematic diagram of the problems of choosing between different educational methods directed towards similar objectives but differing in benefits and costs (Reprinted from Peter H. Rossi and Bruce J. Biddle, editors, The New Media and Education *(Chicago: Aldine Publishing Company, 1966); copyright 1966 by National Opinion Research Centre)*

expect) this is not the case, then can comparative costs be readily established? Furthermore, is there a minimum desired performance, whatever the cost, or does the cost determine what performance will be acceptable? (*see Figure 4.5*). Finally, in relation to teaching, it can be observed that comparative cost studies are particularly difficult to carry out because of the problems involved in calculating the cost of 'conventional' instruction. Kay *et al.* (1968) point out that 'this is particularly true of training, where the major cost is probably to be found in the hidden long-term effects of inefficient methods'.

Attempts, of course, have been made to estimate and compare the costs of different teaching systems. The figures given by Duke (1968)

Table 4.9 Estimates of the cost of computer-assisted instruction (From Duke, 1968, Courtesy: New Education)

Number of Students sharing course	Processor	Terminal	System Software	Total	Instructional material per 1 000 hrs.	Hardware cost per annum (write off over 5 years)	Software cost per annum (write off over 5 years)	Total cost per annum	Cost per Student hour
				Cost in thousands of pounds					
10	20	5	50	75	100	15	40	55	£5·50
100	50	50	100	200	100	40	40	80	£0·80
1000	250	500	150	900	100	180	40	220	£0·22

are shown in *Table 4.9.* Duke concluded that the figures he arrived at compared effectively with those given for conventional instruction in Great Britain (£0·07½ per hour for primary schools, £0·13 per hour for secondary schools, and higher (unspecified estimates for industrial training, higher and further education). He argued that with an expected increase in efficiency from automated instruction, then 'the cost benefit is probably in favour of the computer'. Perhaps it should be pointed out that Duke's figures appear to be based on uncompleted research projects

Table 4.10 The cost benefits of programmed instruction

Investigators	Cost of Program	Cost of Conventional Instruction	Estimated Savings
American Bankers Association (Ofiesh, 1965)	—	—	20%–50% of training time
American Telephone and Telegraph Co. (Ofiesh, 1965)	$218 per student hour	$309 per student hour	29% of instruction 27% of trainee time
Union Carbide Chemicals Co. (Ofiesh, 1965)	—	—	$90 000 in training to date ($30/man.)
Holme and Mabbs (1967)	£1 500	£1 500	£1 500 per yr
Hall and Fletcher (1967)	£20 000	—	1 week's trainee time Approx. £10 000 per yr
Oates and Robinson (1968)	£12 500	—	8·2% of training time £24 700 after 2 yrs
Watson (1968)	—	—	3 hrs. per supervisor $90 000 per course
Mills (1968)	£550	—	£1 275 annually
Howe (1969)	£13 500	—	£1 000 for every 3 courses
Jones and Moxham (1969)	—	—	10 weeks trainee time Labour turnover reduced from 70% to 30%. Retention of skilled labour

rather than on any ongoing use of computer-assisted instruction, and that the calculations are made 'in the light of certain reasonable assumptions' (presumably those listed in *Table 4.9*). A more comprehensive study of the costs of CAI in America has been provided by Kopstein and Seidel (1968). These investigators, after careful discussion, indicating that 'the provisional nature of the comparisons cannot be stressed enough', finally conclude that 'on the assumption that the software costs and instructional programming costs can be very widely distributed and thus become negligible, an economic forecast of CAI at $0·11 per student hour becomes a probability'.

Cost benefits. The aim of a cost benefit analysis is to calculate in terms of money the various benefits and costs, both direct and indirect, to be realised from pursuing a certain course of action, and to set the cost of these against the cost of the initial outlay, or capital invested. Again, it goes without saying that for education such a comprehensive analysis is difficult to do. However, in industrial settings attempts have been made to calculate the

Table 4.11   The indirect benefits of programmed instruction

'We now have quality standard expressed in meaningful terms .... The new defined standard will mean a fall in the number of cigars rejected. Even a drop of 2% of total production would mean annual savings running well into tens of thousands of pounds .... There should be fewer complaints, few customers changing to other brands .... We can virtually leave the training system to look after itself.'

—Newark (1968)

'Such training does improve the knowledge level of a factory and, more important, creates interest in what is often a somewhat stagnant situation.'

—Blunden (1968)

'One of the overwhelming advantages to be gained from considering the use of programmed learning is that it forces you to think about your training objectives, and the increased efficiency offered by the use of programmed material will more often than not justify the cost. Basically, the problem seems to me to be not one of whether the conventional method costs X shillings per student hour as opposed to Y shillings per student hour for programmed material, but rather, what are the financial advantages of having well trained students?'

—Lambert (1968)

'... Subject to having about 2 000 learners before the product-knowledge, programs become obsolete, the program cost should not exceed 10s. per hour. But even here the comparison fails; a program-hour is usually much more productive than a lecture-hour. It almost looks as though one should really calculate the cost of not training, and then see if programmed learning looks economic.'

—Young (1967)

---

cost benefit of introducing programmed instruction, and a survey of results obtained is given in *Table 4.10.*

Perhaps, however, what is more important to note, particularly with reference to education, are indirect, less tangible benefits. Whilst many industrialists are reluctant to calculate the costs involved, this has not prevented them from making statements of the kind listed in *Table 4.11.* Some of these statements re-echo the thoughts expressed in Chapter 1.

In this section it has been argued that estimating the costs of new methods of instruction presents many problems and that the analyses of cost benefits referred to above must be based to a considerable extent on 'reasonable assumptions'. It is important on the one hand to be aware of the tailor-made cost effectiveness study drawn up to justify a certain project but, on the other hand, to recognise that a careful analysis of the problem involved is likely to lead to a better decision than one made by an intuitive guess. Decisions about the effectiveness of a certain strategy may remain for some time largely value-judgments, but the bases for these judgments should be open to inspection, and improvement.

CONCLUSION

In Chapter 1 it was stated that the authors of this book felt that 'educational technology' was synonymous with 'scientific improvement', where 'scientific' implied a systematic, methodological approach which based its decisions on facts rather than value judgments. This chapter has indicated the realities of the situation as opposed to the ideals. In fact, the chapter demonstrates that 'evaluation' is not a simple procedure which involves the quick administration of a pre- and post-test, but that it raises a number of issues which must be seriously considered if instruction is to be improved.

5

Research Strategies for an Educational Technology

JOHN ANNETT

This chapter discusses some of the research that has been done in the field of programmed instruction, and some that might be done in the future. It is not a review of the literature but rather points out some of the trends which should continue to grow, and is somewhat critical of other types of research. The title refers to an 'educational technology' for this is what programmed learning can be said to be, a technology rather than either a pure science or a mysterious art. This basic premise that programmed learning is a technology has implications for research strategies. A technology has fairly immediate goals, it has problems here and now belonging to the real world, problems about teaching and learning which must be met and dealt with. A few years ago a committee of the American Educational Research Association, consisting of Dr. Clark, E. R. Hilgard and L. G. Humphreys, described educational research under six categories, ranging along a continuum from basic or pure research on the learning process to actual utilisation of new techniques in the schools (*see Figure 5.1*). Research relevant to programmed learning is undoubtedly spread along this continuum, much of it unfortunately falling into the category of somewhat haphazard and premature utilisation in the schools. At the same time we are all very conscious of the fact that programmed learning is a science-based technology, so this chapter will begin at this end of the continuum considering the function of basic research in the technology of teaching.

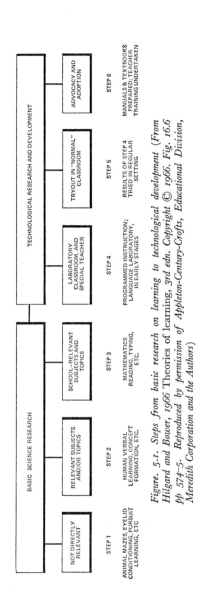

Figure. 5.1. Steps from basic research on learning to technological development (From Hilgard and Bower, 1966 Theories of learning, 3rd edn. Copyright © 1966. Fig. 16.6 pp 574-5. Reproduced by permission of Appleton-Century-Crofts, Educational Division, Meredith Corporation and the Authors)

BASIC RESEARCH

The layman should beware of the idea that research is 'basic' because it is carried out in a laboratory and uses rats and pigeons. Animals are used either because there is some interest in the species as such, or because the variables under investigation, for example hereditary endowment, prior experience, motivational state and so on, can be fairly easily controlled. It cannot be stressed too often that, except in a very general way, comparative psychologists do not use animals on the naive assumption that they are simpler versions of the human species. It is true that the nervous systems of the primates do have many resemblances to that of man but they are not necessarily identical in function, nor are they necessarily simpler. One might mention the olfactory system of the dog and the ultrasonic echo-ranging system of the bat as two outstanding examples of different and functionally superior mechanisms. Comparative psychology is so full of pitfalls that most comparative psychologists refuse to make any but the most general comparisons between man and the particular species under investigation. Although the comparative psychologist is often better able to control his variables, there is no built in guarantee that these are the variables most directly relevant to human studies. Some people may have been led, by the frequent references to rats and pigeons in the literature, to over-estimate the precision with which these results of 'basic' research can be applied to normal human learning. In the physical sciences we have become used to the logical and theoretical continuum between pure and applied science. In the behavioural sciences, however, one can draw analogies between species but one cannot deduce the behaviour of one species from that of another (*see* Bitterman, 1960).

Turning more specifically to the problem of learning theory and its relationship to a technology of teaching, most research is done in the context of a theory. Experiments are set up to verify predictions derived from the theory, and to have a theory is one of the most powerful determinants of the appropriate research strategy. Yet Skinner, from whose work programmed learning is largely derived, claims not to have a theory in the normally accepted sense (Skinner, 1950).

Hypothesis testing

Now a great deal of the work which has been done has been of the hypothesis testing type, undertaken to support or refute a supposed theory of reinforcement. The usefulness of much of this research has been questioned by Skinner and his supporters, notably Holland (1965), who claim that since there is no theory, hypothesis testing research is inappropriate. Educational technology should know where it stands on this issue—is it based on a testable theory, and if not, what is it based on?

The Skinnerian position on reinforcement is essentially that learning in animals occurs when a response is made in the presence of a discriminative stimulus followed by reinforcement. This is an empirical statement rather than a theory. It is a statement of what in fact happens in certain types of laboratory experiments, and as such it is generally and indisputably true. A pigeon not provided with food for pecking a disc will not learn to perform this act. The factual statement does not require any theoretical statement to support it, and Skinner is not professionally interested in elucidating the physiological mechanisms underlying this phenomenon. However, when we get out of the laboratory and watch a child learning we are often at a loss to identify any reinforcing agent. If we introduce supposed reinforcers, as for example in the verbal learning experiments of Greenspoon (1955), or Verplanck (1955), we seldom get a clear-cut result. If, therefore, we wish to stress the analogy between pigeons and men, we are in the position of having to postulate a process of reinforcement by some unknown reinforcer. Thus what was a statement of fact in relation to the rat and the pigeon becomes a hypothesis and a theory when applied to human learning: in this case Skinner must be said to be responsible for a theory about human learning. It is only fair to say, however, that in research on human learning one is often manipulating rather different variables, and people in the position of a hungry pigeon may tend to behave more like one. Nevertheless there are many other experiments adequately controlling other types of variable (for example, type and amount of material, presentation rate, competing tasks, etc.) from which systematic relationships—if you like, 'laws of learning'—do emerge.

The position adopted by the Skinnerians is that in an experiment in programmed learning of the classical knowledge of results versus no knowledge of results type, the finding of no significant difference between the two does not warrant a rejection of the reinforcement hypothesis. It merely shows that response confirmation is not in this case the effective reinforcer. Holland (1961) has argued that research should be directed to identifying appropriate reinforcers. Using this sort of criterion it would be hard to find any experiment which could explicitly reject the hypothesis that learning depends on reinforcement. A hypothesis which cannot in principle be rejected is of course of very little scientific value—it is in effect a tautology.

One cannot sum up the significance of 'basic' research for a technology of teaching in a few words, but I would like to reiterate a few of the points I have been making. I am in complete agreement with Holland that the sort of research which attempts to confirm or disconfirm the Skinnerian position has been virtually fruitless. Certainly the results as summarised for example by Schramm (1964) and Holland (1965) himself have provided neither proof nor disproof of the central feature of Skinner's work—the concept of reinforcement—one of the reddest of red herrings in modern psychology.

PRACTICAL RESEARCH PROBLEMS

This leads on to some rather more practical points in relation to the type of research which examines dichotomies such as *overt* versus *covert* responding, *constructed response* versus *multiple choice, short* versus *long* steps, and so on. In order to test a hypothesis it is essential that the experimenter should systematically vary the relevant conditions holding others constant. The number of relevant variables in any real teaching situation is enormous. Fry (1963) in his introductory book lists no fewer than 26 classes of variables, and Hodge (1967) has reordered and reclassified these (and to some extent extended the original classification). In view of the enormous number of interacting variables, extremely painstaking systematic research is required, in such a situation, if results are not to be contradictory and inconclusive. Typically published work has used rather short chunks of program, student populations have been inadequately sampled, and novelty effects have been almost impossible to control.

Many of these research hypotheses have to do with the detailed interaction of the student with the learning material. Frames are written in order that they should be used in a precise way, response modes are chosen such that the student's response will be of a particular kind. However, having written a program of a particular kind the experimenter often leaves it at that and makes no further effort to control the student's behaviour. Much of this work is done with texts rather than machines, but even a machine cannot always guarantee the kind of control implied by the hypothesis under test. Take the case of multiple choice or constructed response. Even a cheat-proof machine cannot prevent the pupil from constructing his answer when faced with a multiple-choice question. The way is open for a whole range of behaviour from constructed response, followed by selection of the appropriate answer, to random guessing.

Inadequacy of measures

Programmed learning research has also suffered from another important basic difficulty to which attention was drawn several years ago—that is the general inadequacy of the measures of performance gain (*see* Chapter 4). The fault is partly due to the consistently negative attitude of Skinnerians towards the technology of mental testing. However, there are signs that this attitude is changing. Hypothesis testing requires the use of ratio scales and most statistical techniques involve assumptions about the distribution of scores along a given dimension. However, the post-tests commonly used constitute little more than an enumeration of the tasks the learner can perform, or at best, ordinal scales. They specify that the student has learned this and this and this, but not that or that; that student A has learned more of the selected sample of behaviour than student B. Yet such results are often treated like ratio scales to which numbers, such as percentages, can be applied. When a student answers 9 out of 10 questions correctly we have no real grounds for asserting that he has learned 90 per cent. The famous 90–90 criterion is essentially bogus. Annett (1967) observed that the absence of standardised achievement scales was one of the most serious handicaps to educational research, including programmed learning, and it is pleasing to report that British research on the development of such scales is now going on.

So far the remarks have been largely negative. It has been argued that programmed learning is a science-based technology but that the relationship between the practice and the basic theory and research is not at all straightforward. Along with people like Holland, the author has argued that the hypothesis testing research strategy has not been very fruitful and this is for two reasons:

(a) Because the relationship between the supposed theory and the method of testing the theory has often been misunderstood.
(b) Because the research techniques have more often than not been inadequate through poor control of the independent variables and inadequate measurement of the dependent variables.

Research strategies

At this point it will be useful to say something more positive about research strategies which are more promising for a technology of teaching. Holland (1961) suggests that programmed learning depends on three principles, gradual progression, control of the students' observing or mediating behaviour and variations in the material, and he goes on to say 'the specific form that the application will take will be an experimental matter to be worked out by careful experiment analysis'. This view is entirely compatible with the notion of a technology of teaching which fosters its own experimental work rather than relying on crude analogies from supposedly 'basic' research. Take for example the first and third principles—the gradual progression and variation of material. This is in effect the area of task analysis as described by Duncan in Chapter 2. Here, as he implies, much more work needs to be done on the structure of complex skills and the interrelations between sub-skills. Many subject matters are said to have a logical structure of which the subject matter expert is aware, but logical structure can be elusive even in a subject like mathematics. One might have said that counting is 'prior to' mensuration but for the fact that children learn to count by manipulating different sizes of blocks. Indeed it seems to be the feature of modern mathematics that the old order of things has been very readily upset. In language teaching a new priority is being given to the phonic aspects of language as opposed to beginning with grammar and vocabulary lists. In motor skills one might ask what importance should be attached to the fact that events occur in a given sequence, when the differential difficulty of component sub-skills suggests a different order of teaching based on the gradual progression of difficulty. Then there is the whole problem of the relationship between theory and practice. Here there are a set of problems of immediate and crucial importance to a technology of teaching to which the attention of researchers is now being draw. Some parts of psychological research seem relevant but as yet no real frontal attack has been made on these problems.

The second principle, the control of observing and mediating behaviour, is also in need of a great deal more research. This is an aspect of the area of research discussed by Davies in Chapter 3. In many of the early draft programs it appeared that programmers were primarily interested in getting what they believed to be the subject matter content down on paper in almost any form. Some of these programs were little more than transliterated text-books and the programmer had made little effort to control the students' observing behaviour by manipulating the structure of the individual frames. There is need for more of the sort of work done, for example, by Rothkopf (1963) and Frase (1968) on how students learn from written sentences, and for more imaginative efforts, such as Schaefer's (1963) use of redundancy for teaching foreign language vocabulary. But it is difficult to control a learner's behaviour by means of the printed text alone. The reaction of many school children to early programmed textbooks has been surprisingly frank—they simply did not want to sit and read all day. There is room for a much more imaginative use of materials and devices other than the programmed textbooks. As an outstanding example, O. K. Moore's 'talking typewriter' is a fascinating exercise in behavioural control (*see* Hill and Cavanagh, 1969) and some of the work which Mager has reported, (Mager, 1964; Mager and Clark, 1963) on the control of learning environment, needs pursuing. One has to think beyond the text for other means, social as well as electromechanical, for directing the learner's attention to the relevant aspects of the task and getting him to respond in appropriate ways. Work with discovery programs with students learning in pairs or small groups is of value here (*see* Hartley, 1968).

Teaching machines

There is at least one important type of research which has been seriously neglected in developing what Pressey called 'the industrial revolution in teaching'. In Skinner's classic article (1954) he gave one essential reason for introducing teaching machines, and this reason was straightforwardly technological. Assuming that something like 25 000 reinforcement experiences are necessary to build up a reasonable repertoire of mathematical behaviour, it was quite obvious that the unaided teacher could not provide this 'treatment'. The machine was essentially a technological aid to this supposedly necessary process. Skinner's argument was in so many ways reasonable and obvious that he and everyone else has skipped over the implications of this kind of reasoning. He did not actually count the number of 'reinforcements' he believed necessary nor the rate at which these can normally be delivered. The result of such a simple sum was too obvious. At the same time this sort of argument implies that much more detailed and thorough investigation of actual teaching situations are desirable if rational decisions are to be made about the kind of mechanical aids the teacher needs. One, therefore, could argue that there is a case for a new series of observational studies on

N

what happens in real teaching situations as a highly necessary basis for the introduction of techniques as radically new as programmed learning. Indeed it appears that there has been of late a rapid increase in such studies (*see Figure 5.2*).

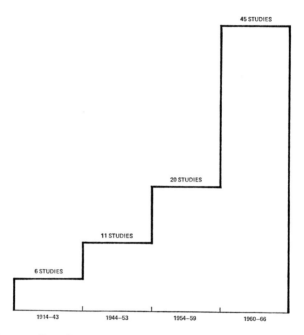

Figure 5.2. Expanding research on classroom observation (After Campbell, 1968)

Observation studies

Medley and Mitzel (1963) and Campbell (1968) have produced a useful survey of the methods and findings of classroom observation studies. Much of this research has been concerned with attempts to measure effective teacher behaviour and to develop measures of teacher effectiveness. The Wisconsin studies by Barr (1961) and his associates are probably well known. Many different measures of teacher performance were taken, including ratings by supervisors, peers and pupils, and teacher aptitude tests. Many thousands of correlations were obtained and the overall result was essentially negative. Research of this kind has so far failed to find any way of assessing teacher behaviour and characteristics which correlates with actual student performance as measured by gain scores. (This should be of some consolation to those of us who are disappointed at the relatively high proportion of negative results when different varieties of teaching systems are compared.) Classroom observation studies have, on occasion, been used to measure dependent variables in methods experiments. For example, Urban (1943) observed and counted the number of times pupils sucked pencils, sneezed without a handkerchief or picked their noses during English lessons, one group of pupils having been given lessons on hygiene and another control group not. With the advent of more sophisticated methods of observation and recording, we may expect the number (and the quality) of such studies to increase.

Direct observation studies have not been the most exciting or the most rewarding of educational researches, but I believe that techniques of direct observation can prove of considerable value to programmed learning research. A teaching machine, or for that matter a simple visual aid, must inevitably have an effect on the behaviour of both pupils and teachers and it is important to know what the effects are, especially since it is sometimes argued that the new and different activities like threading strip projectors and unjamming teaching machines, are bothersome, disrupt the class and are in any case beneath the dignity of the teacher (Butler and Cavanagh, 1969).

But there is a more dramatic approach suggested by Time and Motion Study and Human Engineering. Gilbreth observed the method of laying bricks, and based on his observations he developed new methods which gave enormous increases in output without a corresponding increase in effort. More recent studies in Human Engineering have enabled workplaces to be redesigned, communication channels to be shortened, resulting not only in increased efficiency but in reduced fatigue and accidents. The method of direct observation of classroom behaviour is the most natural starting point for an analysis and reshaping of teaching processes. The *feedback classroom* (Holling, 1967) was clearly designed with something of this in mind; by introducing a small degree of automation the process of question and answer can be made much more efficient in terms of pupil participation even though it may have drawbacks with respect of the limited kind of participation the system permits. In the same way the Pressey machines automate the process of grading pupils with the added bonus of providing for further practice. It seems probably that some gains so far obtained by the use of teaching machines and programs have been principally due to the more efficient use of pupil time.

The variety and quantity of data to be collected by direct

observation studies is enormous and although some of the methods have been tried and developed, these can now be conducted with an essentially new aim in mind, that of diagnosing the inefficiencies in teaching. I have little doubt that systematic study of this kind will throw up not only problems which are at present unsuspected but also new solutions.

COMPUTER-ASSISTED INSTRUCTION

Since 1967 the field of computer-assisted instruction (sometimes called computer-based instruction or computer-assisted learning— CAI, CBI, CAL) has grown rather rapidly. The literature has been reviewed by Hickey (1968) and a number of general statements of the problems and possibilities are available (Annett, 1969). CAI poses some of the old problems and some new. Briefly, the computer is envisaged as being capable of doing all the things a teaching machine can do and much more besides. For example, more or less conventional linear or branching programs can be presented but more elaborate constructed responses can be automatically scored and more complex forms of branching can be used. But there are some important additional features. For example, with the use of time sharing, large numbers (50 or even more) students at separate terminals can use the same program. Computers can allow more varied instruction with the subject matter in several ways. In a simple case, the computer may permit the student to have access to any information he needs almost instantaneously retrieved from a large central store, this is sometimes called the enquiry mode. In other cases, the computer's memory can be used together with rapid access facilities, not only to provide information but to check any inference the student wishes to make on the basis of the information given. This 'Socratic' mode is shown in Feuerzeig's (1964) medical diagnosis system. In certain cases, the computer can be used to create new examples, and to grade these according to student performance.

Another special facility of CAI is in adaptive teaching of the kind demonstrated by Pask some years ago (Pask, 1960, 1969). Yet again, the computer can perform certain administrative functions, storing data on the progress of individuals or groups and even issuing suitable remedial prescriptions. All these possibilities invite new kinds of research. Much of what has been going on recently consists of attempts to demonstrate the potential of CAI. For example, how feasible are various systems of response recognition, how many students can time-share a central computer of given size, how effective are Socratic or adaptive systems and to what subject matter are they suited, how big is the problem of programming for CAI? By and large, the old type of comparative study which turned out to be so fruitless in conventional programmed instruction has been abandoned. With whom or what does one compare a CAI system? 'Is a computer better than a human teacher?' is hardly a meaningful question. In general, we ought to ask other questions, such as under what circumstances is a 'Socratic' dialogue a suitable teaching tool and can a computer do it? On what kinds and amounts of educational data must decisions of a certain kind be based and can a computer collect and use such data?

But overall hangs the problem of cost effectiveness. It could be argued that there is not much point in conducting exploratory research unless there is a hope that the computer will at some foreseeable time achieve equivalent or better results at lower costs. At the present time, computers seem enormously expensive in relation to conventional teaching equipment. Attempts to produce a suitable economic analysis at this stage are speculative and thus one of the most important areas for research lies in developing methods of analysing the costs and benefits of CAI in relation to present and future educational systems. This applies, of course, to all aspects of educational technology and it is unfortunate that these questions have not been asked often enough in relation to conventional programmed instruction. Whilst, superficially, the emphasis is on costs, the heart of the problem is really the analysis of educational and training systems. If we know how a system works, whether it be automated or not, we should be able to identify its strengths and weaknesses and make reasonable predictions of the benefits likely to result from modifying various components. To take an over-simplified example, a system of lecturing to large audiences might be improved by the installation of an amplifier, or a project system might be made more effective by investment in a 'resources centre'. CAI above all invites investigation from the 'systems' point of view because it is too expensive to be used as a mere aid to be taken out of the cupboard as needed.

CONCLUSION

Returning finally to the types of research which can most usefully contribute to a technology of teaching, this chapter has not tried to cover the whole spectrum or to provide a complete review,

but rather to compare some of the different strategies which
could be adopted. It has briefly, clarified what seems to be an
important source of confusion about the nature and purpose of
some of the so-called basic research and to put the view that a
technology must develop its own characteristic methods and
concepts out of the problems with which it is faced. Annett
(1967) drew attention to three areas of research which were
not receiving all the attention that they merited. These were:

(a) The basic and continuing problem of task analysis and the
'structure' of subject matter.
(b) The detailed control of learner behaviour either through
program design or other means.
(c) The use of direct observation studies as a basis for the
(human) engineering of teaching systems.

There is evidence that research is now expanding in each of
these three areas. CAI is introducing new problems, some of
which this chapter has briefly touched on. The old comparative
type of research has now virtually disappeared and at the present
time many workers are happily demonstrating some of the capabilities of CAI in investigating techniques which were not
previously possible, but overall hangs the question of economic
viability. This is now leading us into the position where we have
to ask basic questions about the structure and functioning of
educational systems, and it is these problems that future research
must tackle.

6

Writing a Program:
A Case History

JAMES HARTLEY

This chapter illustrates with one program the main processes that have been described in each of the earlier chapters. Before this, however, the background that led to the construction of the program is outlined, for this background dominated much of its writing and, in addition, it demonstrates how practicalities can intrude on theory.

BACKGROUND

During 1967 a new approach for students studying the phenomenon of 'one-trial learning' in the laboratory was being considered. In the past, a study by Rock (1957) had simply been replicated, and this, because of its weaknesses, had usually generated considerable discontent. Rock had compared the performance of a group of students learning a list of twelve paired-associates (e.g. AA 52) with that of another group in which associates that were not correctly recalled on each trial were replaced with new ones. He found (to most people's surprise) that both groups took the same median number of trials to learn the twelve associates to a criterion of one correct recall, and that the mean number of trials taken, and the mean number of errors made by the two groups were not significantly different. Rock concluded, therefore, that associations were learned on one trial, or not at all, rather than incrementally.

As noted above, this experiment was open to a number of serious criticisms which, as far as this chapter is concerned, are largely irrelevant (*see* Postman, 1963). More recent work (Warr, 1965) suggests that one of the many factors involved in one-trial learning is the difficulty of the items involved. Thus, in the search for a new laboratory task for his students, the author was trying to think of materials which could be graded in difficulty in order to test out predictions based on Warr's position. Typical laboratory material for such experimentation would be the nonsense-syllable (e.g. XAF) which could be classified in terms of varying degrees of association level or difficulty. However, students on the whole do not take kindly to learning nonsense-syllables.

What was required, then, was a set of materials rather like paired-associates in form, which could be graded in difficulty, and which would be meaningful to learn.

Through making the error of misdirecting a driver to turn left against the traffic in a one-way street, it became clear that traffic signs might provide suitable material for future experiments.

At the beginning of the winter term it was discovered that a school being visited was entering pupils for the cycling proficiency test, and that part of this test involved demonstrating knowledge of certain traffic signs. This gave the author the opportunity to measure this particular knowledge. Coloured slides (2in. x 2in.) of some seventy signs were prepared and what appeared to be two sets of signs equivalent in difficulty (thirty-three in each) were drawn up. One of these sets was presented to the pupils, who were asked to write the meaning given by each sign as it was presented. The questions of interest at that time were (a) would there be a gradient of difficulty in the material; and (b) although the comparison would have to be done later, how would such a gradient compare with that obtained from university students? (At that time the author was committing the fallacy of equating 'familiarity' with 'difficulty'.)

The results from the twenty children involved were quite startling. Of thirty-three signs, only one (roadworks) was known by all of them. Several common signs (e.g. pedestrian crossing) were known by only half the children, and some signs were dangerously misunderstood (e.g. half of the children interpreted 'cyclists only' as 'no cycling'). The results, in fact, reflected quite faithfully, only in more detail, the rather dismal findings of Mackie (1966 and 1967), whose surveys of adult knowledge of new traffic signs have indicated that many signs are not understood by more than 50 per cent of motorists. Accordingly, therefore, the author dropped his interest in experiments on one-trial learning, and set about tying to devise a program to teach new traffic signs. It is perhaps also important to note at this point that he had been reading a preliminary copy of Davies's (1969a) thesis on Mathetics. Interestingly enough, Davies had concluded his experimental studies with a one-trial learning explanation of his results. These two concepts—one-trial learning and Mathetics—influenced much of the writing of the traffic signs program.

WRITING THE PROGRAM

The process of programming can be considered as a series of procedures, as shown in *Figure 1.4* (p. 13). In brief, these are:

(a) Determining the objectives with respect to the students (or target-population') for whom the program is written.
(b) Preparing materials to test the achievement of these objectives.
(c) Analysing the subject matter, the task and the behaviours required.
(d) Determining strategies for presenting the material to be taught.
(e) Evaluating the results.

How each of these main stages was set about is described below.

Objectives
The objectives of a program should be stated in a way that is precise and measurable. For the traffic signs program this appeared fairly straightforward, and the objectives were formulated as follows: 'At the end of the program students will be able to write down (or verbalise) the information conveyed by any of the traffic signs contained in the program.' This was a simple formulation, and more precise objectives could have been drawn up (e.g. signs should be recognised immediately, and with 100 per cent accuracy).

These objectives, although simple enough to state, are interesting in that they required the student to *recognise* and not necessarily to recall the signs. Such objectives (which match what drivers do on the road, rather than what they do in the driving test) have implications for tests designed to measure their achievement.

Target population
In theory, the program should be capable of being used by anyone

who uses roads—that is, practically everyone. In addition, it could be assumed that people using the program would have a wide range of knowledge of the signs. Such assumptions have, of course, direct implications concerning optimal strategies of presentation (see below). In brief, it was decided that it would be impractical to design a program suitable for everyone, but that wide applicability should be aimed at, and that the limits of the program's suitability would be determined by testing.

Test materials

Objectives demanding recognition imply that materials must be presented for students to identify. Signs could be presented 'in context' or 'in abstract': this could be done by using slide presentations, or by test-sheets asking students to write down or to indicate verbally the meanings of signs provided. It was decided, for convenience of reproduction, to use (and to teach) the signs 'in abstract'. A selection of signs had to be used, as it would be impractical to ask students to give the meanings of all the signs available. To determine which signs to include in the test the sets of thirty-three signs referred to earlier were each reproduced on 5in. x 3in. cards and initial testing was done using these: responses were tape recorded. Following this, two shorter sets (10 signs each) were drawn up which appeared equivalent in form, and in difficulty. The scoring of these tests was done initially by allocating one mark to each sign correctly identified, but this has led to some difficulties. A more complex scoring system (weighting 'difficult' signs) has now been developed (Hartley, 1971).

The tests were developed in parallel with the ongoing evaluation of the program, the aim being to establish tests which were valid and reliable.

Task-analysis

In producing programmed materials it is customary to analyse the subject matter in order to determine its structure, its relationships, and what the student must do in order to master the material. *Table 6.1* illustrates the structure of the new traffic signs, and *Table 6.2* lists a rule sequence (i.e. a set of relationships) drawn from the former. The aim of this analysis is twofold: it serves (a) to indicate an appropriate teaching sequence, and (b) to suggest appropriate teaching strategies.

Table 6.1 Subject matter analysis (with enumerated sequence)

Material	Traffic Signs										
Topics	Signs which warn (1)			Signs which forbid (2)		Signs which command (3)		Signs which inform (5)		Waiting, Parking signs etc. (6)	
Sub-topics	Junctions	Bends	Hazards (4)	Positive	Negative	Directions	Others	Directions	Others	Waiting	Un-loading
Elements (examples)	Cross-roads	Series of bends	Falling rocks	No entry	Clear-way	Keep left	Cyclists only	One-way street	Services	Road markings	Road markings

Table 6.2 The Rule Sequence

---

1. Traffic signs convey information.
2. Some traffic signs warn of danger ahead.
3. Traffic signs which warn of danger ahead have a special shape.
4. Some traffic signs forbid certain actions.
5. Traffic signs which forbid have a special shape.
6. Some traffic signs command certain actions.
7. Traffic signs which command have a special shape and colour.
8. Some traffic signs inform.
9. Traffic signs which inform have a special shape (and colour).
10. Special signs and road markings convey rules about waiting (and other things).

Sequencing

It is customary to talk in programmed instruction of using a logical teaching sequence (without defining exactly what this means). *Table 6.2* lists one such sequence, a sequence which was not in fact checked by using the matrix technique (*see* Thomas *et al.*, 1963). Had such a matrix been drawn, it presumably would have indicated that the subject matter of the new traffic signs was composed of a set of main concepts, each one to be discriminated from the others. The implications for sequencing from such a matrix would be to either (a) teach major concepts and discriminations together; or (b) teach each concept in turn. In fact, the sequence decided upon was mainly the latter (*see* enumerated sequence, *Table 6.1*): concept blocks were taught in turn, but meshed together by interim tests and by discriminations made at the element level of actual signs. Actually, the main factor determining the sequence used was a practical one: most signs are warning signs, and it was hoped that by introducing later the more spectacular of these (e.g. falling rocks, tank crossing) student interest in the program would be maintained.

Presentation

A wide number of possibilities suggested themselves (largely as a consequence of having to produce material in four colours). It was decided, however, that whatever form the final version of the program might take (e.g. filmstrip) it would be best to produce it first of all in a text format, and to do preliminary trials with this form. Of the available 'programming styles' the linear program was chosen (i.e. all students work through the same sequence of items). It is perhaps worth commenting at this stage why this type of program was chosen as opposed to a branching one (i.e. where students take material necessary for them). It would appear initially that a branching program would be most suitable, as it would cater better for the large individual differences expected, both in ability and pre-knowledge. However, a linear program was chosen for three main reasons:

(a) (the most crucial) it is simple to operate—this is important with respect to the target population;
(b) (relatedly) material that is well known can be skipped over, or briefly reviewed by the reader;
(c) the objectives of the program are such that this is a situation where Skinner's views about errors may possibly be correct (*see* Skinner, 1961).

There seemed to be no point in presenting students with plausible, alternative answers from which to choose the correct one: if

CROSSROADS

Figure 6.1. Crossroads

students consider the sign in *Figure 6.1* to mean 'Hospital', they will be corrected when reading the caption underneath it 'Crossroads': if they know the sign means 'Crossroads', why confuse them with the choice of 'Hospital'?

This decision made, the program was then written using a number of basic principles. These, with additional comments, were as follows:

Easy items can be learned in one-trial. This idea, based on one-trial learning, meant that many of the more familiar signs could be presented once only and not referred to again (e.g. bends). Perhaps better expressed, the principle would be 'familiar items need presenting once only'.

Easy, familiar items can be presented together, thus enlarging the size of step. Thus, for example, signs on minor road junctions, direction signs, etc. were all presented together. By this means (an influence of the large 'exercise formats' of the mathetics system), the relatedness of signs to each other was demonstrated.

More difficult items need strengthening by subsequent repetition. This principle (again based on one-trial learning studies) implied that less familiar signs received more repeated testing: this principle was particularly applied with respect to discriminations (*see* the next principle). Later it was decided that 'difficult' signs could be 'strengthened' by asking students to recall them, or produce them. (The objectives demand recognition as the final behaviour: if students can recall, then it is assumed that they can recognise.) This strategy was one kept 'in reserve': if evaluation showed a certain sign to be proving difficult to learn, then the program could be revised, pupils being asked on one of the sectional tests to draw that particular sign. This strategy strengthened weaknesses without increasing the length of the program.

Discriminations are difficult and confusing: they should be taught together on one page. (This idea was borrowed from Mathetics.) Some signs are very similar to one another (*see Figure 6.2*). Such signs can be introduced together, and the student left to work out for himself differences between them. One of the signs can then be tested, the other later on in a sectional test, and so on. (This also applied to signs to be discriminated across concepts—e.g. 'cyclists only' versus 'no cycling'.)

Overt responses are not necessary on every frame. Written responses were used only when more difficult signs were being presented or tested. It was felt that much could be achieved by simply presenting information and asking the student to learn it.

Knowledge of results is not necessary for every response. This principle follows from the former. Knowledge of results should be given when it is going to be useful—for example, after the testing of difficult items.

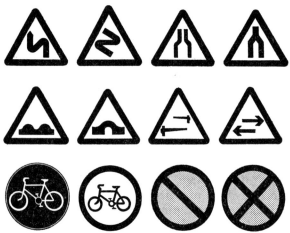

Figure 6.2. Potentially confusing traffic signs

Words should be avoided. In view of the target population of the program, this was imperative. Instructions were reduced to a minimum, and basically they were 'Study each page carefully and learn the information given: you will be tested regularly on the material'. The layout of the program was designed to regularise the procedure, and each page designed to impose a structure on the subject material and to place the material under the control of the learner (ideas again based upon Mathetics). Later, in a slide version of the program, a synchronised tape recording was added to verbalise the written parts of the text.

The program thus took the form of six main sections (*see Table 6.1*), each followed by a sectional test (of 6–8 signs) which sampled the material taught in all previous sections. The more difficult signs and the discriminations came in for more repeated testing. It was felt that such tests would not only make the student aware of his progress, but they would also serve to relate the various sections to each other. Futhermore, they would regularise the procedure: students would become aware that they must learn if they were to be able to answer tests correctly. When evaluating the program (see below) pre- and post-tests were used in addition to these sectional tests.

Using the principles described above, the program taught over one hundred signs in approximately sixty frames.

EVALUATION

The evaluation of the program was done in five stages.

1. The first hand-written draft of the program was tested in the course of its development with individuals readily available— parents, students, secretaries. The results obtained suggested various modifications, such as the splitting up of certain frames that appeared to contain too much information, and the strengthening, by repetition, of certain signs.

2. A typed version was then produced with printed signs taken from an H.M.S.O. pamphlet. This version was tried out with four sixteen-year-old Junior Firemen (who had left school with no 'O' level qualifications). Each one worked through the program and was then shown thirty-three signs and asked to give the meaning of each one. The responses were tape recorded. The results, the time taken, and the retest scores after one month are shown in *Table 6.3.* Such results were taken as encouraging, and a few minor modifications following these students' suggestions were made.

Table 6.3 Results from four Junior Firemen on initial version
of the program. (One mark given for each sign correctly identified)

Student	1	2	3	4
Time taken to study the program	45 min	50 min	55 min	55 min
Time to do test	3·11 min	4·78 min	3·17 min	3·22 min
Post-test/33	30	21	30	31
Retest (1 month later)	30	26	30	27

3. The program was next photographed and put on to 2in. x
2in. slides. A sound-track was recorded, and the program tested
with a group of university students. The pacing of the sound-track
was determined by 'guess'. Two tests were devised, of ten signs
each, which it was hoped would be matched in difficulty, and
an experiment was carried out to measure the effects of pretesting
on post-test performance. The results of this experiment (*see Table
6.4*) showed learning from the program to be so good that no
conclusions about this particular issue could be drawn. The main
points of relevance to be observed here, however, were the high
pretest scores, the success of the group manipulation, and the
favourable comments of many of the students.

Table 6.4 Results from university students using group-presented
program

		Pretest A (out of 10)	Post-test B (out of 10)	Post-test A and B (out of 20)
Group 1	median range (N = 15)	7 5–10		20 16–20
Group 2	median range (N = 16)		6 4–10	20 18–20
Group 3	median range (N = 19)			20 18–20

4. The group program was next tried out with a group of remand home boys (aged between 14 and 16, and with an IQ range of 74–116). The pacing of the program was determined by observation of the group, progressing at what seemed to be an appropriate speed. The students wrote their responses on specially designed response sheets. The program appeared to be enjoyed (novelty effect?) and was moderately successful. It appeared, though (*see Table 6.5*), that an IQ of 90 might be a cut-off point below which it would be unwise to expect good results from the program as it existed at that time. However, the results shown in *Table 6.5* were obtained when using a very heterogeneous group of students.

Table 6.5 Results from Remand Home boys

Student	Age	IQ	Pretest/10	Post-test/20
1	15:5	116	5	18
2	16:7	105	6	19
3	16:0	105	9	18
4	16:4	104	7	20
5	15:7	103	4	16
6	15:3	96	2	8
7	16:5	96	8	20
8	14:7	93	3	17
9	16:9	93	4	15
10	14:0	90	2	9
11	14:1	81	0	2
12	14:3	79	3	9
13	15:4	77	2	4
14	14:5	74	4	15
15	14:8	—	7	16
16	—	—	6	17
17	—	—	2	15
18	—	—	1	14

5. To find out more about this level of student (IQ 80–90) the group program was next tried with groups of 'fourth year leavers' in a number of secondary schools. To determine a suitable pacing rate one class was used in a pilot study, pacing being based (as above) on observation. In addition, however, a master tape of the time intervals used was recorded, and from this a synchronised tape/slide version of the program (omitting section six) was prepared. This program was then tried by Neil Rackham in schools in Sheffield, and some results from his studies are shown in *Table 6.6*.

o

Table 6.6 Results from '4th year leavers'
(Data supplied by Rackham)

		Pretest *(out of 10)*	Post-test *(out of 10)*
School 1	Mean score (N = 38)	4·3	8·1
School 2	Mean score (N = 20)	3·3	7·8

The results in *Table 6.6* concludes this account. It can be seen that the program can be used by a wide variety of students with a wide range of ability, but that certain sections of it need further modification. It is also clear that the group method of presentation is a viable one, although one might expect a textbook version to have certain other advantages. The Road Research Laboratory, Crowthorne, have now printed copies of the program for experimental purposes, and the next stage in the history of this program will be, in fact, to explore further the effectiveness of this technique of presentation.

CONCLUSIONS

Firstly, the same program seems to have been well accepted by almost all who have used it—adults, university students and schoolchildren. Admittedly, it is a short program, but experience shows it has been difficult to persuade people, particularly adults, to have a rest from using the program.

Secondly, the procedure of people looking at the textbook for the first time is most interesting. They open it at the beginning, then they turn to the back, and then they flip backwards and forwards, commenting on the signs as they appear: they seem reluctant to use it in a 'programmed' way. The textbook version thus appears to have lost much of the control over the learning situation held by the slide version.

Finally, despite general scepticism concerning the validity of one-trial learning, it does seem that, together with Mathetics, the principles derived have been of value in writing the program. The slide version has shown itself to work well with a remarkable range of students. It remains, of course, to be seen how far the principles listed above are generalisable to other subject matters.

7

A Guide for Users of Programmed Material*

PETER HODGE

CHOOSING THE PROGRAM

Whatever the reason for using programmed or self-instructional materials, your primary concern will be that they teach the subject matter effectively to your students. *It is therefore important to choose the program carefully before using it.* In the first place you may find it useful to ask the following questions:

1. Do I really need a program at all? Is this a topic which students should be able to learn about for themselves if suitably well-prepared teaching materials were available? Or could this program be used as an additional aid to my normal course or with those students who have difficulty with particular parts of the course? In other words, is the program to be used for:

(a) Basic information?
(b) Remedial instruction?
(c) Enrichment, or as an additional topic to the main course?

2. In choosing a program particular attention should be given to the following points:

(a) Subject matter *content*: is it factually correct?

* Reproduced, with permission, from CAVANAGH, P. and JONES, C. (1969) *Yearbook of Educational and Instructional Technology*, 1969–70, Association for Programmed Learning and Educational Technology, London.

O *

(b) Teaching *approach* : is it in line with modern trends?
(c) *Syllabus relevance* : is it an essential part of the syllabus?
(d) Student *target population* : for whom is it suitable?
(e) Length of *time* the program takes to teach the material.
(f) Does the *test* for the program actually cover what the program sets out to teach? Is this test of a standard comparable to one that you would normally give to your students?
(g) What *results* were obtained when the program was tried out with students prior to or since publication?
(h) What *additional materials* does the program require? For example, will the student need an atlas, log-tables, or a micrometer, etc?

A program should give the following essential information at the front (or in an accompanying Teacher's Manual) if it is to be any good :

(a) A statement of teaching *objectives* which tells you what the student will be able to *do* at the end of the program.
(b) A *test* designed to cover these objectives.
(c) A statement of the *target population* for whom the program is intended (e.g. age range, I.Q.).
(d) A set of *results* obtained in an evaluation study of the program with students.
(e) An indication of the *time* takes the average student to work through the program.

If any of these items are omitted, you should either contact the publishers direct, or get in touch with a local adviser on programmed learning.

3. CAUTION : UNLESS YOU ARE FAMILIAR WITH PROGRAMMED LEARNING TECHNIQUES, DO NOT ATTEMPT TO CRITICISE THE PROGRAM FOR PROGRAMMING STYLE OR METHOD! By all means reject a program if it does not answer the criteria listed above, but do not confuse this with the actual method of teaching.

Some common problems met in choosing a program

1. It does not cover one or two points which you feel it should teach. Possible solution :
Use the program and either write additional material to cover the points omitted, or give it orally.

2. There is no test of what the program teaches.

Possible solution :

Write to the publisher and demand to see a copy of the test. If this is not practicable, you might consider drawing up a test of your own based on what the program teaches. To do this, list the teaching points covered and test only these. Do not expect a program to produce a rabbit out of a hat!

3. The program requires written answers and you do not wish to buy a new set of programs each year.

Possible solution :

either (a) get your students to write their answers in normal exercise books,

    or (b) consider preparing a duplicated answer sheet, which might also serve as a summary for revision and be helpful for evaluation purposes.

4. What happens at the end of the program if students want to revise?

Solution :

either (a) as in 3(b),

    or (b) prepare duplicated sheets of notes based on the content of the program simply for revision purposes. You can often get a good idea of this from the revision tests scattered throughout some programs, or from the over-all test of the program objectives.

5. Does the use of a program exclude additional work by the instructor/teacher?

Answer :

Emphatically no! The purpose of the program is usually for students to be able to work through it on their own. But this does not exclude the teacher from afterwards taking students further or developing certain aspects of the work taught. This may involve the use of practical materials, laboratory work, reference to other books, and group discussion. While the student is working through the program the teacher should not need to intervene except where there is some real difficulty (and proper evaluation of a program is designed to reduce such difficulties to a minimum). You will find yourself with more time to devote to those individuals who most require your help. You may also feel like using additional films or visual materials and these can often be linked to the use of a program very effectively.

6. Different students will work at different speeds. What happens when students finish at different times?

Answer :

 This is an organisational problem and one which will be dealt with under the heading of program use. It should not be allowed to interfere with your choice of program as such. After all, you . have exactly the same problem with conventional teaching, though it may be accentuated by the use of self-instructional materials.

USING THE PROGRAM

Before using the program

 1. Check that all the materials to be used are prepared in sufficient numbers to allow each student to work unhindered. These will include :

(a) Test(s).
(b) Answer sheets or workbooks.
(c) Additional materials (e.g. maps, diagrams, apparatus).

 2. *Before* you hand out the progam to students, it is essential to give them the *test* of the material that is to be taught.
The purpose of this is twofold :

(a) To see if the student needs the program at all.
(b) To assess later how much the student has actually learned.
  If a student scores more than 40% on the test before reading the program, it is clear that he needs only to work through certain parts. The teacher is the best judge of those parts on which he is weak. A useful guide, however, can be obtained in many cases by getting the student to work through the revision or self-tests that appear at the end of each section or chapter of many programs. The student should work through these tests until he gets two or more answers wrong. He should then go back to the *previous* section and continue working through to the end.

 3. ALWAYS MAKE SURE THAT YOUR STUDENTS HAVE THE NECESSARY PRE-KNOWLEDGE FOR THEM TO BE ABLE TO WORK THROUGH THE PROGRAM. A good program will usually state what the student must know or be able to do before reading the program (e.g. he should be able to calculate the

answer to simple problems, using log tables). Some programs have a test to check that a student is equipped with the necessary knowledge before he starts. If the program you are using does not have such a test, it may be wise to draw up your own test of those particular points which your experience has shown to be necessary for a student to be able to tackle this topic.

How to use the program

This will depend on whether it is to be used for :

(a) Basic instruction.
(b) Remedial instruction.
(c) Additional work of 'enrichment'.

Each of these teaching situations will require a different kind of classroom organisation. As a guide, below are some suggestions as to how classes might be organised for each type of situation.

Programs for basic instruction

1. Decide how many periods the students should take to complete the program. This will vary according to the length of the program and the kind of student with whom it will be used.

2. Give each student a target to aim at—for example, finish one section or chapter by the end of two sessions, or by the end of the week if the section is a long one. This target should take into account the hares as well as the tortoises !

3. Make sure that students know what to do if they finish early. As soon as each student finishes he should do the test of the material taught (*see* section entitled—After the Program). He might then do one of the following things :

(a) Revise notes made during the program.
(b) Follow up the lesson in another book.
(c) Do a practical exercise or a laboratory experiment.

4. NEVER USE A PROGRAM IN ISOLATION. It should be used as an integrated part of your course and cannot be expected to produce satisfactory results if simply thrown at the student.

5. Record data for evaluating the effectiveness of a program. If the program is being used for the first time, it is useful to make a record of certain features, apart from the scores on tests before and after. These will be useful if you are using the program again, and may include :

(a) The average *times* taken by students to complete each section, as well as the total time taken to complete the program.

(b) Particular pages or frames which students found *difficult* and which need to be modified slightly.
(c) Any *additional materials* which were used during the program and any supplementary exercises done afterwards.

6. If you are using *equipment*, such as a teaching machine or a slide projector, it is essential to check that :

(a) There is a *power point* available in the room.
(b) The equipment is in *working order.*
(c) Students *know how to use it.*
(d) Arrangements are made for *quick repair* if anything goes wrong, so that time is not lost. (Always check with the supplier about services for repair or replacement.)

Programs for remedial instruction
The same practical considerations as those above should be borne in mind. As regards the overall organisation, there are two ways in which the program may be used :

(a) Where a student is finding a particular part of his normal course difficult, the teacher may direct him to a program which will ensure that he receives the additional help he requires. This means having the relevant program(s) handy and in sufficient numbers to ensure that any student who needs one can find it. The best place for this may be at the back of the class.
(b) Where a number of students are having difficulty with class work, and the teacher almost needs to treat them as a separate class. In such cases it may be advisable to group these students at the back of the classroom or direct them to a study room (e.g. the library), if supervision is available, where they can work through the program without disrupting the rest of the class and ask questions if they have any difficulties.

Programs for additional work or 'enrichment'
It may be useful to have copies of programs on specialist topics which students can work through if they finish a class exercise and wish to carry their study further. These may be programs which are being used with another class at a higher level, or individual programs on a particular point which has been referred to in class (e.g. programs on mitosis, meiosis and Mendelian theory in biology, which may be used with advanced classes or as 'enrichment' material for brighter students lower down the school). These might

be left at the back of the classroom or be readily available in the library.

After using the program

1. As each student finishes the program, he should be given the *test* he was given before starting, or one very similar. Try to give students the test immediately they finish, if possible, before going on to do further work.
2. Mark these test answers using the key at the back of the program or in the accompanying Teacher's Manual.
3. Enter the pre- and post-program test scores for each student on a mark sheet or in your record book.
4. Make a note of the time each student took to complete the program and of any difficulties he encountered in the program. In the latter case, write down the number of the page(s) he found difficult.
5. Check that any wrong answers to the test are put right.
6. Make sure that students follow up the work done in the program with further revision or practical work.

Some typical problems of using programs

1. Students finish early and then have nothing to do.
Cause : You have not planned the organisational aspects carefully. Look at page 203.
2. Students find the program too easy and become bored or disruptive.
Possible causes :

    (a) You did not choose the program carefully enough to see if it was suitable for this level of student.
    (b) You did not give them a test beforehand to see if they needed the program.
    (c) There is too much verbal material involved and you need to provide additional exercises during the program or use visual material.
    (d) It is just a bad program ! This happens.

3. You have difficulty with equipment.
Causes :

    (a) Bad planning, e.g. not enough power points, no arrangements for repairs, no instruction in how to use it, no provision of space for students to use the equipment in, so as not to disrupt the class.

(b) Not sufficient numbers of machines to allow for individual use the whole time. This again requires planning to enable students to book a time when they can each use the equipment. A simple sheet for booking a time is probably the best idea, provided it is flexible enough to allow the student having real difficulties to use it when he needs it most.

4. Students who fail to complete a section of the program in normal classroom hours.
Solution :

either (a) Insist that they complete it in their own time or in a study period.
  or (b) Cut down the amount of work you expect each student to do at a time.

There is now good evidence to show that some external 'pacing' by the teacher is often more effective than letting students finish in their own time.

5. Students score well on the test immediately after doing the program but do rather poorly on an end-of-term test.
Possible causes :

(a) The two tests are not comparable.
(b) The program was not followed up by further work and revision.

This chapter cannot cover all the contingencies that may arise with the use of programs, although it covers some of the main problems experienced by teachers and other users of programs. More information about programs at present available is provided in the Appendix.

Appendix

RESOURCES FOR PROGRAMMED INSTRUCTION

Catalogues of Programs

CAVANAGH, P. and JONES, C. W. (1969) *Yearbook of Educational and Instructional Technology*, 1969–70, Association for Programmed Learning and Educational Technology, London

(Supplements to this bibliography are published in *Visual Education* and *Programmed Learning and Educational Technology*. The bibliography also lists the addresses of publishers, teaching machine companies and researchers in the field.)

CALDER, J. R. and PAXTON, W. F. (1968) *Programmed Learning: Catalogue of Programmed Text and Films*, Moray House College of Education, Edinburgh

(Copies of programs may be borrowed for inspection.)

Information Centres

National Council for Educational Technology,
160 Great Portland Street,
London, W1N 5TB

Programmed Instruction Centre for Industry,
Department of Psychology,
The University,
Sheffield

The Association for Programmed Learning and Educational Technology,
33 Queen Anne Street,
London, W1M 0AL

Abstracts

The Department of Educational Studies, Open University, Walton Hall, Walton, Bletchley, Bucks. provides a most useful abstracting service covering all, but particularly industrial, aspects of educational technology. (Until December 31st 1971 this service was provided by the Department of Employment and Productivity Training Division.)

Useful textbooks

(i) *General*

DAVIES, I. K. and HARTLEY, J. (Eds.) (1972) *Contributions to an Educational Technology*, Butterworths, London

KAY, H., DODD, B. T., and SIME, M. E. (1968) *Teaching Machines and Programmed Instruction*, Penguin, Harmondsworth

LANGE, P. C. (Ed.) (1967) *Programed Instruction*, N.S.S.E. Univ. Chicago Press

(ii) *Research Reviews*

GLASER, R. (Ed.) (1965) *Teaching Machines and Programmed Learning*, Vol. II, *Data and Directions*, N.E.A., Washington

UNWIN, D. and LEEDHAM, J. (Eds.) (1967) *Aspects of Educational Technology*, Methuen, London

TOBIN, M. J. (Ed.) (1968) *Problems and Methods in Programmed Learning*, Parts I–V, National Centre for Programmed Learning, University of Birmingham

DUNN, W. R. and HOLROYD, C. (Eds.) (1969) *Aspects of Educational Technology*, Vol. II, Methuen, London

MANN, A. P. and BRUNSTROM, C. K. (Eds.) (1969) *Aspects of Educational Technology* Vol. III, Pitman, London

BAJPAI, A. and LEEDHAM, J. (Eds.) (1970) *Aspects of Educational Technology*, Vol. IV, Pitman, London

(Volume V of *Aspects of Educational Technology* is in press. These volumes present papers given at the Annual Conference of the Association for Programmed Learning and Educational Technology.)

Journals

Programmed Learning and Educational Technology (Quarterly). Published by Sweet and Maxwell Ltd., 11 New Fetter Lane, London, E.C.4

Journal of Educational Technology (3 issues per year). Produced and distributed on behalf of Books for Schools Ltd. by Councils and Education Press Ltd., 10 Queen Anne Street, London, W1M 9LD

Journal of the National Society of Programmed Instruction (Monthly). Published by the National Society for Programmed Instruction, Trinity University, 715 Stadium Drive, San Antonio, Texas, 78212

Educational Technology (Monthly). Published by Educational Technology Publications Inc., 140 Sylvan Avenue, Englewood Cliffs, New Jersey, 07632

Audio-visual Communication Review (Quarterly). Published by the Department of Audio-visual Instruction, 1201, Sixteenth Street, N.W., Washington D.C. 20036

Visual Education (Monthly). Published by the National Committee for Audio-visual Aids in Education, 33 Queen Anne Street, London

Industrial Training International (Monthly). Published by Pergamon Press Ltd., Oxford

Education and Training (Monthly). Published by Turnstile Press Ltd., Great Turnstile, London WC1V 7HJ

Industrial and Commercial Training (Monthly). Published by John Wellens Ltd., Guilsborough, Northampton NN6 8PY.

Bibliography

ADDISON, R. M. and HOMME, L. E. (1966) 'The reinforcing event (RE) menu', *J. Natn. Soc. Programmed Instruc.*, **5** No. 1, 8–9

AMERICAN EDUCATIONAL RESEARCH ASSOCIATION (1952) 'Report of the committee on the criteria of teacher effectiveness,' *Rev. Ed. Res.*, **22** 238–262

ANASTASI, A. (1968) *Psychological Testing*, 3rd edn, Macmillan, New York

ANDERSON, J. A. (1969) 'Single-channel and multi-channel messages: a comparison of connotative meanings', *Audio-vis. Commun. Rev.*, **17** No. 4, 428–434

ANGELL, D. and LUMSDAINE, A. A. (1962) 'Retention of material presented by auto-instructional programs which vanish and which do not vanish verbal cues', Abstracted in Schramm, W. (1964) *The Research on Programmed Instruction*, U.S. Dept. Health, Education and Welfare, Washington

ANGELL, D., SHEARER, J. W. and BERLINER, D. C. (1964) 'A study of training performance evaluation techniques,' Tech. Rep. NAVTRADEVCEN 1449–1. U.S. Naval Training Device Center, New York

ANNETT, J. (1964) 'A low-cost, cheat-proof teaching system', *Programmed Learning*, **1** No. 3, 155–158

ANNETT, J. (1967) 'Research strategies for a technology of teaching,' Unwin, D. and Leedham, J. (Eds.) *Aspects of Educational Technology*, Methuen, London

ANNETT, J. (1968) 'Simulators and teaching machines,' Rolfe, J. M. (Ed.) *Vehicle Simulation and Training Research*, I.A.M. Report No. 442, R.A.F. Institute of Aviation Medicine, Farnborough, Hants

ANNETT, J. (1969) 'Computer-assisted instruction,' *S.S.R.C. Newsletter*, No. 6, 12–14 (June)

ANNETT, J. and DUNCAN, K. D. (1967) 'Task analysis and training design,' *Occup. Psychol.*, **41** 211–221

ANNETT, J. and DUNCAN, K. D. (1968) 'Task analysis: a critique', Barnes, J. and Robinson, N. (Eds.) *New Media and Methods in Industrial Training*, British Broadcasting Corporation, London

ANTIOCH COLLEGE (1960) *Experiment in French Language Instruction: 2nd Report*, Antioch Press, Yellow Springs, Ohio

APTER, M. J. (1968) 'The development of audio-visual instruction', *Programmed Learn. (& Educ Technol.)*, **4** No. 4, 302–315

AUSTWICK, K. (1963) 'Teaching machines and programmed learning', Unpublished Ph.D. thesis, University of Sheffield

AUSTWICK, K. (1965) 'The revision of constructed-response programs', *Programmed Learning*, **3** No. 1, 34–46

AUSUBEL, D. P. (1961) 'Learning by discovery: rationale and mystique', *Bulletin of the National Association for Secondary School Principals*, **45** 18–58

AUSUBEL, D. P. (1963) *The Psychology of Meaningful Verbal Learning*, Grune and Stratton, New York

AUSUBEL, D. P. (1967) 'A cognitive-structure theory of school learning', Siegel, L. (Ed.) *Instruction: Some Contemporary Viewpoints*, Chandler, San Francisco

BAKER, J. D. (1969) 'The uncertain student and the understanding computer', De Brisson, A. (Ed.) *Programmed Learning Research: Major Trends*, Dunod, Paris

BALDWIN, E. D. (1964) 'The effectiveness of different forms of supplementation as adjuncts to programmed learning', *Dissertation Abstracts*, **25** No. 2, 994–995

BANKS, B. (1969) 'An experimental autoinstructional course in mathematics', Davies, I. K. and Hartley, J. (Eds.) (1972) *Contributions to an Educational Technology*, Butterworths, London

BARLOW, J. A. (1967) 'Note: student cheating in studying programed material', *Psychol. Rec.*, **17** 515–516

BARNES, R. M. (1957) *Work Sampling*, 2nd edn, John Wiley, New York

BARR, A. S. *et al.* (1961) 'Wisconsin studies of the measurement and prediction of teacher effectiveness: a summary of investigations', *J. Exp. Educ.*, **30** 1–155

BARRY, W. J. (1967) 'Programmed instruction in B.E.A.', *Progr. Instr. Ind.*, Pergamon, London

BARTZ, W. H. and DARBY, C. L. (1965) 'A study of supervised and non-supervised programed instruction in the university setting', *J. Ed. Res.*, **58** 208–211

BASKIN, S. (1961) 'Quest for quality: some models and means', *New Dimensions in Education*, No. 7, U.S. Dept. Health, Education and Welfare, Washington

BECKER, J. L. (1963) *A Programmed Guide To Writing Autoinstructional Programmes*, R.C.A., Camden, N.J

BELBIN, E. (1965) 'Problems of learning for the over-40s', *Geront. clin.*, **7** 61–68

BELBIN, E. and BELBIN, R. M. (1969) 'Retraining and the older worker', Pym, D. (Ed.) *Industrial Society*, Penguin, Harmondsworth

BELL, N. T., FELDHUSEN, J. F. and STARKS, D. D. (1965) *Adjunct Programs And Instructional Quizzes To Accompany Course In Educational Psychology*, Purdue University, Lafayette

BENSEN, J. (1968) 'Utilizing adjunct programs for flexible and improved instruction', *J. Industrial Teacher Education* **5** No. 4, 27–32

BERTRAND, C. A. (1966) 'An experimental development of programmed instructional material for the vocational education department of the Texas Department of Corrections', *Dissertation Abstracts*, **26** 7139

BIENVENISTE, G. (1967) 'The new educational technologies and the developing countries', Bereday, G. and Lauwerys, J. A. (Eds.) *The World Yearbook of Education: Educational Planning*, Evans, London

BIRAN, L. A. and PICKERING, E. (1968) 'Unscrambling a herringbone: an experimental evaluation of branching programming', *Research Reports on Programmed Learning*, No. 25, School of Education, Birmingham University

BITTERMAN, M. E. (1960) 'Toward a comparative psychology of learning', *Am. Psychol.*, **15** No. 11, 704–712.

BJERSTEDT, A. (1964) 'Mapping the pheno-structure of didactic sequences', *Didakometry*, No. 1, School of Education, Malmo, Sweden

BJERSTEDT, A. (1965) 'Mapping the effect-structure of self-instructional materials', *Programmed Learning*, **2** No. 2, 99–109

BLACK, H. B. (1962) 'Improving the programming of complex pictorial materials:

discrimination learning as affected by prior exposure to and relevance of the figural discriminandi', University of Indiana School of Education Memorandum, Bloomington

BLAKE, C. S. (1966) 'A procedure for the initial evaluation and analysis of linear programs', *Programmed Learning*, **3** No. 2, 97–101

BLOOM, B. S. (Ed.) (1956) *Taxonomy of Educational Objectives*, Longmans, New York

BLOUNT *et al.* (1967) Reported by Evans, D., Ripple, R. E. and Treffinger, D. (1969) 'Programmed instruction and productive thinking: a preliminary report of a cross-national comparison', Dunn, W. R. and Holroyd, C. (Eds.) *Aspects of Educational Technology* **2** Methuen, London

BLUNDEN, B. W. (1968) 'From craftsman to technician—a P.I.R.A. experiment', *Progr. Instr. Ind.*, **2** No. 3, Pergamon, London

BOWDEN, B. V. (1968) 'Education', *Social Science Research Council Newsletter* No. 2, 11–12 (February)

BROOKS, L. O. (1967) 'Note on revising instructional programs', *Psychol. Rep.*, **20** 117–118

BROWN, G. H. *et al.* (1959) 'Development and evaluation of an improved field radio repair course', Technical Report No. 58, Human Resources Research Office, Alexandria, Virginia

BROWN, G. H. and VINEBERG, R. (1960) 'A follow-up study of experimentally and conventionally trained field radio repairmen', Technical Report No. 65, Human Resources Research Office, Alexandria, Virginia

BRUNER, J. S. (1966) *Toward a Theory of Instruction*, Harvard University Press, Cambridge, Mass

BUTLER, F. and CAVANAGH, P. (1969) 'The role of the teacher in theory and practice in classroom programmed instruction', Dunn, W. R. and Holroyd, C. (Eds.) *Aspects of Educational Technology*, **2** Methuen, London

CAMPBELL, W. J. (1968) 'Studies of teaching', *New Zealand J. Educ. Studies*, **3** No. 2, 97–124

CARROLL, J. B. (1963) 'Research on teaching foreign languages', Gage, N. L. (Ed.) *Handbook of Research on Teaching*, Rand McNally, Chicago

CAVANAGH, P. (1967) 'Research report', *New Education*, **3** No. 10, 18–21 and p. 38

CAVANAGH, P. and JONES, C. W. (1968) 'An evaluation of the contribution of a program of self-instruction to management training', *Programmed Learn. (& Educ, Technol.)*, **5** No. 4, 294–300.

CHAPANIS, A. (1959) *Research Techniques in Human Engineering*, Johns Hopkins Press, Baltimore

CHERIS, B. (1964) 'On comparing programming and other teaching methods', *J. Medical Educ.*, **39** 404–410

CHITTICK, R. A., ELDRED, D. M. and BROOKS, G. M. (1966) 'The use of programmed instruction with disturbed students', USPHS Grant No. MH-01076, *Final Progress Report, National Institute for Mental Health*

COGSWELL, J. F., BRATTEN, J. E., EGBERT, R. E., ESTAVAN, D. P., MARSH, D. G. and YETT, F. A. (1966) 'Final Report: Analysis of Instructional Systems: Report of a project New Solutions to Implementing Instructional Media through Analysis and Simulation of School Organisation', *Technical Memorandum* TM–1493/201/80, System Development Corporation

COHEN, J. (1960) *'Chance, Skill and Luck'*, Penguin, Harmondsworth

COOK, J. O. (1963) 'Superstition in the Skinnerian', *Am. Psychol.*, **18** 516–518

COTTERMAN, T. E. (1959) 'Task classification: an approach to partially ordering information on human learning', WADC TN 58–374, Wright Air Development Center, Dayton, Ohio

COVINGTON, M. V. and CRUTCHFIELD, R. S. (1965) Programmed learning and creativity, Davies, I. K. and Hartley, J. (Eds.) (1972) *Contributions to an Educational Technology*, Butterworths, London

COX, J. A. and BOREN, L. M. (1965) 'A study of backward chaining', *J. educ. Psychol.*, **56** 270–274

COX, R. C. (1965) 'Item selection techniques and evaluation of instructional objectives', *J. Educ. Measurement*, **2** 181–187

CRONBACH, L. J. (1960) *Essentials of Psychological Testing*, 2nd edn, Harper and Row, New York

CROWDER, N. A. (1960) 'Automatic tutoring by intrinsic programming', Lumsdaine, A. A. and Glaser, R. (Eds.) *Teaching Machines and Programmed Learning*, N.E.A., Washington

DALE, H. C. A. (1958) 'Fault finding in electronic equipment', *Ergonomics*, No. 1, 356

DAVIES, I. K. (1965a) 'A design for programmed learning', *Programmed Learning*, **2** No. 2, 71–73

DAVIES, I. K. (1965b) 'The analytical and synthetic stages of program writing', *Programmed Learning*, **2** No. 2, 76–87

DAVIES, I. K. (1967a) 'Mathetics: a functional approach', Unwin, D. and Leedham, J. (Eds.) *Aspects of Educational Technology*, Methuen, London

DAVIES, I. K. (1967b) 'Frame writing: an algorithm for decision making', *J. Nat. Soc. Programmed Instruc.*, **6** No. 6, 15–18

DAVIES, I. K. (1969a) 'Mathetics: an experimental study of the relationship between ability and practice in the acquisition of basic concepts in science', Unpublished Ph.D. thesis, University of Nottingham

DAVIES, I. K. (1969b) *Structure And Strategy: A Model For Instructional Decision-making*, School of Education Paper, University of Indiana, Bloomington, Indiana

DAVIES, I. K. (1972) 'Some aspects of measurement in educational technology', Davies, I. K. and Hartley, J. (Eds.) *Contributions to an Educational Technology*, Butterworths, London

DAVIES, I. K. and PACKER, D. C. L. (1970) 'Decision tables and the communication of complex rules and instructions', *Anticipatory Training for New and Re-organised Tasks*, Proceedings of the Ergonomics Research Society One-Day Conference, Ergonomics Research Society, London

DAVIS, L. E. (1957) 'Job design and productivity: a new approach', *Personnel*, **33** 418–430

DAVIS, L. E. (1966) 'The design of jobs', Document T.736, Tavistock Institute of Human Relations, London

DENO, S. L. and JENKINS, J. R. (1969) 'On the "behaviourality" of behavioural objectives', *Psychology in the Schools*, **6** 18–24

DEPARTMENT OF EDUCATION AND SCIENCE (1968) 'Secondary School Design: Modern Languages', *Building Bulletin*, No. 43, H.M.S.O., London

DICK, W. (1963) 'Retention as a function of paired and individual use of programed instruction', *J. Programed Instruction*, Vol. II No. 3, 17–23

DODD, B. T. (1967a) 'A diagnostic branching system for remedial training in the manipulation of vulgar fractions', *Programmed Learn. (& Educ. Technol.)*, **4** No. 1, 28–37

DODD, B. T. (1967b) *Programmed Instruction for Industrial Training*, Heinemann, London

DOLEJSI, I. (1969) 'On the problems of "purposeful wrong manipulation" of programmed texts', Dunn, W. R. and Holroyd, C. (Eds.) *Aspects of Educational Technology*, Vol. II, Methuen, London

DUBOIS, P. H. (1965) 'The design of correlational studies in training', Glaser, R. (Ed.) *Training Research and Education*, Wiley, New York

DUKE, J. F. (1968) 'Computer-based learning', *New Education*, **4** No. 4, 23–24

DUNCAN, C. and HARTLEY, J. (1969) 'The effect of mode of presentation and recall upon a simple learning task', *Programmed Learn.* (& *Educ. Technol.*), **6** No. 3, 154–158

DUNCAN, K. D. (1964) 'Experiments with an inexpensive device for programmed instruction in the multiple choice branching style', *Programmed Learning* **1** No. 3, 145–155

DUNCAN, K. D. (1969) 'Task analysis evaluated', De Brisson, A. (Ed.) *Programmed Learning Research: Major Trends*, Dunod, Paris

DUNCAN, K. D. (1971) 'Evaluation of training design for a complex industrial task', Annett, J. and Duncan, K. (Eds.) *The Analysis of Industrial Skill*, (In press).

DUNCAN, K. D. and GILBERT, T. (1967) 'Effects of omitting branches and questions from a scrambled text', *Br. J. educ. Psychol.* **37** No. 3, 314–319

DUNN, W. R. and HOLROYD, C. (Eds.) (1969) *Aspects of Educational Technology*, Vol. II, Methuen, London

DWYER, F. M. (1967) 'Adapting visual illustrations for effective learning', *Harv. Educ. Rev.*, **37** 250–263

DWYER, F. M. (1968) 'The effect of varying the amount of realistic detail in visual illustrations designed to complement programmed instruction', *Percept. Mot. Skills*, **27** 351–354

DWYER, F. M. (1969) 'An analysis of the instructional effectiveness of visual illustrations presented via television', *J. Psychol.*, **72** 61–64

EDWARDS, W., LINDMAN, H. and PHILLIPS, L. D. (1965) 'Emerging technologies for making decisions', Newcomb, T. (Ed.) *New Directions in Psychology*, Vol. II, Holt, Rinehart and Winston, New York

ELLAMS, J. J. P. (1969) 'The development of a student attitude questionnaire for use in programmed learning investigations', Dunn, W. R. and Holroyd, C. (Eds.) *Aspects of Educational Technology*, Vol. II, Methuen, London

ERAUT, M. R., (1969) 'The design of learning systems with variable input', Dunn, W. R. and Holroyd, C. (Eds.) *Aspects of Educational Technology*, Vol II, Methuen, London

ESBENSEN, T. (1968) *Working with Individualized Instruction: The Duluth Experience*, Fearon Press, Palo Alto

EVANS, J. L., GLASER, R. and HOMME, L. E. (1962) 'An investigation of teaching machine variables using learning programmes in symbolic logic', *J. Educ. Res.*, **55** 433–452

EVANS, J. L., HOMME, L. E. and GLASER, R. (1962) 'The ruleg system for the construction of programmed verbal learning sequences', *J. Educ. Res.*, **55** 513–518

FERSTER, M. B. (1965) *Programmed College Composition*, Appleton-Century-Crofts, New York

FEUERZEIG, W., MUNTER, P., SWETS, J. A. and BREEN, M. (1964) 'Computer-assisted teaching in medical diagnosis', *J. med. Educ.*, **39** 746–754

FITTS, P. M. (1964) 'Perceptual motor skills learning', Melton, A. W. (Ed.) *Categories of Human Learning*, Academic Press, New York

FLANAGAN, J. C. (1954) 'The critical incident technique', *Psychol. Bull.*, **51** 327–358

FOLLEY, J. D. (1964a) 'Development of an improved method of task analysis and beginnings of a theory of training', NAVTRADEVCEN 1218-1, U.S. Naval Training Device Center, New York

FOLLEY, J. D. (1964b) 'Guidelines for task analysis', NAVTRADEVCEN 1218-22, U.S. Naval Training Device Center, New York

FRASE, L. T. (1968) 'Questions as aids to reading: some research and theory', *J. Am. Educ. Res.*, **5** No. 3, 319–332

FRASE, L. T. (1969) 'Cybernetic control of memory while reading connected discourse', *J. educ. Psychol.*, **60** No. 1, 49–55

FREEDMAN, M. (1968) 'The application of programmed learning to blind children', (Personal Communication)

FREY, S. H., SHIMABUKURO, S. and WOODRUFF, A. B. (1967) 'Attitude change in programed instruction related to achievement and performance', *Audio-vis. Commun. Rev.*, **15** No. 2, 199–205.

FRY, E. B. (1960) 'A study of teaching machine response modes', Lumsdaine, A. A. and Glaser, R. (Eds.) (1960) *Teaching Machines and Programmed Learning*, N.E.A., Washington

FRY, E. B. (1963) *Teaching Machines and Programmed Instruction*, McGraw Hill, New York

GAGNÉ, R. M. (1962a) 'The acquisition of knowledge', *Psychol. Rev.*, **69** 355–365

GAGNÉ, R. M. (1962b) 'Simulators', Glaser, R. (Ed.) *Training Research and Education*, University of Pittsburgh Press, Pittsburgh

GAGNÉ, R. M. (1963) 'Learning and proficiency in mathematics', *Maths. Teacher*, **56** 620–626

GAGNÉ, R. M. (1965a) 'The analysis of instructional objectives for the design of instruction', Glaser, R. (Ed.) *Teaching Machines and Programmed Learning*, Vol. II, N.E.A., Washington

GAGNÉ, R. M. (1965b) *The Conditions of Learning*, Holt, Rinehart and Winston, New York

GAGNÉ, R. M. (1968) 'Contributions of learning to human development', *Psychol. Rev.*, **75** 177–191

GAGNÉ, R. M. (1969) 'Learning categories and instructional strategies', De Brisson, A. (Ed.) *Programmed Learning Research: Major Trends*, Dunod, Paris

GAGNÉ, R. M. and BOLLES, R. C. (1959) 'A review of factors in learning efficiency', Galanter, E. (Ed.) *Automatic Teaching: The State of the Art*, Wiley, New York

GAGNÉ, R. M. and DICK, R. W. (1962) 'Measures in a self-instructional programme', *Psychol. Rep.*, **10** 131–146

GEDYE, J. L. (1967) 'A teaching machine programme for use as a test of learning ability', Unwin, D. and Leedham, J. (Eds.) *Aspects of Educational Technology*, Methuen, London

GILBERT, J. E. (1966) 'Comparative programmed instruction research', *J. Natn. Soc. Programmed Instruc.*, **5** No. 6, 7–10

GILBERT, T. F. (1960) 'On the relevance of laboratory investigation of learning to self-instructional programming', Lumsdaine, A. A. and Glaser, R. (Eds.) *Teaching Machines and Programmed Learning*, N.E.A., Washington

GILBERT, T. F. (1962) 'Mathetics: the technology of education', *J. Math.*, **1** 7–73 and **2** 7–56

GILBERT, T. F. (1967) 'Praxeonomy: a systematic approach to identifying training needs', Davies, I. K. and Hartley, J. (Eds.) (1972) *Contributions to an Educational Technology*, Butterworths, London

GLASER, R. (1962) 'Some research problems in automated instruction', Coulson, J. (Ed.) *Programmed Learning and Computer-Based Instruction*, Wiley, New York

GOLDBECK, R. A. and CAMPBELL, V. N. (1962) 'The effects of response mode and difficulty level on programmed learning', *J. educ. Psychol.*, **53** No. 3, 110–118

GOLDBECK, R. A. et al. (1962) 'Integrating programmed instruction with conventional classroom teaching', *Audio-vis. Commun. Rev.*, **12**

GOLDSTEIN, L. S. and GOTKIN, L. G. (1962) 'A review of research: teaching machines vs. programmed textbooks as presentation modes', *J. Progr. Instr.*, **1** 29–36

GREAT BRITAIN (1963) *Higher Education*, Report of the Committee on Higher Education, H.M.S.O., London

GREEN, E. J. (1967) 'The process of instructional programing', Lange, P. C. (Ed.) *Programed Instruction*, National Society for the Study of Education, Chicago

GREENSPOON, J. (1955) 'The reinforcing effect of two spoken sounds on the frequency of two responses', *Am. J. Psychol.*, **68** 409–416

GREENWAY, A. (1965) 'A systematic procedure for the internal evaluation of branching instructional programmes', SP(N) Report 2165, Division of Senior Psychologist (Naval), Naval Manpower Dept., Ministry of Defence, London

GRIFFITHS, H. and EDWARDS, G. (1967) 'An attempt to use an overhead projector as a means of developing and evaluating intrinsic programming', Tobin, M. J. (Ed.) *Problems and Methods in Programmed Instruction, Part 2*, National Centre for Programmed Learning, University of Birmingham

GRISWOLD, E. (1968) 'Programmed instruction production and cost', *J. Natn. Soc. Programmed Instruc.*, **7** No. 7, 16–17

GRONLUND, N. E. (1965) *Measurement and Evaluation in Teaching*, Macmillan, New York

GROPPER, G. L. (1967) 'Does programmed television need active responding?', *Audio-vis. Commun. Rev.*, **15** No. 1, 5–22

GROPPER, G. L. *et al.* (1961). *An Evaluation of Television Procedures Designed to Stimulate Extra-curricular Science Activities*, American Institutes for Research, Pittsburgh

GRUBB, R. E. (1968) 'Learner-controlled statistics', *Programmed Learn.* (& *Educ. Technol.*), **5** No. 1, 38–42

GUILFORD, J. P. (1956) *Fundamental Statistics in Psychology and Education*, McGraw Hill, New York

GUTHRIE, E. R. (1952) *The Psychology of Learning*, Harper and Row, New York

HALL, C. and FLETCHER, R. N. (1967) 'Programmed techniques in the G.P.O.', *Progr. Instr. Ind.*, **1** Pergamon, London

HAMILTON, N. R. (1965) 'Increasing long-term retention of knowledge', American Institutes for Research, Palo Alto

HAMILTON, N. R. (1967) 'Programs for initial instruction and review: some effects on retention', *J. Natn. Soc. Programmed Instruc.*, **6** No. 2, 12–13

HANDEL, S. (1967) *The Electronic Revolution*, Penguin, Harmondsworth

HANSEN, D. N. (1966) 'Computer assistance with the educational process', *Rev. Educ. Res.*, **36** No. 5, 588–603

HANSON, L. F. (1963) 'The carbon-paper ear', *J. Progr. Instr.*, **2** No. 3, 5–8

HARBISON, F. and MYERS, C. A. (1964) *Education, Manpower and Economic Growth*, McGraw Hill, New York

HARPER, W. W. (1969) 'A programmed case-study', *Training and Development Journal*, **23** No. 2, 42–44

HARTLEY, J. (1964) 'A study in programmed learning', Unpublished Ph.D. thesis, University of Sheffield

HARTLEY, J. (1965) 'Linear and skip-branching programmes: a comparison study', *Br. J. educ. Psychol.*, **35** No. 3, 320–328

HARTLEY, J. (1966a) 'Some guides for evaluating programmes', Cavanagh, P. and Jones, C. (Eds.) *Programmes in Print*, 171–193, Association for Programmed Learning, London

HARTLEY, J. (1966b) 'Optional and controlled branching: comparison studies', *J. Progr. Instr.*, **3** No. 4, 5–11

HARTLEY, J. (1966c) 'Research Report', *New Education*, **2** No. 1, 29–35

HARTLEY, J. (1968) 'Some factors affecting student performance in programmed learning', *Programmed Learn.* (& *Educ. Technol.*), **5** No. 3, 206–218

HARTLEY, J. (1971) 'Programmed instruction as "propaganda": two methods of publicising traffic signs compared', Road Research Laboratory Report (In press)

HARTLEY, J. and CAMERON, A. (1967) 'Some observations on the efficiency of lecturing', *Educ. Rev.*, **20** No. 1, 30–37

HARTLEY, J. and FRANKLIN, G. B. (1965) 'The functional analysis of frames: proposed systems', *Programmed Learning*, **2** No. 2, 93–99

HARTLEY, J. and HOGARTH, F. (1971) 'Programmed Learning in Pairs', *Educational Research*, **13** No. 2, 130–134

HARTLEY, J., HOLT, J. and SWAIN, F. (1971) 'The effects of pretests, interim tests and age on post-test performance followin gself-instruction', *Programmed Learn.* (& *Educ. Technol.*), **7** No. 4, 250–256

HARTLEY, J. and WOODS, P. M. (1968) 'Learning poetry backwards', *J. Natn. Soc. Programmed Instruction*, **7** No. 10, 9–15

HASLERUND, G. M. and MEYERS, S. (1958) 'The transfer value of given and individually derived principles', *J. educ. Psychol.*, **49** 293–298

HEINICH, R. (1965) *The Systems Engineering Of Education, II: Application Of Systems Thinking For Instruction*, Instructional Technology and Media Project, University of Southern California, Los Angeles

HENDRIX, G. (1947) 'A new clue to transfer of training', *Elem. School J.*, **48** 197–208

HICKEY, A. E. (1968) 'Computer-assisted instruction: a survey of the literature'. 3rd edn, Tech. Rep. No. 8, ONR Contract N0014-68-L-0236, Entelek Inc., Newburyport, Mass

HICKEY, A. E. and NEWTON, J. M. (1964) *The Logical Basis of Teaching: I. The Effect, of Subconcept Sequence on Learning*, Entelek Inc., Newburyport, Mass

HILGARD, E. R. and BOWER, G. H. (1966) *Theories of Learning* 3rd edn, Appleton-Century-Crofts, New York

HILL, A. B. and THICKETT, J. M. B. (1966) 'Batch size, cycle time and setting time as determinants of productivity in skilled machining work', *Occup. Psychol.*, **40** 83–89

HILL, J. and CAVANAGH, P. (1969) 'Some explorations of the use of the E.R.E. as an aid to teaching reading to adults', Dunn, W. R. and Holroyd, C. (Eds.) *Aspects of Educational Technology*, Vol. II, Methuen, London

HILTON, B. D. (1969) 'Development of a diagnostic test to enable maximum use to be made of an available mathematics program at the Army School of Education', Dunn, W. R. and Holroyd, C. (Eds.) *Aspects of Educational Technology*, Vol. II, Methuen, London

HOBAN, C. F. (1960) 'The usable residue of educational film research', Schramm, W. (Ed.) *New Teaching Aids for the American Classroom*. Institute for Communication Research, Stanford

HODGE, H. P. R. (1967) 'A proposed model for investigating the instructional process', Tobin, M. (Ed.) *Problems and Methods in Programmed Learning*, Part I, National Centre for Programmed Learning, University of Birmingham

HOLLAND, J. G. (1961) 'New directions in teaching machine research', Coulson, J. E. (Ed.) *Programmed Learning and Computer-Based Instruction*, Wiley, New York

HOLLAND, J. G. (1965) 'Research on programming variables', Glaser, R. (Ed.) *Teaching Machines and Programed Learning*, Vol. II, N.E.A., Washington

HOLLAND, J. G. and SKINNER, B. F. (1961) *The Analysis of Behavior*, McGraw Hill, New York

HOLLING, K. (1967) 'The feedback classroom in use', Unwin, D. and Leedham, J. (Eds.) *Aspects of Educational Technology*, Methuen, London

HOLME, K. and MABBS, D. (1967) 'Programmed learning—an expanding discipline', Tobin, M. (Ed.) *Problems and Methods in Programmed Learning*, Part 4, National Centre for Programmed Learning, University of Birmingham

HOLT, H. O. (1963) 'An exploratory study of the use of a self-instructional program in basic electricity', Hughes, J. L. (Ed.) *Programed Learning: A Critical Evaluation*, Educational Methods Inc., Chicago

HOLZ, W. C. and ROBINSON, J. S. (1963) 'A note on machines in a technology of education', *J. Progr. Instr.*, **2** No. 3, 31–33

HOMME, L. E. (1963) 'Use of the Premack Principle in controlling the behaviour of nursery school children', *J. exp. Analysis Behav.*, **6** 544

HORABIN, I. S., GANE, C. P. and LEWIS, B. N. (1967) *Algorithms and the Prevention of Instruction*, Cambridge Consultants (Training) Limited, Cambridge

HORN, R. E. (1964) 'What programming errors can be discovered by student testing?', *Progr. Instr.*, **4** No. 2, 6–11

HOWE, R. C. (1969) 'Programmed learning—a programmed initial-installation training course', *Post Office Electrical Engineers Journal* (January)

HUGHES, R. J. and PIPE, P. (1961) *Introduction to Electronics*, Doubleday, New York

HUNTER, I. M. L. (1964) *Memory*, Penguin, Harmondsworth

IVES, J. M. and WALLIS, D. (1969) 'The evaluation of a naval arithmetic teaching program with different forms of presentation and supervision', *Programmed Learn. (& Educ. Technol.)*, **6** No. 2, 86–101

JACOBS, P. I. (1962) 'Some implications of testing procedures for auto-instructional programming', RB-62-10 Behavioural Sciences Lab., Wright Patterson Air Force Base, Ohio

JACOBS, P. I., MAIER, M. H. and STOLUROW, L. H. (1966) *A Guide to Evaluating Self Instructional Programs*, Holt, Rinehart and Winston, New York

JEFFELS, A. (1969) 'Engineering apprentice training: programmed learning integrated with skill development', Dunn, W. R. and Holroyd, C. (Eds.) *Aspects of Educational Technology*, Vol. II, Methuen, London

JOHNSON, K. A. and SENTER, R. J. (1965) 'The comparison of forward and backward chaining techniques for the teaching of verbal sequential tasks', AMRL-TR-65-203, Wright Patterson Airforce Base, Ohio

JONES, A. and MOXHAM, J. (1969) 'Costing the benefits of training', *Personnel Manage.*, **1** No. 4, 22–28

JONES, S. (1964) 'Why can't leaflets be logical?', *New Society*, **102** No. 16

KAHN. H. and WIENER, A. S. (1967) *The Year 2000*, Macmillan, New York

KANNER, J, H. (1968) *The Instructional Effectiveness of Colour Television*, Eric Clearinghouse on Educational Media and Technology, Stanford University Press, Stanford, California

KAPEL, D. E. (1966) 'An analysis of "cheating" in programmed instruction', *J. Natn. Soc. Programmed Instruc.*, **5** No. 10, 9–12

KATZ, M. (Ed.) (1961) *Making the Classroom Test: A Guide for Teachers*, Educational Testing Service, Princeton

KAUFMAN, R. A. (1963) 'An experimental evaluation of the role of remedial feedback on an intrinsic program', *J. Progr. Instr.*, **2** No. 4, 21–30

KAY, H. (1968) 'Summary: with pointers to futur e action', Barnes, J. and Robinson, N. (Eds.) *New Media and Methods in Industrial Training*, British Broadcasting Corporation, London

KAY, H., DODD, B. T. and SIME, M. E. (1968) *Teaching Machines and Programmed Instruction*, Penguin, Harmondsworth

KAY, H. and SIME, M. (1963) 'Survey of teaching machines', Goldsmith, M. (Ed.) *Mechanisation in the Classroom*, Souvenir Press, London

KING, S. D. M. (1964) *Training Within The Organisation*, Tavistock Publication, London

KLAUS, D. J. (1961) *High School Physics*, American Institute for Research, Pittsburgh

KNIGHT, M. A. G. (1961) An experimental training course in fault diagnosis, Research report for Task No. 202, R.A.F. Brampton, Huntingdon

KNIGHT, M. A. G. (1964) 'A note on the use of programmed instruction in a fault finding training course', *Programmed Learning*, **1** No. 3, 134–145

KNIGHT, M. A. G. (1965) 'The testing and validation of programs', *Programmed Learning*, **2** No. 2, 109–117

KOMOSKI, P. K. (1966) 'Programed instructional materials 1964–65', *Progr. Instr.* **5** Nos. 3 and 4

KOPSTEIN, F. F. and CAVE, R. T. (1962) 'Preliminary cost comparison of technical training by conventional and programmed learning methods', Tech. Documentary Rep. MRL-TDR-62-79. Behavioural Science Lab., Wright Patterson Airforce Base, Ohio

KOPSTEIN, F. F. and SEIDEL, R. J. (1968) 'Computer-assisted instruction versus

P

traditionally administered instruction: economics', *Audio-vis. Commun. Rev.*, **16** No. 2, 147–175

KRISHNAMURTY, G. B. (1968) 'Application of programmed learning technique in the training of family planning workers', *Newsletter of the Indian Association for Programmed Learning*, **3** No. 1, 29–36

KRUMBOLTZ, J. O. and WEISMAN, R. G. (1962) 'The effect of overt vs. covert responding to programmed instruction on immediate and delayed retention', *J. educ. Psychol.*, **53** 89–92

LAMBERT, P. (1968) 'Computer programmer training in I.C.T.', *Progr. Instr. Ind.*, **2** No. 5, Pergamon, London

LANER, S. (1954) 'The impact of visual-aid displays showing a manipulative task', *J. exp. Psychol.*, **6** 95–106

LANER, S. (1955) 'Some factors influencing the effectiveness of an instructional film', *Br. J. Psychol.*, **46** 280–292

LANKFORD, B. C. (1965) 'Programmed instruction in the junior high school: a study of teacher roles', *Dissertation Abstracts*, **25** No. 10, 5791–2

LEITH, G. O. M. (1968) 'Programmed instruction, acquisition of knowledge and mental development of students', *Proceedings UNESCO Seminar on Programmed Instruction*, Paper ED/ENPRO/6, Varna, Bulgaria. UNESCO, Paris

LEITH, G. O. M. (1968) 'Learning from abstract and concrete and visual illustrations', *Visual Education*, 13–15, (January)

LEITH, G. O. M. (1969) 'Learning and personality', Dunn, W. R. and Holroyd, C. (Eds.) *Aspects of Educational Technology*, Vol. II, Methuen, London

LEITH, G. O. M. and WEBB, C. C. (1968) 'A comparison of four methods of programmed instruction with and without teacher intervention', *Educ. Rev.*, **21** No. 1, 25–31

LEVINE, R. and BAKER L. (1963) 'Item scrambling in a self-instructional program', *J. educ. Psychol.*, **54** 138–143

LEVY, P. (1969) 'New research for new curricula', *J. Curric. Stud.*, **1** No. 2, 101–108

LEWIS, B. N., HORABIN, I. S. and GANE, C. P. (1967) 'Case studies in the use of algorithms', *Progr. Instr. Ind.* **1** No. 8, Pergamon, London

LEWIS, B. N. and WOOLFENDEN, P. J. (1969) *Algorithms and Logical Trees: A Self-Instructional Course*, Algorithms Press, Cambridge

LINDSLEY, D. B. (1957) 'Psychophysiology and motivation', Jones, M. R. (Ed.) *Nebraska Symposium on Motivation*, University of Nebraska, Lincoln

LINDVALL, C. M. (1967) *Measuring Pupil Achievement and Aptitude*, Harcourt, Brace and World, New York

LUMSDAINE, A. A. (1961) *Student Response in Programmed Learning: A Symposium*, National Academy of Sciences—National Research Council, Washington D.C.

LUMSDAINE, A. A. (1962) 'Some theoretical and practical problems in programmed instruction', Coulson, J. E. (Ed.) *Programmed Learning and Computer-Based Instruction*, Wiley, New York

LUMSDAINE, A. A. (1963) 'Instruments and media of instruction', Gage, N. L. (Ed.) *Handbook of Research on Teaching*, Rand McNally, Chicago

LUMSDAINE, A, A, and GLADSTONE, A. I. (1958) 'Overt practice and audio-visual embellishments', Lumsdaine, A. A. and May, M. A. (Eds.) *Learning from Films*, Yale University Press, New Haven, Connecticut

LUMSDAINE, A. A., SULZER, R. L. and KOPSTEIN, F. F. 'The effect of animation cues and repetition of examples on learning from an instructional film', Lumsdaine, A. A. (Ed.) *Student Response in Programmed Instruction*. National Academy of Sciences —National Research Council, Washington D.C.

MACKIE, A. M. (1966) 'National survey of the knowledge of the new traffic signs', Ministry of Transport, *RRL. Report* No. 51

MACKIE, A. M. (1967) 'Progress in learning the meanings of symbolic traffic signs', Ministry of Transport, *RRL Report* No. LR91

MCCUSKER, H. F. and SORENSEN, P. H. (1966) 'The economics of education', Rossi P. H. and Biddle, B. J. (Eds.) *The New Media and Education*, Anchor Books, New York

MCGUIGAN, F. J. (1967) 'The G statistic: an index of amount learned', *J. Natn. Soc. Programmed Instruc.*, **6** No. 9, 14–16

MCGUIGAN, F. J. and PETERS, J. (1965) 'Assessing the effectiveness of programed texts—methodology—some findings', *J. Progr. Instr.* **3** No. 1, 23–34

MAGER, R. F. (1961) 'On the sequencing of instructional content', Davies, I. K. and Hartley, J. (Eds.) (1972) *Contributions to an Educational Technology*, Butterworths, London

MAGER, R. F. (1962) *Preparing Objectives For Programmed Instruction*, Fearon Press, San Francisco

MAGER, R. F. (1964) 'Learner-controlled instruction', 1958–1964, *Progr. Instr.* **4** No. 2

MAGER, R. F. and BEACH, K. M. (1967) *Developing Vocational Instruction*, Fearon Press, Palo Alto, California

MAGER, R. F. and CLARK, D. C. (1963) 'Explorations in student controlled instruction', *Psychol. Rep.*, **13** 71–76

MAGER, R. F. and CLARK, D. C. (1963) 'Normative feedback in automated instruction', *Psychol. Rep.*, **13** 599–616

MAGER, R. F. and MCCANN, J. (1961) *Learner Controlled Instruction*, Varian Associates, Palo Alto, California

MAGNUSSON, D. (1967) *Test Theory*, Addison-Wesley, Reading, Mass

MANN, A. P. and BRUNSTROM, C. K. (Eds.) (1969) *Aspects of Educational Technology*, Vol. III, Pitman, London

MARGULIES, S. and EIGEN, L. D. (Eds.) (1962) *Applied Programed Instruction*, Wiley, New York

MARKLE, D. G. (1968) 'Controlling behavior changers' behavior', *Audio-vis. Commun. Rev.* **16** No. 2, 188–203

MARKLE, S. M. (1963) 'Faulty branching frames: a model for maximising feedback to the programmer', *Progr. Instr.*, **3** No. 1, 4–5

MARKLE, S. M. (1967) 'Empirical testing of programs', Lange, P. C. (Ed.) *Programed Instruction*, National Society for the Study of Education, Chicago

MECHNER, F. M. (1964) *Behavioural Technology and the Development of Medical Education Programs*, Basic Systems, New York

MECHNER, F. M. (1965) 'Science education and behaviour technology', Glaser, R. (Ed.) *Teaching Machines and Programmed Learning*, Vol. II, N.E.A., Washington

MECHNER, F. M. (1967) 'Behavioural analysis and instructional sequencing', Lange, C. P. (Ed.) *Programed Instruction*, National Society for the Study of Education, Chicago

MECHNER, F. M. and COOK, D. A. (1964) *Behavioural Technology and Manpower Development*, Basic Systems, O.E.C.D. and New York

MEDLEY, D. M. and MITZEL, H. E. (1963) 'Measuring classroom behaviour by systematic observation', Gage, N. L. (Ed.) *Handbook of Research on Teaching*, Rand McNally, Chicago

MELARAGNO, R. J. (1967) 'Two methods for adapting self-instructional materials to individual differences', *J. educ. Psychol.*, **58** No. 6, 327–331

METFESSEL, N. S. and MICHAEL, W. B. (1967) 'A paradigm involving multiple criterion measures for the evaluation of the effectiveness of school programs', *Educ. psychol. Measur.*, **27** No. 4, 931–944

MILLER, E. E. (1963) 'A classification of learning tasks in conventional language', AMRL-TDR-63-74. Wright Air Development Center, Dayton, Ohio

MILLER, G. A., GALANTER, E. and PRIBRAM, K. H. (1960) *Plans and the Structure of Behaviour*, Holt, Rinehart and Winston, New York

MILLER, G. A. and MCKEAN, K. O. (1964) 'A chronometric study of some relationships between sentences', *Q. Jl. exp. Psychol.*, **16** 297–308

MILLER, R. B. (1953) 'A method for man-machine task analysis', WADC TR 53–137, Wright Air Development Center, Dayton, Ohio

MILLER, R. B. (1954) 'Suggestions for short cuts in task analysis procedures', AIR-A77-54-SR-42, American Institutes for Research, Pittsburgh

MILLER, R. B. (1956) 'A suggested guide to position-task description', ASPRL TM 56-6, Air Research and Development Command, Lowry Air Force Base, Colorado

MILLER, R. B. (1962a) 'Task description and analysis', Gagné, R. M. (Ed.) *Psychological Principles in System Development*, Holt, Rinehart and Winston, New York

MILLER, R. B. (1962b) 'Analysis and specification of behaviour for training', Glaser, R. (Ed.) *Training Research and Education*, Wiley, New York

MILLER, R. B. (1966) 'Task taxonomy: science or technology?', Conference on the human operator in complex systems, University of Aston

MILLER, W. C. (1969) 'Film movement and affective response and the effect on learning and attitude formation', *Audio-vis. Commun. Rev.*, **17** No. 2, 172–181

MILLS, D. (1968) 'Clerical training in the quality department of Bryce Berger, Ltd.', *Progr. Instr. Ind.*, **2** No. 11, Pergamon, London

MILLS, G. M. (1969) 'The analysis of response errors in the evaluation of technical teaching programs', *Programmed Learn.* (& *Educ. Technol.*), **6** No. 2, 121–132

MOORE, O. K. (1962) *The Automated Responsive Environment*, Yale University, New Haven

MOORE, O. K. and ANDERSON, A. R. (1960) *Early Reading And Writing*, (15 min. 16 mm colour film), Basic Education Inc, Hamden, Connecticut

NEALE, J. G., TOYE, M. H. and BELBIN, E. (1968) 'Adult training: the use of programmed instruction', *Occup. Psychol.*, **42** 23–31

NEIDT, C. O. and SJOGREN, D. D. (1968) 'Changes in student attitudes during a course in relation to instructional media', *Audio-vis. Commun. Rev.*, **16** No. 3, 268–279

NEWARK, J. H. (1968) 'Improved quality control at J. R. Freeman', *Progr. Instr. Ind.*, **2** No. 1, Pergamon, London

NOBLE, G. (1967a) 'An experimental attempt to integrate programmed instruction with classroom instruction', Unwin, D. and Leedham, J. (Eds.) *Aspects of Educational Technology*, Methuen, London

NOBLE, G. (1967b) 'A study of the differences between paired and individual learning from a branching program', *Programmed Learn.* (& *Educ. Technol.*), **4** No. 2, 108–112

NOBLE, G. (1968) 'A study of children's perceptions of intrinsic teaching machines and programmed instruction', *Programmed Learn.* (& *Educ. Technol.*), **5** No. 2, 142–150

NOBLE, G. and GRAY, K. (1968) 'The impact of programmed instruction: a longitudinal attitude study', *Programmed Learn.* (& *Educ. Technol.*), **5** No. 4, 271–282

OATES, A. A. and ROBERTSON, C. F. (1968) 'Programmed learning for clerical work in the G.P.O.', *Progr. Instr. Ind.*, **2** No. 2, Pergamon, London

O.E.C.D. (1965) *The Requirements of Automated Jobs*, Organisation for Economic Co-operation and Development, Paris

O.E.C.D. (1966) *Demographic Trends 1965–80 in Western Europe and North America*, Organisation for Economic Co-operation and Development, Paris

OFIESH, G. D. (1965) *Programed Instruction*, American Management Association, New York

OSGOOD, C. E. (1953) *Method and Theory in Experimental Psychology*, Oxford University Press, New York

OZBEKHAN, H. (1967) 'Automation', *Sci. J.* **3** No. 10, 67–72

PASK, G. (1960) 'Adaptive teaching with adaptive machines', Lumsdaine, A. A. and Glaser, R. (Eds.) *Teaching Machines and Programmed Learning*, N.E.A., Washington

PASK, G. (1969) 'Adaptive machines', Davies, I. K. and Hartley, J. (Eds.) (1972) *Contributions to an Educational Technology*, Butterworths, London

PAYNE, D. A., KRATHWOHL, D. R. and GORDON, J. (1967) 'The effect of sequence on programmed instruction', *Am. Educ. Res. J.*, **4** 125–132

PIAGET, J. and INHELDER, B. (1964) '*The Early Growth of Logic in the Child*', Harper and Row, New York

PIKAS, A. (1967) 'Comparison between traditional and programmed learning as a function of the contents of the comparison test', *Programmed Learn.* (& *Educ. Technol.*), **4** No. 4, 270–283

PINSENT, A. (1941) *The Principles of Teaching Method with Special Reference to Post-Primary Education*, Harrap, London

POULTON, E. C. (1959) 'Effects of printing types and formats on the comprehension of scientific journals', *Nature*, **184** No. 5, 1824

POULTON, E. C. (1960) 'A note on printing to make comprehension easier', *Ergonomics*, **3** 245–248

POULTON, E. C. (1967) 'Skimming (scanning) news items printed in 8-point and 9-point letters, *Ergonomics*, **10** No. 6, 713–716

POULTON, E. C. (1969) 'How efficient is print?', Davies, I. K. and Hartley, J. (Eds.) (1972) *Contributions to an Educational Technology*, Butterworths, London

POULTON, E. C. and BROWN, C. H. (1968) 'Rate of comprehension of an existing teleprinter output and of possible alternatives', *J. appl. Psychol.*, **52** No. 1, 16–21

POSTMAN, L. (1963) 'One-trial learning', Cofer, C. N. and Musgrave, B. S. (Eds.) *Verbal Behavior and Learning*, McGraw Hill, New York

PREMACK, D. (1959) 'Toward empirical behaviour laws: 1. Positive reinforcement', *Psychol. Rev.*, **66** 219–233

PREMACK, D. (1963) 'Rate differential reinforcement in monkey manipulation', *J. exp. Analysis Behav.*, **6** 81–89

PREMACK, D. (1965) 'Reinforcement theory', Jones, M. R. (Ed.) *Nebraska Symposium on Motivation*, University of Nebraska Press, Lincoln, Nebraska

PRESSEY, S. L. (1962) 'Basic unresolved teaching-machine problems', *Theory into Practice*, **1** 30–37

PRESSEY, S. L. (1963) 'Teaching machine and learning theory crisis', *J. appl. Psychol.*, **47** 1–6

PRESSEY, S. L. and KINZER, J. R. (1964) 'Auto-elucidation without programming', *Psychology in the Schools*, **1** No. 4, 359–365

PYATTE, J. A. (1969) 'Some effects of unit structure on achievement and transfer', *Am. Educ. Res. J.*, **6** 241–261

REID, R. L. (1963) 'The simple fixed sequence program', Goldsmith, M. (Ed.) (1963) *Mechanisation in the Classroom*, Souvenir Press, London

REVELLE, R. (1967) 'Population', *Sci. J.*, **3** No. 10, 113–118

RICHMOND, W. K. (1967) *The Teaching Revolution*, Methuen, London

RIPPEY, R. M. (1966) 'A contrast between the teacher and materials', *School Review*, 283–291, (Autumn)

ROCK, I. (1957) 'The role of repetition in associative learning', *Am. J. Psychol.*, **70** 186–193

ROE, K., CASE, H. W. and ROE, A. (1962) 'Scrambled versus ordered sequence in autoinstructional programs', *J. educ. Psychol.*, **53** 101–104

ROEBUCK, M. (1968) 'Evaluating programs in the tropical rainforest', *Bull. Prog. Res. Unit, Glasgow University*, No. 13, 13–16

222   Strategies for Programmed Instruction

ROSSI, P. H. and BIDDLE, B. J. (1966) *The New Media and Education*, Anchor Books, New York

ROTHKOPF, E. Z. (1963) 'A verbal learning theory, inspection behaviour and the response to programmed instruction', *Proc. Berlin Conf. on Programmed Learning and Teaching Machines*, Pedagogische Arbeitstelle, Berlin

ROWNTREE, D. (1967) *Basically Branching: A Handbook for Programmers*, Macdonald, London

ROWNTREE, D. (1969) 'Tutorial programming—an integrated approach to frame writing', Dunn, W. R. and Holroyd, C. (Eds.) *Aspects of Educational Technology*, Vol. II, Methuen, London

RUPE, J. C. (1952) 'Research into basic methods and techniques of Airforce job analysis—I', Human Resources Research Center, Chanute Airforce Base, Illinois

RUPE, J. C. (1956) 'Research into basic methods and techniques of Airforce job analysis—IV', Air Force Personnel and Training Research Center, Chanute Airforce Base, Illinois

RUPE, J. C. and WESTEN, R. J. (1955a) 'Research into basic methods and techniques of Air Force job analysis—II', Air Force Personnel and Training Research Center, Chanute Air Force Base, Illinois

RUPE, J. C. and WESTEN, R. J. (1955b) 'Research into basic methods and techniques of Air Force job analysis—III', Air Force Personnel and Training Research Center, Chanute Air Force Base, Illinois

RYAN, F. L. (1968) 'Teacher inclusion in a programmed instructional sequence involving social studies content', *J. Educ. Res.*, **62** No. 2, 53–57

SCHAEFER, H. H. (1963) 'A vocabulary program using "language redundancy"', *J. Progr. Instr.* **2** 9–16

SCHRAMM, W. (1964) *The Research on Programed Instruction: An Annotated Bibliography*, U.S. Dept. Health, Education and Welfare, Washington

SCHRAMM, W., COOMBS, P. H., KAHNERT, F., and LYLE, J. (1967) *The New Media: Memo to Educational Planners*, UNESCO, Paris

SCOTT, W. E. (1966) 'Activation theory and task design', *Organ. Behav. & Human Perform.*, **1** 3–30

SENTER, R. J., NEIBERG, A., ABAMA, J. S. and MORGAN, R. L. (1964) 'An evaluation of branching and motivational phrases in a scrambled book', *Programmed Learning*, **1** 124–133

SHEFFIELD, F. D., MARGOLIUS, G. J. and HOEHN, A. J. (1961) 'Experiments on perceptual mediation in the learning of organisable sequences', Lumsdaine, A. A. (Ed.) *Student Response in Programmed Instruction*, National Academy of Sciences—National Research Council, Washington D.C.

SHRIVER, E. L. (1960) 'Determining training requirements for electronic system maintenance: development and test of a new method of skill and knowledge analysis', Tech. Rep. 63, Human Resources Research Office, Alexandria, Virginia

SHRIVER, E. L., FINK, C. D. and TREXLER, R. C. (1961) *A Procedural Guide for Technical Implementation of the FORECAST Methods of Task and Skill Analysis*, George Washington University, Human Resources Research Office, Washington, D.C.

SHRIVER, E. L., FINK, C. D. and TREXLER, R. C. (1964) 'FORECAST systems analysis and training methods for electronics maintenance training', Res. Rep. 13, Human Resources Research Office, Alexandria, Virginia

SHRIVER, E. L. and TREXLER, R. C. (1965) 'Application and test of the FORECAST concept of electronics maintenance on Navy LORAN equipment', Tech. Rep. 65-3, Human Resources Research Office, Alexandria, Virginia

SILBERMAN, H. F., MELARAGNO, R. S., COULSON, J. E. and ESTAVAN, D. (1961) 'Fixed sequence versus branching autoinstructional methods', *J. educ. Psychol.*, **52** No. 3, 166–172

SIME, M. E. (1968) 'Computers as test beds for teaching systems', Davies, I. K. and,

Hartley, J. (Eds.) (1972) *Contributions to an Educational Technology*, Butterworths, London

SIME, M. E. and DODD, B. T. (1964) 'Notes on Programme Writing', Mimeographed, Dept. of Psychology, University of Sheffield

SINGLETON, W. T. (1968) 'Some recent experiments on learning and their training implications', *Ergonomics*, **11** 53–59

SKINNER, B. F. (1950) 'Are theories of learning necessary?', *Psychol. Rev.*, **57** 193–216

SKINNER, B. F. (1953) *Science and Human Behavior*, Macmillan, New York

SKINNER, B. F. (1954) 'The science of learning and the art of teaching', *Harv. Educ. Rev.*, **24** 86–97

SKINNER, B. F. (1959) *Cumulative Record*, Appleton Century Crofts, New York

SKINNER, B. F. (1961) 'Teaching machines', *Scient. Am.*, **205** No. 5, 90–102

SMALLWOOD, R. (1962) *A Decision Structure for Teaching Machines*, M.I.T. Press, Cambridge, Mass

SMITH, K. U. and SMITH, M. F. (1966) *Cybernetic Principles of Learning and Educational Design*, Holt, Rinehart and Winston, New York

SMITH, R. G. (1964) *The Development of Training Objectives*, Human Resources Research Office, Alexandria, Virginia

STAINER, F. W. (1967) 'Training for fault diagnosis', *Proc. IEE.*, **114** 400–404

STANLEY, J. C. and BOLTON, D. (1957) Book review section, *Educ. psychol. Measur.*, **17** 631–634

STOLUROW, L. M. (1964) 'A taxonomy of learning task characteristics', AMRL-TDR-64-2, Wright Air Development Center, Dayton, Ohio

STOLUROW, L. M. and DAVIS, D. (1965) 'Teaching machines and computer-based systems', Glaser, R. (Ed.) *Teaching Machines and Programed Learning*, Vol. II, N.E.A., Washington

SULLIVAN, A. M. (1969) 'A structured individualised approach to teaching introductory psychology', Davies, I. K. and Hartley, J. (Eds.) (1972) *Contributions to an Educational Technology*, Butterworths, London

SUPPES, P. (1966) 'The use of computers in education', *Scient. Am.* **215** No. 3, 206–220

TABER, J. I., GLASER, R. and SCHAEFER, H. H. (1965) *Learning and Programmed Instruction*, Addison Wesley, Reading, Mass

TAYLOR, E. A. (1967) 'The use and cost of programmed instruction at Stewarts and Lloyds', *Progr. Instr. Ind.*, **1** Pergamon, London

TAYLOR, W. (Ed.) (1969) *Towards a Policy for the Education of Teachers*, Colston Papers No. 20, Butterworths, London

THIAGARAJAN, S. (1969) Design and development of a program for attitude change, *J. Natn. Soc. Programmed Instruc.*, **8** No. 9, 10–11

THOMAS, C. A., DAVIES, I. K., OPENSHAW, D. and BIRD, J. B. (1963) *Programmed Learning in Perspective*, City Publicity Services, London

THOMAS, L. F. (1968) 'The analysis of skill and training for flexibility', Proc. Brit. Psychol. Soc. (Occup. Psychol. Div.) Annual Conference, Loughborough

THOMAS, W. J. (1966) 'Programme writing teams in technical training command', *R.A.F. Educational Bulletin*, No. 3, 64–70

THORNDIKE, E. L. (1906) *The Principles of Teaching*, New York, Seiler

THORNDIKE, E. L. (1913) *The Psychology of Learning*, Macmillan, New York

TUCKER, G. L. and HARTLEY, J. (1967) 'Experiments with programmed instruction in primary schools', *Visual Education*, 17–23 (December)

TYLER, R. W. (1961) 'Measuring the results of college instruction', Harris, T. and Schwahn, W. E. (Eds.) *The Learning Process*, O.U.P., New York

URBAN, J. (1943) *Behaviour Changes resulting from Study of Communicable Diseases*, Teachers' College, Columbia, New York

VAIZEY, J. (1966) *Education for Tomorrow*, Penguin, Harmondsworth

VAIZEY, J. (1967) *Education in the Modern World*, Weidenfeld and Nicolson, London

VERNON, M. D. (1962) *The Psychology of Perception*, University of London Press, London

VERPLANCK, W. S. (1955) 'The control of the content of conversation: reinforcement of statements of opinion', *J. abnorm. soc. Psychol.*, **51** 668–676

WALL, J. D. (1968) 'The future of educational research', *Educ. Research*, **10** No. 3, 163–169

WALLIS, D. (1964) 'Experiments in the use of programmed instruction to increase the productivity of training', *Occup. Psychol.*, **38** 141–160

WALLIS, D. (1965) 'The technology of military training', *Manpower Planning* (proceedings of NATO Conference on Operational and Personnel Research, Brussels 1965), English Universities Press, London

WANLESS, V. (1969) 'Programmed learning and maladjusted children', Dunn, W. R. and Holroyd, C. (Eds.) *Aspects of Educational Technology*, Vol. II, Methuen, London

WARR, P. B. (1965) 'Repetition and verbal learning', *Br. J. Psychol.*, **56** 147–156

WARR, P. B. and BIRD, M. W. (1968) *Identifying Supervisory Training Needs*, H.M.S.O., London

WARR, P. B., BIRD, M. and RACKHAM, N. (1970) *Evaluation of Management Training*, Gower Press, London

WASON, P. C. and JONES, S. (1965) *The Logical Tree Project*, Mimeographed report of the Department of Psychology, University College, London

WATSON, P. G. (1968) 'An industrial evaluation of four strategies of instruction', *Audio-vis. Instruct.*, **13** No. 2, 156–158

WEBB, C. (1967) 'An investigation into the effects of adaptive linear systems and review procedures upon a programmed learning task in physical geography', Tobin, M. (Ed.) *Problems and Methods in Programmed Learning*, Part 2, National Centre for Programmed Learning, University of Birmingham

WENDT, P. (1967) 'Optional returns from the bypass', *J. Natn. Soc. Programmed Instruc.* **6** No. 2, 4–5

WHEATLEY, R. A. (1969) 'Measurement in programmed learning experiments—problems encountered and some possible solutions', Mann, A. P. and Brunstrom, C. K. (Eds.) *Aspects of Educational Technology*, Vol. III, Pitman, London

WILLIAMS, W. L. and WHITMORE, P. G. (1959) 'The development and use of a performance test as a basis for comparing technicians with and without field experience and the Nike Ajax IFC Maintenance Technician', Tech. Rep. 52, Human Resources Research Office, Alexandria, Virginia

WODTKE, K. H. (1967) 'On the assessment of retention effects in educational experiments', *J. Exp. Educ.*, **35** No. 4, 28–36

WRIGGLE, L. K. (1965) 'The amount and nature of teacher help necessary for optimum achievement through use of programmed learning devices', *Dissertation Abstracts*, **25** No. 10, 5802–3

YOUNG, E. B. (1967) 'A world-wide experiment in staff training', *Progr. Instr. Ind.*, **1** Pergamon, London

ZINN, K. (1967) 'Computer assistance for instruction: a review of systems and projects', Bushnell, D. D. and Allen, D. W. (Eds.) *The Computer in American Education*, Wiley, New York

Index

Tests *continued*
  transfer, 148
  validity of, 134–135
  verbal, 134
  see also Post-test; Pretest
Textbooks, 208
Thomas, C. A. *et. al.*, 37
Time taken, 154–156
Tracking, 74
Traffic signs program, 188–198
Training, generality of, 68–70
Training design, problems of, 68–78
Training problems, 64
Training techniques, 42
Transfer tests, 148
Tyler, R. W., 21

Typefaces, 120
Typewriter typefaces, 120
Typography, 118, 120

U
University education, 5–6

V
Valves, hand-operated, 72, 76, 77, 78
Verbal tests, 134
Visual diagrams, 121
Vocations, 28

W
'Whifs', 121
Woolfenden, P. J., 124